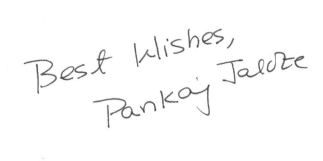

Best Wishes,
Pankaj Jalote

CMM in Practice

CMM in Practice

Processes for Executing Software Projects at Infosys

Pankaj Jalote

Addison-Wesley
An imprint of Addison Wesley Longman, Inc.

Reading, Massachusetts   Menlo Park, California

New York   Don Mills, Ontario   Wokingham, England

Amsterdam   Bonn   Sydney   Singapore   Tokyo

Madrid   San Juan   Paris   Milan

 **Software Engineering Institute**

The SEI Series in Software Engineering

Many of the designations used by manufacturers and sellers to distinguish their products are claimed as trademarks. Where those designations appear in this book, and Addison Wesley Longman, Inc. was aware of a trademark claim, the designations have been printed in initial capital letters or all capital letters.

The author and publisher have taken care in preparation of this book, but make no expressed or implied warranty of any kind and assume no responsibility for errors or omissions. No liability is assumed for incidental or consequential damages in connection with or arising out of the use of the information or programs contained herein.

The publisher offers discounts of this book when ordered in quantity for special sales. For more information, please contact:

Addison Wesley Longman, Inc.
One Jacob Way
Reading, Massachusetts 01867
(781) 944-3700

Library of Congress Cataloging-in-Publication Data

Jalote, P.
    CMM in practice: processes for executing software projects at
Infosys / Pankaj Jalote.
       p. cm.—(SEI series in software engineering)
    Includes bibliographical references.
    ISBN 0-201-61626-2
    1. Software engineering. 2. Capability maturity model (Computer
software) I. Title II. Series.
QA76.758.J354 1999
005.1′068′5–dc21
                                          99–43580
                                          CIP

Text printed on recycled paper.

ISBN 0-201-61626-2
1 2 3 4 5 6 7 8 9—MA—0302010099
First printing, October 1999

Dedicated to
N. R. Narayana Murthy
and his co-visionaries

Contents

Preface

Worldwide, the demand for software is increasing at a rapid pace, with no end in sight for this growth in appetite. The growth has spawned a dramatic increase in software development activity which, in turn, has sharpened the focus on the processes used for building software, collectively known as the software process. Although opinions differ on the nature and formality of the software process, there is now general agreement that use of proper processes is extremely important for an organization that seeks to deliver high-quality software and increase its own productivity.

The heightened importance of the software process has created a need for process improvement, which requires methods for process analysis and assessment. One of the most extensive and influential software process improvement and assessment frameworks is the Capability Maturity Model (CMM) for software developed by the Software Engineering Institute (SEI) at Carnegie Mellon University. The CMM categorizes software process maturity into five levels—from level 1 (the lowest) to level 5 (the highest). For each level, the CMM specifies some key process areas (KPAs), which represent the areas on which an organization should focus if it wants to move to a particular level. Each KPA is associated with goals that represent the requirements to be satisfied by the process for that KPA. The KPAs for different maturity levels can be used for assessing the capability of the existing process as well as for identifying the areas that need to be strengthened so as to move the process from a lower level of maturity to a higher level.

The CMM framework is quite general and not prescriptive. Although organizations can implement CMM in different ways, relating the characteristics mentioned in the CMM to real-life practices and processes can prove difficult. This book describes the set of processes used for executing a project at Infosys Technologies Ltd., a large software house headquartered in Bangalore, India. Infosys was formally assessed at CMM level 4 in December 1997 by two SEI-authorized lead assessors.

Rather than just explaining the various technical and management processes employed by Infosys, this book describes the processes as they appear at various stages in the life cycle of a project. Because the life cycle of a project includes both technical and management processes, this approach ensures that most processes affecting a project are explained. This approach is also one to which both practitioners and students can more easily relate. It does leave out the organization-level processes for supporting and managing the process activities. Some aspects of these processes have been described, wherever their inclusion would not break the flow of the book. In addition, an article describing the management of the CMM framework implementation at Infosys is included as Appendix B.

The book includes 15 chapters. Chapter 1 gives a brief overview of the CMM and describes some organization-level support for processes at Infosys. The remaining chapters focus on project execution and are organized into three parts. Part I (Chapters 2 and 3) deals with processes that are executed before the project formally commences. Part II (Chapters 4 through 10) deals with project planning activities. Part III (Chapters 11 through 15) examines project execution and termination. Most chapters focus on some key task in a project and have been kept as independent as possible of the other chapters.

It is not the intent of this book to provide an extensive coverage of literature or detailed explanations of the CMM. The main goal is to describe the processes of an organization that employs the CMM framework. The book also illustrates how simple and known approaches can be combined effectively to have a highly mature overall process. It does not suggest that Infosys's approach is "optimal" or "better than someone else's" or "an ideal implementation of the CMM." Likewise, it does not recommend that these processes be used by others—that decision is left for the readers.

The positive feedback I received on my earlier textbook, *An Integrated Approach to Software Engineering* (Springer Verlag, 1997), which had a case study running through the book, convinced me of one thing: In software engineering, it is invaluable to have "real examples with real outputs" and a "complete example," if possible, when explaining concepts. This book employs the same approach. Most of the examples are "real" in that they have been picked from real projects, and one actual project—the weekly activity report (WAR) project—is used through much of the book to illustrate how different processes interrelate. Although the processes described are used at Infosys, any sensitive numbers (for example, on quality and productivity) included may have been sanitized to maintain the company's confidentiality.

This book should prove useful to all practitioners who are interested in the software process or the CMM framework. It should be immensely helpful to those practitioners who are trying to implement the CMM in their own organizations. To help ISO organizations in their effort to move to CMM, a general study describing possible gaps in an ISO organization with respect to different levels of the CMM has been provided in Appendix A. As the book discusses how projects are executed in a successful organization, it should also be of interest to professionals who are now managing software projects. For instructors and students, it can serve as a supplementary text for a project-oriented course on software engineering, as the book provides a good view of how software is developed in a business environment, along with a case study.

It is perhaps proper to explain my own involvement with Infosys. As Vice President (Quality) at Infosys, I was one of the main architects behind the company's successful transition from ISO to CMM level 4. It should be pointed out that although Infosys supplied all of the material I requested, I take full responsibility for any mistakes, misrepresentations, and inaccuracies that may be present in the book. Such issues are bound to occur when one tries to describe the "essence" of an organization's process manual, along with a case study, in such a compact book. Any deviations in these descriptions from the actual processes of Infosys are entirely my responsibility, as I decided which portions of processes to include and in what manner.

Any comments or queries about the book are welcome and can be sent to me at jalote@iitk.ac.in. For any information regarding Infosys, visit www.itlinfosys.com or send mail to public-relations@itlininfosys.com.

Pankaj Jalote

Acknowledgments

First and foremost, I would like to express my gratitude to Infosys, whose generous cooperation and help made this book possible. After its assessment was over, I proposed this book to the Directors of Infosys. To their credit, despite the risks associated with making the processes public, they agreed to let me use Infosys's documents related to processes in this work. In particular, I am grateful to Mr. K. Dinesh, the Director responsible for quality and productivity, who gave his full backing to the process activities and to this project.

Many others have contributed greatly to making this book become a reality. My sincere thanks to members of the Quality Department at Infosys, in particular Bhashyam and Raghavan, who manage the process activities, and to all of my colleagues who participated in defining the various processes and provided feedback on chapters. They include Meera, Savita, Ramkumar, Nitya, Subbu, Seshan, Varsha, Dr. Bala, Ram Prasad, Saiju, Vasu, and many others. My special thanks to Devarajan, project leader of the WAR project, who helped me with the case study.

I am particularly grateful to Mark Paulk, Bill Curtis, Ron Radice, Karl Wiegers, George Winters, Kim Caputo, and Anita Carleton for reviewing the manuscript and providing valuable feedback that greatly improved the book. My sincere thanks also go to Lakshmi, who provided invaluable help in compiling the material and typesetting.

With fondness, I acknowledge the help provided by my wife Shikha (who is herself an excellent software engineer) in editing and reviewing, and my daughters Sumedha and Sunanda, who had to do without their legitimate share of my time for many, many months.

1

Introduction

Software organizations in the world employ nearly 7 million engineers and generate annual revenue of more than $600 billion, an amount that has been growing at an annual rate exceeding 25% for the past three years. About half of this revenue is generated by the software products industry, which builds general-purpose software products, and roughly half is generated by the software service industry, which builds customized software products for clients. The software industry today is viewed as one of the most promising industry segments and one holding tremendous future potential.

If we consider developing a software product as a project, then the software industry constantly focuses on project execution. Assuming that the average software project consumes about 7 person-years of effort (during which a software product consisting of 20,000 to 80,000 lines of code can be built), then the software industry, with its more than 7 million engineers, executes in excess of 1 million software projects per year! Clearly, executing software projects efficiently is of paramount importance to the software industry as a whole.

The processes used for executing a software project clearly have a major effect on the quality of the software produced and the productivity achieved in the project. Consequently, a need exists to evaluate processes used in an organization for executing software projects and to improve them. The Capability Maturity Model (CMM) for software developed by the Software Engineering Institute (SEI) is a framework that can be used for both purposes [17]. The CMM classifies the maturity of the software processes in five levels—level 1 to level 5, with level 5 being the highest maturity. Of the more than 700 assessments that were performed between 1992 and 1997 and whose assessment results were formally reported to the SEI, only about 20 organizations worldwide have been assessed at level 4 or level 5 [21].

This book describes the processes used for executing software projects at Infosys, a highly successful software company that has been assessed at level 4. Infosys is a large software house employing more than 3,000 people and having offices and development centers in 6 countries and customers in more than 15 countries. Its total revenue has been growing at a rate of 70% annually for the last five years, and its market capitalization increased more than 25-fold from early 1996 to early 1999. By any yardstick, it is a highly successful software company. By describing the processes used for project execution at Infosys, the book describes one possible implementation of the CMM.

No silver bullets are available that will solve all the problems related to software projects [2]. Nevertheless, many proven and promising techniques for all aspects of software development and project management can be used together to handle projects effectively. This book therefore illustrates how known approaches can be effectively combined to create a highly mature, yet simple-to-use overall process.

In this chapter, we introduce the two topics that are central to the book: the CMM and the process infrastructure of Infosys. The rest of the book deals with processes used for project execution at Infosys, their relationship to the CMM, and examples of their use. First, however, we briefly discuss the role of processes in project execution.

1.1 Process-Based Approach for Project Execution

A software development project is one in which a software product to fulfill some needs of a customer should be developed and delivered within a specified cost and time period. In other words, the three main characteristics of a project are its cost, schedule, and quality, where "quality" represents how well the product satisfies the customer. A project is generally initiated when some estimates for these parameters are established.

A project is successful if it meets or exceeds the expectations on all three fronts—cost, schedule, and quality. The software industry can cite many examples of projects that did not succeed. Although the situation has considerably improved over the years, many projects still fail to reach completion within budget, deliver within schedule, or fulfill quality expectations. One anlaysis of project data [18] shows that about one-third of projects have cost and schedule overruns of more than 125%. Examples of projects that are runaways (that is, out of control) have also been documented [5].

Possible reasons for project failures include improper estimation, loose requirements management, weak project management, improper risk management, and poorly engineered solutions, among others. Many of these reasons can be combined in one category called "process failure." That is, a software project often fails because the process followed in the project was not suitable. For example, the major reasons for runaways are unclear objectives, bad planning, new technology, no project management methodology, and insufficient staff [5]. At least three of these five reasons can be considered as "process failure" (the other two—insufficient staff and new technology—can be considered as risks whose management is also a part of the process). For a project to succeed, a key success parameter is the set of processes followed in the project. If suitable process models are chosen for the important tasks in the project, and the chosen processes are executed properly, then the chances of a project succeeding become extremely high.

As having a high productivity can generally reduce cost and minimize the schedule for a project, high quality and productivity (Q&P) can be viewed as the twin aims of a project for delivering a software product. Although processes are needed to satisfy the project goals, they are also essential for satisfying the objectives of an organization that is in the business of executing software projects. Of course, the organization will want all of its projects to succeed. It is larger than its projects, however, and has some desired objectives over and above the twin objectives of a project. First, an organization generally wants predictability. That is, it is not enough that a project have high Q&P; the organization also seeks a predictable Q&P. Without predictability, good estimation is not possible, and building reasonable estimates is essential to any project-oriented business. Second, an organization desires continuous improvement in Q&P.

Q&P of an organization depends on three factors: process, people, and technology. This relationship, which is sometimes called the quality triangle, is depicted in Figure 1.1 [24]. The quality triangle is similar to the process-technology-leadership triangle, also known as the iron triangle [13].

As the process has a major effect on the Q&P delivered by an organization, one way to improve Q&P is to improve the processes used by the organization. In much of this book, as well as in much of the CMM for software, the focus is on the process aspect. (The personal software process proposed by Humphrey concentrates on improving the estimation and software development capability of individual software engineers [9], whereas the People Capability Maturity

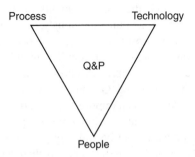

Figure 1.1   The process, people, and technology triangle

Model [22] focuses on improving the human resources in an organization. Many factors that affect the productivity of people are discussed in [4].)

Technically, a process for a task comprises a sequence of steps that should be followed to execute that task. The software process consists of various processes that should be followed to perform different tasks in a project. For an organization, however, the processes are much more than a sequence of steps— they encapsulate the collective experience of that organization. That is, the processes capture past experience in executing projects, enabling the organization to leverage this experience in future projects. Essentially, processes incorporate what the organization has learned about successfully executing projects. By capturing the "recipes" for success in the form of processes, and then following the processes in future projects, an organization ensures continued successes in its projects. The encapsulation of the experience of successful and effective engineers and managers and its dissemination to others allow the benefits of experience to be conferred on even a newcomer in the organization. As a result, processes also play a key role in effectively managing the growth of an organization.

An established approach for improving the processes of an organization is to enhance the processes based on experience gained from successful and failed projects, such that the enhanced processes prevent failures in future and help emulate the successes. If an organization hopes to take software process improvement seriously, a considerable effort must be invested in capturing the experience with processes and plowing it back into the processes for leveraging the experience. Learning and leveraging experience with processes constitute an important aspect of CMM level 3.

Although learning and process improvement are always possible, identifying successes and failures and determining their causes become easier and less subjective if quantitative data are available about the performance of the process on projects. The organization's ability to monitor a project's process and apply proper control to ensure success is also considerably enhanced if the project goals are set in quantitative terms and quantitative information is available about the progress of the project. If quantitative information is available about the process capability, then improvements in the organization's Q&P over time can also be determined unambiguously. This measurement can help quantify the return on the investments made in process improvement by the organization. In general, an organization's ability to effectively plan and manage projects and to manage and improve its process is significantly enhanced if a quantitative approach is employed. Quantitatively managing the process is the focus of level 4 of the CMM and an important aspect of this book.

Many problems must to be faced while improving the process of an organization, and different strategies can be followed to overcome the hurdles that arise along the way. Many of these issues relate to change management (process improvement introduces changes), and many books address the issue of how to handle these problems (for example, [3, 6]). This book focuses primarily on processes, rather than change management issues.

1.2 Capability Maturity Model for Software

Once it is accepted that proper processes are essential for an organization to consistently deliver high quality and have high productivity, a question immediately arises: What are the desirable characteristics of an organization's processes for executing software projects? The next issue is, How can the organization improve the processes for improving the Q&P, and what are the characteristics of the improved process? This area is where process frameworks play an important role.

A process framework specifies some characteristics that the process must have to "qualify" as a process of some maturity. The maturity of a process may be classified in some levels, and a framework may characterize a process in two or more levels. A framework specifies only the characteristics that processes at different levels should have; it does not prescribe any process. Thus different processes can fulfill the requirements of the framework. By specifying characteristics of processes for different levels of maturity, frameworks also provide guidance regarding the improvements needed to move from one maturity level to the other.

Many frameworks are available for software processes, including ISO 9001, CMM, Trillium, SPICE, and BOOTSTRAP. Currently, the two most widely used and most influential models are ISO 9001 [10] and the CMM [17].

ISO 9001 is a general standard for providing service; it has been specifically interpreted for software in ISO 9000-3 [11]. TickIT provides further guidelines on how software organizations should use ISO 9001 [12]. ISO 9001 has 20 clauses that an organization must satisfy to qualify as "ISO certified." The "ISO certified" category does not contain any additional distinctions (further improvement is generally handled through the auditing process). In other words, the ISO 9001 framework includes only two levels. The model is general and considers the working of the entire organization—not just its software projects. More discussion on the ISO model is included in Appendix A. More detailed discussion is given in [16].

The CMM for software is a framework that focuses on processes for software development. It was developed by observing best practices in software organizations as well as non-software organizations. Hence, it reflects the collective process experience and expectations of many companies. It can be used both to evaluate the software process of an organization and to plan process improvements. The foundations of CMM were laid down in [8], and the framework itself is described completely in [17]. We briefly discuss the CMM framework here, based on the descriptions in [17].

1.2.1   Maturity Levels in CMM

One objective of the CMM is to distinguish mature processes from immature or ad hoc processes. In a software organization that has immature software processes, projects are executed without many guidelines, and the outcome of a project depends largely on the capability of the team and the project leader. Consequently, the result is not predictable. On the other hand, in an organization with mature processes, a project is executed by following various processes that the organization has set up for software projects. In this case, the outcome of the project is less dependent on the team capability and more controlled by the processes. It follows, then, that the more mature the processes, the better the control on the projects and the more predictable the results.

The range of results that can be expected in a project when it is executed using the software process of an organization is the *software process capability*. The actual result achieved in a project executed using the software process is the *software process performance* (on that project). Clearly, the process performance depends on the process capability. To improve process performance consistently on projects, the process capability must therefore be enhanced; that is, the process must become more mature.

The path to higher maturity includes some well-defined plateaus that are viewed as *maturity levels* by the CMM. Each maturity level specifies certain characteristics for processes, with higher maturity levels having more advanced characteristics that are found in more mature software processes. Hence, the CMM framework describes the key elements of software processes at different levels of maturity. Consequently, it also specifies the path that a software process follows in moving from immature and ad hoc process to highly mature process. This path includes five maturity levels, as shown in Figure 1.2 [17].

In level 1, an organization executes a project in a manner that the team and project manager see fit. At the defined level (level 3), the processes are used on an ad hoc basis. The repeatable level (level 2) applies to an organization in which project management practices are well established, although organization-wide processes may not exist. At the defined level (level 3) the software processes for the organization have been precisely defined and regularly followed. With organization-wide processes, the organization may learn from different projects and subsequently improve the processes to benefit future projects. At the managed level (level 4), quantitative understanding of the process capability makes it possible to quantitatively predict and control the process performance on a project. Once the foundation of quantitative process management exists, then the process capability can be improved in a controlled manner and the improvement can be evaluated quantitatively. At the optimizing level (level 5), the process improves continuously,

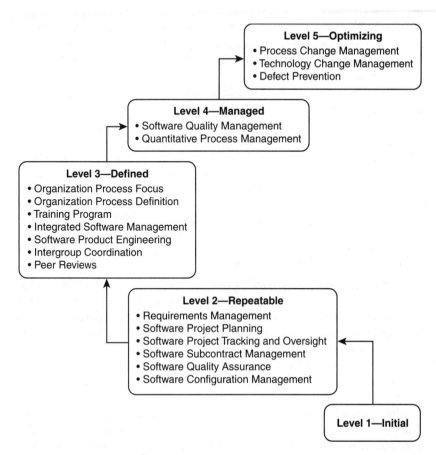

Figure 1.2 Maturity levels in the CMM

with level 4 providing the mechanisms to quantitatively evaluate the effectiveness of process enhacement initiatives.

Several reasons exist for selecting these levels [8]:

- They represent the phases observed in organizations as their processes evolve and mature.
- Each level represents some reasonable process improvement from the previous level.
- The levels provide guidance in defining a set of process improvement areas, once the current level of the organization is determined.

Each maturity level (except level 1) is characterized by some key process areas (KPAs), which specify the areas on which the organization should focus to elevate its processes to that maturity level. The KPAs for the different levels are also shown in Figure 1.2. As can be seen in the figure, most of the KPAs at level 2 focus on project management, whereas the KPAs in level 3 target institutionalization of processes and some additional processes for engineering of software. The KPAs at level 4 revolve around quantitatively managing the process and projects, and the KPAs at level 5 focus on process improvement through defect prevention, technology introduction, and process enhancements.

Maintaining processes at higher levels of maturity is a challenging task requiring commitment from the organization and a proper work culture. Of the 700 assessments that were conducted between 1992 and 1997 and whose assessment results were provided to the SEI, approximately 165 organizations were assessed at level 2, 105 at level 3, 16 at level 4, and 4 at level 5 [21]. That is, of the 700 organizations, only about 20 were at level 4 or 5. The number of high-maturity organizations is growing rapidly, however.

1.2.2 KPAs in Different Levels

The KPAs for a particular level can be considered as the requirements for achieving that maturity level. For an organization to achieve a level, all of the KPAs at that maturity level as well as the KPAs at all lower maturity levels must be satisfied by the processes of that organization. Each KPA specifies some goals that the processes of the organization must meet to satisfy that KPA.

In addition, each KPA specifies a group of activities, called key practices, that can collectively satisfy the goals of that KPA. The key practices are organized into various groups called *commitment to perform, ability to perform, activities performed, measurements and analysis,* and *verifying implementation.* The activities under "commitment to perform" describe the actions that the organization must take to support the particular KPA. "Ability to perform" activities focus on issues like training, resource requirements, and control structures, all of which are important for developing the ability in specific personnel and the organization as a whole to perform activities for that KPA. "Activities performed" describes the actual process activities that are recommended. "Measurements and analysis" targets the measurements that should be done for the activities of the KPA, and "verifying implementation" activities focus on ensuring that the implementation of the processes is verified through independent persons and senior management.

In many senses, the goals for each KPA capture the essence of that KPA. They specify the objectives that the CMM has set for the processes relating to the KPA. Although the goals can be satisfied by an organization performing the key practices, they can also be satisfied by alternative practices that differ from the key practices specified in the CMM. To give an idea about the different KPAs, we briefly discuss here the goals of the different KPAs. These goals are taken from the CMM [17], albeit with some minor changes in the wording of some goals.

Table 1.1 lists the goals for KPAs at level 2. The goals of RM ensure that the requirements are properly documented and the requirement changes are properly managed in the project. Note that the process for analyzing and specifying requirements is not a goal of RM. Goals of SPP ensure that proper planning is done for a project, which includes an estimation and a listing of activities to be performed, and that the plan is documented. Goals of SPTO ensure that, during the project execution, the actual performance of the project is evaluated against the plans and actions are taken when the actual performance deviates from the plans significantly.

SQA focuses on reviews and audits carried out to ensure that proper processes are followed (rather than on quality control activities like testing). Its goals also make sure that quality assurance activities are planned and that proper actions are taken when the project fails to comply with the established standards and processes. Goals of SCM ensure that programs and documents that must be controlled in the project are identified, that changes to them are controlled, and that these activities are properly planned. The SSM KPA is applicable when the organization that is developing software subcontracts some parts of the development effort to another organization. This KPA is usually not applicable to organizations that handle all activities relating to the project themselves.

Table 1.2 details the goals of the KPAs at level 3. The goals of OPF ensure that process definition and improvement activities are executed in a planned manner in the organization, which requires the formation of a group dedicated to process activities. OPD goals require that the processes are defined and documented and that information about the use of the process is collected and is made available to other projects. That is, the KPA ensures that, in addition to having defined processes, the experience of other projects about how to make the best use of the processes becomes available, so a new project can leverage past experience.

The goals of TP ensure that the organization has identified the training needs for the various roles and that project people receive necessary training in a planned manner. The goals of ISM require that the process used for a project be tailored from the standard process; the defined processes are then used for managing the project. The goals of SPE focus on the engineering tasks being performed in the project, with engineering tasks being performed properly and the different work products remaining consistent, even under the face of changes. The IC KPA becomes more of an issue when multiple engineering groups are involved (for example, when a system is being built that may require mechanical, electrical, and software systems). In a general sense, however, it tries to ensure that the interfaces between the different groups that contribute to a project are properly defined and work smoothly. The goals of PR ensure that the peer review activities are properly carried out in a project and that sufficient support for conducting peer reviews and followup activities is provided.

Table 1.1 Goals for KPAs at Level 2 (Repeatable)

KPA	Goals
Requirements Management (RM)	• Software requirements are controlled to establish a baseline for software engineering and management activities. • Software plans, products, and activities are kept consistent with requirements.
Software Project Planning (SPP)	• Estimates are documented for use in planning and tracking the project. • Project activities and commitments are planned and documented. • Affected groups and individuals agree to their commitments related to the project.
Software Project Tracking and Oversight (SPTO)	• Actual results and performances are tracked against the software plans. • Corrective actions are taken and managed to closure when actual results and performance deviate significantly from the software plans. • Affected groups and individuals agree with the changes to commitments.
Software Subcontract Management (SSM)	• The prime contractor and the subcontractor agree to their commitments. • The prime contractor tracks the subcontractor's actual results against its commitments. • The prime contractor and the subcontractor maintain ongoing communication. • The prime contractor tracks the subcontractor's actual performance against its commitments.
Software Quality Assurance (SQA)	• Software quality assurance activities are planned. • Adherence of software products and activities to the applicable standards, procedures, and requirements is verified objectively. • Affected groups and individuals are informed of software quality assurance activities and results. • Noncompliance issues that cannot be resolved within the project are addressed by senior management.
Software Configuration Management (SCM)	• Software configuration management activities are planned. • Selected software work products are identified, controlled, and available. • Changes to identified software work products are controlled. • Affected groups and individuals are informed of the status and content of software baselines.

Table 1.2 Goals of KPAs at Level 3 (Defined)

KPA	Goals
Organization Process Focus (OPF)	• Software process development and improvement activities are coordinated across the organization. • The strengths and weaknesses of the software processes used are identified. • Organization-level process development and improvement activities are planned.
Organization Process Definition (OPD)	• A standard software process for the organization is developed and maintained. • Information related to the use of the organization's standard software process by the software projects is collected, reviewed, and made available.
Training Program (TP)	• Training activities are planned. • Training for developing the skills and knowledge needed to perform software management and technical roles is provided. • Individuals in the software engineering group and software-related groups receive the training necessary to perform their jobs.
Integrated Software Management (ISM)	• The project's defined software process is a tailored version of the organization's standard software process. • The project is planned and managed according to the project's defined software process.
Software Product Engineering (SPE)	• The software engineering tasks are defined, integrated, and consistently performed to produce the software. • Software work products are kept consistent with each other.
Intergroup Coordination (IC)	• All affected groups agree to the customer's requirements. • All groups agree to the commitments between different groups. • The groups identify, track, and resolve intergroup issues.
Peer Reviews (PR)	• Peer review activities are planned. • Defects in the software work products are identified and removed.

Table 1.3 shows the goals for the KPAs at level 4. Level 4 includes only two KPAs: QPM and SQM. The goals of QPM ensure that the capability of the organization process is understood quantitatively and that the process capability is employed to set quantitative goals for a project. Data on actual performance of

Table 1.3   Goals for KPAs at Level 4 (Managed)

KPA	Goals
Quantitative Process Management (QPM)	• The quantitative process management activities are planned. • The process performance of the project's defined software process is controlled quantitatively. • The process capability of the organization's standard software process is known in quantitative terms.
Software Quality Management (SQM)	• The project's software quality management activities are planned. • Measurable goals for software product quality and their priorities are defined. • Actual progress toward achieving the quality goals for the software products is quantified and managed.

the current project are collected and then compared with data on past performance; if significant deviations are observed, proper corrective actions are applied to bring the project back in control. In QPM, it is expected that monitoring and corrective actions will take place on an ongoing basis. The goals of SQM require that the project set quantitative quality goals and have suitable plans for achieving these goals. In this KPA, the actual performance of the project is also measured and compared with the planned progress. Significant deviations "trigger" corrective actions.

The three KPAs at level 5 focus on improving the capability of the process. Goals of these KPAs appear in Table 1.4. The DP KPA requires that the defect

Table 1.4   Goals for KPAs at Level 5 (Optimizing)

KPA	Goals
Defect Prevention (DP)	• Defect prevention activities are planned. • Common causes of defects are sought and identified. • Common causes of defects are prioritized and systematically eliminated.
Technology Change Management (TCM)	• Incorporation of technology changes is planned. • New technologies are evaluated to determine their effects on quality and productivity. • Appropriate new technologies are transferred into normal practice across the organization.
Process Change Management (PCM)	• Continuous process improvement is planned. • Participation in the organization's software process improvement activities is organization-wide. • The organization's standard software process and the project's defined software process are improved continuously.

prevention be done proactively—by systematically analyzing the causes of defects and then eliminating those causes. If defects can be prevented from entering the software, then the effort spent in removing them can be reduced, thereby improving quality and productivity. Similarly, TCM focuses on the proactive introduction of technology in the organization to improve quality and productivity. Goals of PCM require that process improvement take place continuously, in a planned manner, and with the involvement of a large cross-section of the organization. Although not explicitly mentioned in the goals, the fact that level 5 comes after level 4 implies that effects of defect prevention, technology, and process change be measured quantitatively at level 5.

1.2.3 Assessment Method

One goal of standards or frameworks is to provide some consistency in evaluation so that the framework can be used as a basis for comparison with a different organization. Achieving this goal requires that the evaluation of processes with respect to the framework must be standardized such that the outcome of evaluation is independent of the evaluator. Guidelines for assessment have been discussed in [8], and detailed instructions for conducting an assessment appear in the SEI's handbook for assessors [15]. Here we give a brief description of the assessment process, which is based on the author's experience as a member of an assessment team.

The approach that organizations use for their process assessment and improvement is called the CMM-based appraisal for internal process improvement (CBA-IPI). Another form of assessment, called software capability evaluation, usually takes place at the request of someone (typically, a customer) outside the organization being evaluated. The CBA-IPI is intended to help the organization being assessed improve its processes. It therefore evaluates the strengths and weaknesses of the software process in addition to evaluating the satisfaction of the different goals of the different KPAs.

The assessment is performed by an assessment team, which is led by an SEI-authorized lead assessor, and consists of 6 to 10 experienced people from the organization under scrutiny. The team members must be familiar with CMM and processes-related issues and receive assessment training from the lead assessor. During the course of the assessment, the team members collect information about the software process of the organization. There are three main sources of information:

- Maturity questionnaires
- Documentation
- Interviews

A *maturity questionnaire* is an instrument that is used to get some feedback regarding the process being used in the organization [23]. It contains a set of questions for each KPA, most of them based on the key practices under the

KPA. The questions ask whether a practice is being followed (the possible answers to the questions are "yes," "no," "don't know," and "does not apply"). As a first step in assessment, the questionnaire is given to project leaders, their supervisors (middle managers), and some project team members. The answers are then compiled. If the answer to a question is overwhelmingly "yes," then the statement in the question could be treated as an *observation* about that practice. The assessment process requires at least two independent observations from two different sources before confirming that a practice is being followed. Frequently, however, a maturity questionnaire is used as an aid for further exploration during interviews and document examination.

For the assessment, four to six projects are selected. These projects should be representative of the project profile of the organization. Documentation from these projects is made available to the assessment team, and their project leaders are interviewed individually to obtain more observations and seek any necessary clarifications. Besides documents of the selected projects, documents describing the processes are examined for the purpose of making observations.

In addition, groups of technical personnel representing different functions are interviewed. These groups are called functional area representative (FAR) groups. In an assessment, 4 to 6 FAR groups may be interviewed, with each FAR group having 4 to 10 people. Possible FAR groups include the following:

- Project leaders (of projects other than the selected ones)
- Middle managers to whom project leaders report
- Configuration controllers
- Software Engineering Process Group members
- Training personnel
- Developers
- Testers
- Analysts

The interviews attempt to obtain evidence regarding the usage of key practices of the different KPAs. Generally, the maturity questionnaire and the examination of the project documents and the documents regarding the processes and policies will yield some evidence for most key practices. Interviews therefore become a means for clarifying doubts and as additional sources of information. Between the information-gathering sessions, the team consolidates whatever information it has gathered and reaches agreement on which key practices can be considered as satisfied (a key practice is considered as satisfied if two independent information items support it). Agreement requires consensus of the entire team. Figure 1.3 depicts the overall assessment process.

To consolidate the information on a KPA, a coverage sheet is used which lists all requirements for the KPA and provides space for making observations. For consolidation, the assessment team might be organized into multiple mini-teams, with each mini-team handling a few KPAs. After consolidating the available information, the mini-team responsible for a KPA presents the results to the

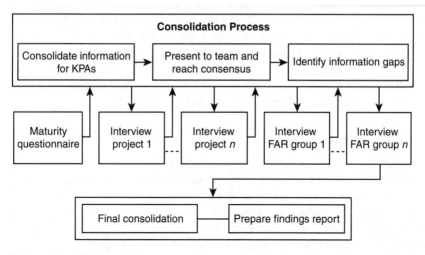

Figure 1.3 The assessment process

entire assessment team. As noted earlier, a key practice is considered as "satisfied" only when all team members agree. If doubts persist, then these "gaps" are identified and clarified during the interview sessions through appropriate questions and requests for documents. As we can see, the information-gathering steps in the process are interleaved with consolidation activity to allow proper assimilation of information. If all key practices are satisfied, then the goals for those KPAs are satisfied. Otherwise, goal satisfaction requires the team to determine whether an alternative practice exists that satisfies the goal. If all goals of a KPA are satisfied, then the KPA is satisfied. An organization is considered to have reached a level if it satisfies all KPAs for that level and for all levels below it.

During consolidation, the strengths and weaknesses for each KPA are noted. In the presentation of the final findings, the goal satisfaction for all KPAs is presented, along with the strengths and weaknesses information. In this manner, the final findings not only report the maturity level of an organization, but also delineate the areas in which improvement is possible. These areas can then be used to plan additional process improvement activities.

1.3 Processes at Infosys

The purpose of this book is to explain the implementation of the CMM framework up to level 4, as done at Infosys. It is therefore important to give some background about Infosys. Processes in an organization evolve within the business context of the organization and are deployed primarily to satisfy some of its business objectives. This section provides a brief background about Infosys and gives a brief overview of how processes are defined and deployed at that company. It also discusses the overall project management process; details of various components of this process make up much of the rest of this book. As will be pointed out during the course of the discussion, some elements of these processes also help satisfy some requirements of the CMM.

1.3.1 Background

Infosys is a software house that has its headquarters in Bangalore, India. Its stated mission is "to be a globally respected corporation that provides best-of-breed software solutions delivered by best-in-class people." It currently employs approximately 3,000 people, with offices and development centers located in more than 18 cities in 6 countries. It was founded in 1981 by a group of seven software professionals with an equity base equivalent to $300. The basic aim of the company was to provide software services to customers all over the world. Today, Infosys has a market capitalization of more than $3.5 billion (based on market rates in April 1999). Its revenue has grown from $9.5 million in 1994 to more than $120 million in 1999. It has customers in more than 15 countries across the world. These customers include major corporations in the world—more than 30 of them being *Fortune* 500 companies—that are engaged in diverse businesses such as banking, retailing, manufacturing, telecommunications, financial services, insurance, and transportation.

As a high rate of growth is a part of the business strategy at Infosys, good processes are critical. Without well-defined and tightly controlled processes at all levels, it would not be possible to absorb the envisaged rate of growth, as a high growth rate also implies the hiring of a large number of software engineers in the organization every year and the execution of an ever-larger number of projects every year. In such a situation, direct control by senior and experienced people is clearly not possible. Instead, the organization must rely on processes to ensure that quality and productivity are maintained and improved, despite the high growth rate. Consequently, processes are defined for most tasks that are performed regularly and process orientation and process improvement have been made part of the work culture.

To provide software services to its clients, the company is organized into strategic business units, with each business unit focusing on a different application domain. Special services are also offered, depending on the market demand—for example, packaged services for the Year 2000 problem and conversion from UNIX to Windows NT. Another service offering is distinguished by the business paradigm it uses—the off-shore development center (OSDC). In the OSDC model, an organization that has a core competency in executing software projects agrees to set up a dedicated development center for a (usually large) client. The personnel in this OSDC execute projects for that client only, providing the client organization with its own dedicated software development facility without any management overhead.

Although the application domains and the clients may differ, from the point of view of project execution, the main services can be divided into three major categories: development, maintenance, and reengineering. In development projects, the basic contract is to develop and deliver new software, which may or may not eventually become part of a larger system. In maintenance projects, the project team takes over the maintenance of some existing software, which may or may not have been developed by Infosys. In reengineering projects, an existing system that uses some languages, databases, operating systems, and so on is reengineered into a system using newer languages, architectures, databases, or operating systems.

The nature of each type of project is different from that of the other types of projects, and different issues exist for all three types of projects. A separate life-cycle process has therefore been defined for each type of project. In this book, we will focus primarily on development projects.

The organization plays an important role in the nature of processes and the way in which processes change. Here we briefly discuss some aspects of Infosys that help in deploying and changing processes and in implementing the CMM framework. Many of these factors provide the organizational support that is critical for any process initiative to succeed.

1. **Senior managers who are software professionals.** All the six director-promoters of the company are software professionals who have executed software projects in the past. As a result, the senior management can appreciate the need for process initiatives, which helps in winning their backing for such initiatives.

2. **Process orientation and adoption of ISO.** A process orientation characterizes the entire organization, and processes are defined and used not only for software projects but also for all important activities being performed in the organization, including human resource management, finance, travel, and so on. The use of these processes is audited in the same manner as the use of processes in projects. Early adoption of ISO (Infosys received its ISO certification in 1993), which looks at all aspects of an organization, helped build and strengthen the process culture.

3. **A strong commitment to measurement and transparency.** Infosys fosters a high degree of transparency in all of its operations. Having such data available makes decisions transparent and less subjective. Hence, the company has a strong desire to measure all important factors (for example, besides external customer surveys, it conducts surveys to measure employee satisfaction and internal customer satisfaction). Due to this orientation, it is easy to introduce metrics programs.

4. **A training program.** Infosys recruits mostly engineers, but only after strict screening through tests and interviews (only about 8% of the applicants are offered jobs). All new recruits go through a rigorous, three-month training program, which also includes mock projects, before they undertake a real project. Besides the training for entry-level engineers, the company provides continuing education and skill-upgrading programs on new technologies, project management, soft skills, team building, and so on. This training is conducted by a full-fledged training department with more than 30 faculty members, about one-third of whom have Ph.D.s. (A training program is a KPA at level 3 of the CMM. As it is not directly in the workflow of a project, it will not be discussed in this book.)

5. **Use of technology.** Not only does the organization develop software, but it also uses technology heavily for its own operations. It employs an integrated system for enterprise management, built via SAP, through which it manages many of the finance, human resource development, project, and personnel activities. Every worker is provided with a personal workstation, and various platforms are available for use. Video and audio conferencing facilities are also available for interacting with customers and geographically separated team members. This technology orientation ensures that Infosys enjoys a continuous drive to use tools and technology to improve the working of the organization.

1.3.2 Process Architecture and Documentation

For an organization, the standard processes followed on a project must be properly specified and documented. This requirement is also part of the Organization Process Definition KPA of CMM level 3. The specification of the process reflects its architecture. A process can be organized in two ways: bottom-up and top-down. In the bottom-up approach, mini-processes are defined for the major phases. In addition, allowable life cycles specify how these mini-processes can be arranged to form a process. In a top-down approach, the process is broken into stages, stages into substages, substages into activities, and so on.

Infosys's processes are organized in a top-down manner. Each process is organized in a four-tier architecture. A process consists of stages or phases, a stage (phase) consists of activities, and each activity could be further broken down into subactivities. A subactivity is usually the smallest schedulable activity in a project. The formal process definition specifies the top three levels only—further details are specified as checklists. IBM Rochester also follows a similar approach for process specification [14]. Figure 1.4 depicts this process architecture.

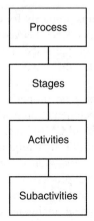

Figure 1.4   Process architecture

Each process definition uses a standard template that reflects this architecture. A process definition generally starts with the process overview and gives the stages for the process, along with references. The definition for each stage generally follows the ETVX (Entry, Task, Verification, and eXit) model [19]. For each stage, the following terms are specified:

1. **Overview:** A brief description of the stage

2. **Participants:** All participants who take part in executing the various activities in the stage

3. **Entry Criteria:** The prerequisites that must be satisfied before this stage can be started

4. **Inputs:** All inputs needed to execute the stage

5. **Activities:** All activities (and sometimes important subactivities) that are performed in this stage

6. **Exit Criteria:** The conditions that the outputs of the stage must satisfy to consider the stage completed

7. **Outputs:** All outputs of the stage

8. **Measurements:** All measurements that must be taken during the execution of the stage

9. **Special Considerations**

10. **References**

With such a specification for each stage, the dependence between stages is explicitly detailed in the form of entry criteria. The order in which the stages appear in the process definition is primarily for documentation convenience; it need not necessarily imply dependence between stages. In this book, for the sake of brevity, we will focus on the stages and activities when specifying a process. The other attributes for the stages will be mentioned only briefly, where needed.

All process definitions must be properly documented so that they are accessible to the users. This documentation is also a requirement of the Organization Process Definition KPA of CMM level 3. At Infosys, the Quality System Documentation (QSD) fulfills this requirement. One volume in QSD describes all engineering processes—that is, processes dealing directly with tasks in executing projects. These processes are divided into two groups: life-cycle processes and management processes. Life-cycle processes include process definitions for development, maintenance, reengineering, and product projects. Management processes contain the different processes related to project management. Table 1.5 lists some of the important processes in this volume.

Some of these processes will be discussed later in the book. For many of the activities in these processes, "guidelines" have been proposed. For some, detailed "checklists" or "work instructions" are given. These guidelines and checklists are specified in a separate volume, which also contains the templates for the various documents that need to be produced in a project, forms that are used for various activities, and standards. Table 1.6 gives some examples of guidelines, checklists, and templates found in this volume.

Table 1.5   Engineering Processes

Life Cycle

- Development process
- Maintenance process
- Reengineering process
- Product development process

Management

- Obtain project process
- Project management process
- Requirements change management process
- Configuration management process
- Product management process
- OSDC management process

Table 1.6   Guidelines, Checklists, and Templates for Selected Activities

Guidelines	Checklists	Templates/Forms
• Effort and schedule estimation guidelines	• Requirements analysis estimation guidelines	• Requirements specification document
• Group review procedure	• High-level design procedure checklist	• Functional design document
• Process tailoring guidelines	• Build checklist	• Unit test plan document
• Defect estimation and monitoring guidelines	• Unit test and system test plan checklist	• Acceptance test plan document
• Guidelines for measurements and data analysis	• Configuration measurements checklist	• Project management plan
	• Status report checklist	• Configuration management plan
• Risk management guidelines	• Requirements review checklist	• Milestone analysis report
• Guidelines for requirement traceability	• Functional design review checklist	• Status report
• Defect prevention guidelines	• Code review checklist	• Process definition template

Most processes are driven by policies that are laid down by Infosys. The document that contains the policies for various tasks is called the Quality Manual. It lists the various high-level tasks performed in a project and the policies that the processes for these tasks must support. Policies are important in CMM—for many KPAs, the CMM requires the existence of documented policies. Why are documented policies required? Process definitions work in a business context, and processes aim to achieve some business objective. What the business objectives require from processes are stated as policies, which the processes must support. In other words, policies state some high-level guidelines or objectives that must be achieved through the processes. They can also be viewed as abstraction of the processes that provides visibility into processes to the senior management and gets commitment toward processes from them.

Policies are high-level, general statements of the organization's intent. Some examples follow:

"The process capability shall be quantitatively analyzed periodically and a new capability baseline issued"

"Data and artifacts regarding usage of process and tools on projects shall be collected from projects and made available for process capability analysis and process improvement efforts, and for aiding other projects in process implementation and tool selection"

"Significant deviations, beyond organizational norms, in the project's actual performance with respect to its plans, shall be reviewed by the business manager and shall trigger corrective actions"

One policy states that "metrics data shall not be used for performance appraisals," reinforcing a necessary foundation for all measurement systems for software. This assurance is particularly important for a level 4 organization, as it is committed to, and places a heavy reliance on, reliable data collection from projects.

Thus the process infrastructure consists of policies, processes, and documents such as guidelines and checklists. Policies are statements at the highest level of abstraction that are implemented by processes. The processes themselves are supported by guidelines, checklists, templates, and other documents that provide further details about steps or activities in the process. Figure 1.5 illustrates this structure.

Within the process support infrastructure, the process database and the process capability baseline play key roles in project planning. These two components provide metrics and other information about the use of processes on projects. We will discuss them in more detail in Chapter 5.

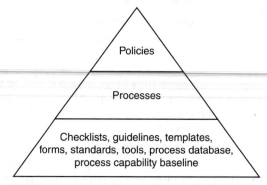

Figure 1.5   Process infrastructure

1.3.3   SEPG and Software Process Improvement Planning

Many factors are essential if process improvement initiatives are to succeed in an organization. Some of these factors have been discussed elsewhere [6, 8]. One success factor, which is also a key practice of the Organization Process Focus KPA of CMM level 3, is the formation of a core group that takes responsibility for coordinating the process activities in the organization. This core group is commonly called the Software Engineering Process Group (SEPG) [20]. At Infosys, the SEPG consists of quality professionals whose sole duty is monitoring and improving the processes for improving the Q&P in the organization. It includes approximately 1.5% of the company's software engineers.

Process definition and enhancement are key activities of any SEPG. To increase the involvement of other people and to improve the acceptability of processes, SEPG rarely defines a process by itself. Instead, whenever a new process must be defined or a major enhancement implemented, a task force of the users of the processes (that is, personnel from projects), and at least one SEPG member is created. This task force defines the process, pilots it (as discussed later in this chapter), and then hands the process over to the SEPG for deployment. The SEPG then maintains the process. This approach also reduces the need for full-time personnel to staff the SEPG.

As "processes won't stick by themselves" [8], a conscious effort must be made after the processes are defined to ensure that the processes are implemented and become "standard practice." For this reason, besides offering training on processes, an SEPG member is associated with a project as a quality advisor. The quality advisor provides assistance in defining and following processes, ensures that the processes are followed, aids in analyzing the data, and provides specific training on some aspects of processes, if needed. This job is a well-defined and structured activity for which sets of tasks that the advisor must execute at different stages of the project have been clearly specified. A quality advisor typically spends a few hours each week on one project. To involve other people in process activities, as well as to reduce the load on SEPG members, software engineers also serve as quality advisors for projects other than their own, after getting the required training from the SEPG. The feedback collected from the projects shows that the quality advisor plays a very helpful and effective role. The tasks of the quality advisor also help in satisfying some requirements of the Software Quality Assurance KPA of CMM level 2.

In addition, one senior SEPG person is assigned as group leader to look after the process activities of a business unit. The quality advisors working with projects in that business unit report to the group leader, rather than to the project leader. In this way, the quality advisor provides an independent channel for reporting on process-related issues. Besides planning and monitoring the quality advisory work, the group leader handles overall metrics and other analysis for the entire unit; he or she also undertakes process improvements for the unit, presenting the results to the business unit head. With this approach for process deployment, the SEPG structure mimics the organization structure. This relationship enhances collaboration between the business units and the SEPG.

Overall, the major tasks of the SEPG focus on process management (definition, analysis, modification, and so on), training, process deployment, and audits. Figure 1.6 provides distribution indicating where the SEPG spends its effort. The "miscellaneous" category includes activities such as consulting, internal SEPG training, attending conferences and courses, self-study, travel, leave, internal meetings, and presentations to customers.

If we omit the miscellaneous activities in Figure 1.6, the process management and process implementation tasks consume most of the effort of the SEPG. If training and audits are also considered as aspects of deploying

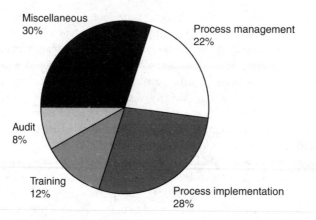

Figure 1.6 Effort distribution of SEPG

processes on projects, then almost half of the SEPG effort goes toward imple-menting processes. This fact is worth noting, because process definition, mod-eling, and analysis are often treated as the SEPG's main task. Although they do form the backbone of the SEPG activities, the deployment of processes is actu-ally the most costly step. Unless proper structures exist for process deployment and sufficient attention is given to this task, the defined processes are likely to stay on paper only. Translating the processes from paper to practice requires considerable effort.

The process management effort is largely spent in process improvement activities, as new processes are defined only infrequently. The head of the SEPG maintains a process improvement plan, which contains the initiatives to be taken in the near future. Planned analysis and improvement of processes are expected by the Organization Process Focus KPA of CMM level 3. The initia-tives in the process improvement plan are mostly based on information from two sources: suggestions for improvements from users of the processes and oth-ers, and strategic planning done by the SEPG.

Any person in the organization, including quality advisors and other SEPG members, can suggest process improvements. An improvement suggestion is evaluated and, if considered useful, might be incorporated directly in the next release of the process. Alternatively, a task force might be set up to develop the suggestion further. In such a case, the idea becomes an initiative in the improve-ment plan that is maintained by the SEPG.

Strategic planning represents a major source of process improvement ini-tiatives. A strategic plan is obtained from the business objectives and goals of the organization. For example, when Infosys adopted the CMM framework, its strategic plan contained the process initiatives that had to be taken to implement the framework. These initatives were identified by doing a "gap analysis" for the organization processes with respect to the framework and then deciding which enhancements were needed to make the process compliant with the framework. Only then were task forces formed to actually create or upgrade the processes. Appendix B discusses this issue further.

Strategic planning is also driven by quantitative analysis of metrics data and the organization's goals for improvement. If the organization identifies some goal for improvement, or if the metrics data suggest that room for improvement exists in some area, then an improvement target is set. Process initiatives are then determined that will help achieve the target. For example, one year the organization's goal was to achieve a 10% improvement in quality and productivity in the next year. This goal was established based on business needs and trends in the industry, and the SEPG was given the responsibility for improving the processes to achieve this goal. First, using existing quality and productivity data (obtained from the process capability baseline and process database), the target productivity and quality levels were decided. Next, metrics data were analyzed to determine potential areas of improvement, for which improvement initiatives were devised. In this case, the basic strategy to achieve the objective involved two steps:

1. Increase defect removal rates at early stages.
2. Reduce defect injection rates through defect prevention and usage of tools.

In terms of increasing the defect removal rates, an examination of the current defect removal rates determined that the following should be achieved:

- Increase the defect detection rate of design review and specification review by 3% to 5%.
- Increase the defect removal rate of code walkthrough and unit testing by about 5%.

If these goals could be achieved, then the defects found in the system testing would decline, which would in turn reduce the main testing effort and thereby increase the productivity. Furthermore, it would reduce the number of defects delivered and thereby increase the software quality. Different approaches for achieving these goals by projects were then identified. For reducing the defect injection rate, it was decided that an across-the-board reduction of 5% in defect introduction for all phases should be targeted. Upgrading of checklists and usage of tools were considered as the possible implementation strategies.

The SEPG monitors the execution and progress of the process improvement. Sometimes, a steering team might be formed to monitor the progress.

1.3.4 Senior Management Involvement

Senior management involvement and commitment to processes are also institutionalized at Infosys. Commitment from, and visibility to, the senior management regarding the process activities are expected by the Organization Process

Focus KPA of CMM level 3. As mentioned earlier, the policy direction for processes is set in the Quality Manual document, which is approved by Infosys's CEO. In addition, the SEPG is under the direct supervision of a director, and the group reports and discusses its monthly performance indicators to him. These indicators reflect the performance of the SEPG in quantitative terms. A total of about a dozen performance indicators are reported, including the following:

- Number of projects that have quality advisors associated with them
- Number of project closure analyses done
- Number of audits done and summary of their outcome
- Summary of training activities conducted by the SEPG
- Number and summary of internal assessments done
- Number and summary of process changes done

Furthermore, the SEPG reports a summary of process activities and results of metrics analysis on a quarterly basis to the management council, the highest governing body, which contains all directors and business unit heads. This report generally includes an analysis of customer complaints, an analysis of noncompliance with processes in projects (and other departments), trends in quality, productivity, and schedule slippage for different category of projects, and a summary of process improvement initiatives. It provides a clear and regular indication of what is happening on the process front in the organization. The management council also approves all major proposals for process change, sets the improvement goals for the organization, and sorts out any unresolved issues for the SEPG that need senior management intervention. As discussed earlier, a metrics analysis for each business unit is also done quarterly, the results of which are discussed with the business unit head.

This system of reporting to the director, business unit head, and management council has undergone a substantial change over the years. Before overall data collection and analysis steps were in place, the reports to senior management essentially contained a summary of completed activities. As the metrics program became institutionalized, these reports changed from primarily a summary of activities to a summary of metrics data analysis. Now senior management has a clear view, in quantitative terms, of the effects of process initiatives and improvements in the organization's quality and productivity. The need for quantitative visibility into some key parameters by senior management was a key motivation for adopting the CMM framework and for implementing a comprehensive metrics program.

In addition to this regular interaction, senior management members are also roped in for special initiatives. For example, when the CMM level 4 initiative began, a steering team was formed from the most senior personnel and headed by the CEO. The SEPG and all working groups reported every month to this steering team. All issues facing the initiative were also resolved in the steering team meetings, which frequently lasted half a day. Appendix B discusses this effort in greater depth.

1.3.5   Process Life Cycle

Although we will look at different processes throughout the book, let us briefly discuss the process of defining and managing the processes themselves. This meta-process specifies how processes are defined and maintained. Most mature software organizations will perform this activity. It is also expected by the Organization Process Definition KPA of CMM level 3. As this process does not directly affect the execution of a project, it does not show up in the set of processes used while executing a project.

Process improvement is not a one-time-only activity, but rather a continuous process. Different models for implementing process improvements exist—for example, the quality improvement paradigm [1], the IDEAL model of SEI [6, 17], and the spiral model [9]. All of these models are based on Deming's PDCA (Plan-Do-Check-Act) cycle. Infosys uses a simpler model for process management, which also is a derivative of the PDCA cycle. The general life cycle of a process at Infosys is shown in Figure 1.7.

As can be seen in Figure 1.7, a process is initially defined. It is then implemented in the organization. In this phase, the usage of the process becomes institutionalized. Once the process is implemented, it may be changed, and the changed process may again need to be implemented. This cycle turns process improvement into a continuous process. As Figure 1.7 shows, this life cycle has three major stages: process definition, process implementation and deployment, and process analysis and change.

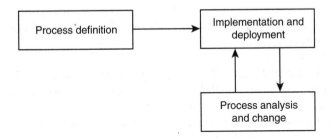

Figure 1.7   Process life cycle

Process Definition.   A process is defined for a task that transforms some inputs to outputs. The goal is to specify a process that will perform the task in an "optimal" manner. Generally, for any task for which a process might be defined (that is, where the task is not straightforward or trivial), a divide-and-conquer approach will perform it effectively. This strategy results in a process being defined as a set of stages, with each stage being a set of activities, as discussed earlier.

Generally, a new process is defined when existing processes are inadequate for a class of projects. Initially, for such a project, the process that most closely matches the needs of the project is modified suitably. When more such projects are executed and it is felt that this approach is inefficient and might lead to sub-optimal solutions, a new process is defined for that class of projects. The task of defining a process consists of the following activities:

> Initiate process definition
>> Create a draft sketch of the process
>> Obtain authorization from senior management
> Define process
>> Identify life-cycle stages
>> Identify activities to a sufficient level of granularity
>> Identify inputs and outputs
>> Identify entry and exit criteria
>> Identify measurements, participants, and references
>> Write overview
>> Establish cross-reference to ISO and CMM, if necessary
> Define tailoring guidelines
> Review with users and senior management
> Generate process definition following organization standards

The main participants in this stage are the SEPG members, the members of the task force, process users, and senior management. The entry criteria state that the new process (or the process update) that needs to be defined has been identified, and the exit criteria state that the process definition in the required format is available and has been reviewed. The effort spent in this process definition phase is logged.

Process Implementation.   Process implementation includes those activities that must be carried out to implement new processes or to implement changes to an existing process, across the organization. Changes to a process are classified as either minor or major. In the case of minor process changes, the process definition and proposed changes are reviewed, and a notification is sent to all users. Some orientation may be provided to the users, if needed. In contrast, the implementation of major changes resembles the implementation of a new process. That is, it requires a properly planned piloting of the process before it is released for organization-wide implementation.

Before the process is "launched," it is introduced to the organization's senior and middle management and to some potential users. This step helps win management's backing and commitment, and it creates an understanding among both them and the users about the significance and need for change. It also helps obtain commitments from the users for piloting and implementation.

Piloting starts with the preparation of a plan for the pilot, which includes setting the objectives of the pilot, project selection criteria, mechanisms for evaluating the process, and so on. Volunteer projects satisfying the selection criteria are then identified, and the process is executed on these projects. At the end of the pilot, a post-pilot analysis is performed, which includes gathering users' feedback on the process. This information is then used to update the process, if needed. If the pilot is considered successful, the process may be released to the organization through formal release notes and procedures (which entails sending some approved copies to some senior management, making the processes available on the intranet, announcing the release, and so on). Major activities in this phase of the process management process are as follows:

> Launch the process
> Pilot the process
>> Plan for piloting
>> Identify pilot projects
>> Define data collection and analysis plan for the pilot
>> Provide orientation to pilot project teams
>> Monitor pilot
>> Collect data, feedback, issues, and other information
>> Perform post-pilot analysis
>> Close pilot
> Update draft process definition, if needed
> Baseline updated process definitions
> Release formally
> Conduct training
> Deploy the process organization-wide

After a process has been piloted and released, training on its use is conducted to aid its implementation across the organization. Although training is necessary for institutionalization of processes, however, it is not sufficient. With software projects, the processes have to be executed by people. Compliance with processes therefore becomes difficult to achieve, particularly given that the processes are not static. To ensure that processes are properly deployed, some model is needed to aid deployment. As noted earlier, Infosys handles this issue by attaching an SEPG member—the quality advisor—to the project. This advisor does not directly take part in the project activities, but helps the project along by defining the necessary processes and following them. The advisor also monitors whether the standard processes of the organization are being followed properly.

The participants in this phase are SEPG, senior management, process users, and pilot projects. The input is the draft process definition, and the outputs consist of the final process definition, results of piloting, training material, and feedback. The exit criterion is that the process has been released and training has been imparted. During this stage, the effort spent is measured, along with the feedback from pilots and training feedback.

Process Analysis and Change. Process analysis and change includes those activities which are carried out to identify a need for changes to existing processes and to handle the change request. Such changes are primarily driven by the desire to improve the process. They may be triggered by tool changes, introduction of new methods, lacunae in existing processes, data analyses, feedback from internal and external audits and assessments, user requests for changes, implementation of models like ISO and CMM, feedback obtained from projects, and so on. An important source of change is the metrics analysis done for each project and the process capability analysis done on the data from multiple projects. Regular analysis of data helps identify areas for improvement.

A process change request is made by filling out the modification request form. Anyone in the organization can submit a change request through this form. Changes that have little or no effect on current project activities constitute minor process changes. Changes that have a dramatic effect on the current project activities constitute major process changes and need senior management review and authorization. Minor changes are accumulated, and every six months (or more frequently) they are analyzed to determine their suitability for incorporation in the processes. The approved changes are then weaved into the process definitions, and new processes are released. Major change requests form process improvement initiatives, the implementation of which has been discussed earlier.

The input to this stage consists of the change requests, and the main output is the changed process. The entry criterion states that there are enough change requests or it is time for the next release of the processes. The number of change requests incorporated is the main measurement, a summary of which is reported to the senior management, as discussed earlier.

1.3.6 Project Management Process

An engineering project has two important dimensions: one dealing with the engineering activities that must be performed to build whatever the project aims to accomplish, and the other dealing with the project management. Despite the presence of adequate technical competence and inputs to properly perform the engineering tasks, a project may nevertheless fail due to poor project management. Project management is an integral part of executing a project and must be properly done to successfully complete a project. In a software project, where the engineering activities are executed by people and can be viewed as processes, the entire project execution can be considered as a process that is followed to build the software. Effectively managing this process, which can include hundreds of tasks with various interdependencies, becomes extremely important for success. The set of activities needed to manage the process for a project is specified in the project management process. The project management process is fairly standard, having three main stages:

- Project planning
- Project execution
- Project closure

The *project planning* stage involves reviewing contractual commitments and creating a plan to meet those commitments. Creating a project plan involves defining a life-cycle process to be followed in the project, estimating the effort and schedule for the project, and preparing a detailed schedule for tasks to be performed. It also includes planning for quality and configuration management, as well as doing risk management planning for the project. The major activities in this phase of the process are as follows:

> Become familiar with the project
> Create a project plan and schedule
>> Define project objectives
>> Plan for human resources
>> Define project organization
>> Identify a suitable standard process for project execution
>> Tailor the standard process to meet project requirements
>> Identify the methods, tools, templates, and standards to be used
>> Identify risks and define plans to mitigate them
>> Estimate effort
>> Define project milestones
>> Create a schedule for the project
>> Define a quality plan
>> Define a measurement plan for the project
>> Define a training plan for the project
>> Define project-tracking procedures
>> Define assumptions made in project planning
> Perform group review for the project plan and schedule
> Obtain authorization from senior management
> Define and review the CM plan
> Provide orientation to the project team

The participants in this phase are the project leader (who is responsible for developing the project plan), the customer, an SEPG representative, and the business manager for the project. The entry criterion is that the contract or project authorization is available. The main inputs are the proposal or the contract plus the process capability baseline and the process database. The exit criterion is that the project plan has been defined and group reviewed. The main outputs consist of the plan documents and review records. The effort spent and the defects found during the review are the main measurements for this phase.

The *project execution* phase involves executing the project plan and making corrections whenever the project goes outside the path laid down in the project plan. In other words, it involves tracking and controlling the implementation of the project process. This phase is the longest in the project management process, incorporating many periodic tasks, such as monitoring project status and quality and taking corrective steps, if necessary. The main activities in this phase are as follows:

> Track project status
> Review project status with senior management
> Manage requirement changes
> Monitor compliance to defined project process
> Conduct milestone reviews

The participants in this stage are the same as the participants in the previous stage, with the addition of the project team. The entry criterion is that the project plan is complete and approved. The main inputs consist of the project plan and project-related documents such as a contract, request for proposal, software requirements, and so on. The exit criterion is that all work products delivered are accepted by the customer. The outputs are plan documents, review records, status reports, and similar documents. The effort spent in this stage is the main measurement.

The last stage of the project management process, *project closure,* involves a systematic wind-up of the project after customer acceptance. The main goal here is to learn from the experience so that the organization process can be improved. Post-project data analysis constitutes the main activity in this stage, with metrics analysis being performed, process assets being collected for future use, and lessons learned being recorded. The participants are the project leader, the project team, the quality advisor for the project, and the business manager. The main inputs consist of the metrics data collected during the project, the record of customer complaints, and project plans. The entry criterion states that the customer has accepted the work products. The exit criterion is that a post-project meeting has been conducted. The outputs are the project closure report and the process assets collected from this project.

In the remainder of this book, we will discuss various elements of the management process. Part I describes some activities that can be considered as part of project initiation. Part II includes separate chapters for some planning activities, such as process definition and tailoring, risk management, effort and schedule estimation, quality planning, and CM planning. The other tasks in the planning phase (such as human resource planning, project organization, tools to be used, project tracking procedures, and so on) are discussed briefly in Chapter 9. Part III includes chapters that focus on life-cycle execution, peer reviews, project monitoring and controlling, monitoring compliance, and project closure.

1.4 Summary

This chapter briefly introduced the two topics that are central to this book—the Capability Maturity Model of the SEI, and processes at Infosys. The CMM for software specifies five maturity levels, with each level being characterized by some key process areas. For each KPA, a few goals that need to be satisfied are given, along with a list of key practices that can be used to satisfy these goals. To ensure that the evaluation of process maturity is uniform across different organizations, the SEI has also specified the process for maturity assessment.

Infosys is a highly successful software house with headquarters in Bangalore, India, whose revenues have been growing at an annual rate of more than 70% for the last five years. It employs in excess of 3,000 people, has customers in 15 countries, and receives more than three-fourths of its revenues from customers for which it has executed projects in the past. To manage its huge growth, and to ensure a high degree of customer satisfaction, Infosys is committed to a process-based approach to organization management and project execution. This ISO-certified organization has been assessed at level 4 of the CMM.

To aid proper process deployment and improvement, a well-defined process management scheme deals with process definition, deployment, and analysis. The Software Engineering Process Group manages most of the process activities, with the help and involvement of others. The SEPG also provides assistance to projects to ensure the proper deployment of processes in them. Senior management sponsors the process activities and sets the goals for improvement. The SEPG reports regularly to senior management on trends in quality and productivity and other process-related information.

The overall project management process was also briefly discussed. It consists of three stages: planning, execution, and closure. Planning entails all activities that must be completed before starting the execution of the project. The execution phase focuses on monitoring and controlling the execution. The last phase ensures that lessons learned in the project can be properly captured for future use. In the rest of the book, different activities of the project management process are discussed in greater detail.

References

[1] V. R. Basili and H. D. Rombach. The experience factory. In: *The Encyclopedia of Software Engineering.* John Wiley and Sons, 1994.

[2] F. Brooks. No silver bullets—essence and accidents of software engineering. *IEEE Computer,* pp. 10–18, April 1987.

[3] K. Caputo. *CMM Implementation Guide: Choreographing Software Process Improvement.* Addison-Wesley, 1998.

[4] T. DeMarco and T. Lister. *Peopleware—Productive Projects and Teams.* Dorset House Publishing, 1987.

[5] R. L. Glass. *Software Runaways, Lessons Learned from Massive Software Project Failures.* Prentice Hall PTR, 1998.

[6] R. Grady. *Successful Software Process Improvement.* Prentice Hall PTR, 1997.

[7] J. Gremba and C. Myers. *The IDEAL model: A practical guide for improvement.* http://www.sei.cmu.edu/ideal/ideal.bridge.html.

[8] W. Humphrey. *Managing the Software Process.* Addison-Wesley, 1989.

[9] W. Humphrey. *A Discipline for Software Engineering.* Addison-Wesley, 1995.

[10] International Standards Organization. *ISO 9001, Quality Systems—Model for Quality Assurance in Design/Development, Production, Installation, and Services.* 1987.

[11] International Standards Organization. *ISO 9000-3, Guidelines for the Application of ISO9001 to the Development, Supply and Maintenance of Software.* 1991.

[12] U.K. Dept. of Trade and Industry and British Computer Society. *TickIT: A Guide to Software Quality Management System Construction and Certification Using EN29001.* 1992.

[13] C. Kaplan, R. Clark, and V. Tang. *Secrets of Software Quality.* McGraw Hill, 1995.

[14] S. H. Kan. *Metrics and Models in Software Quality Engineering.* Addison-Wesley, 1995.

[15] S. Masters. *CMM Based Appraisal for Internal Process Improvement (CBA-IPI): Method Description.* Technical Report, Software Engineering Institute, CMU/SEI-96-TR-007, 1996.

[16] O. Oskarsson and R. L. Glass. *An ISO 9000 Approach to Building Quality Software.* Prentice Hall PTR, 1996.

[17] M. Paulk, et al. *The Capability Maturity Model for Software: Guidelines for Improving the Software Process.* Addison-Wesley, 1995.

[18] L. H. Putnam and W. Myers. *Industrial Strength Software—Effective Management Using Measurement.* IEEE Computer Society Press, 1997.

[19] R. A. Radice, et al. A programming process architecture. *IBM Systems Journal,* 24 (2), 1985.

[20] Software Engineering Institute. *Software Engineering Process Group Guide.* Technical Report, CMU/SEI-90-TR-24.

[21] Software Engineering Institute. Maturity profile report, http://www.sei.cmu.edu/sema/profile.html.3.download.html.

[22] *People Capability Maturity Model (P-CMM),* http://www.sei.cmu.edu/cmm-p/.

[23] Software Engineering Institute. *Maturity Questionnaire.* Special Report. CMU/ SEI-94-SR-7.

[24] Software Engineering Institute. *CMM Based Appraisal for Internal Process Improvement (CBA IPI),* Team Training Material, 1996.

PART I

Project Initiation

2

Proposals and Contracts

In the software services business, vendors provide software services (such as developing or maintaining software) to customers who want these services. Infosys is a vendor organization that provides services to customers across the world. Whenever a vendor is to develop some software for a customer, a clear understanding is needed between the two parties for transacting this business. In a business setup, usually all understandings between parties taking part in a transaction are formalized in a contract that forms the basis of the transaction and has legal implications (that is, it can be used in a court of law).

Frequently the contract contains general terms and conditions, and the specific terms for a particular project for providing some software service might be specified in a proposal for that project. Generally, a vendor proceeds with the project only when the proposal has been accepted and the contract signed. (If the customer and the vendor have good understanding and confidence in each other, the actual work might commence, based on some oral, electronic, or other informal "go-ahead" signal, with the formal contract signed later.)

Many issues have to be handled in a contract and a proposal, including legal concerns, commercial arrangements, and intellectual property rights. These two documents form the starting point of a business transaction or relationship. Contracts and proposals usually are outside the scope of software engineering, although they do set the context in which a software project is executed. This chapter gives a brief overview of the contents of proposals and contracts and the processes that take place before the project activity commences. Although these do not directly implement any KPAs—except some aspects of the Requirements Management KPA—a clearly agreed-on contract and proposal help immensely in building a good working relationship between the customer and the vendor. This, in turn, impacts project execution.

2.1 Customer and Vendor Interaction

One needs first to understand how an organization becomes a customer for a software vendor. The first step for the customer organization that wants some software services is to get in touch with the vendor. This contact is initiated either by the customer organization itself or by the sales staff of the vendor. The customer, through its own information network, finds out about various vendors and then contacts the most promising ones. Alternatively, the sales personnel of the vendor, through their information network, might establish contact with the customer.

After the initial contact is established, the customer usually requests information from the vendor about itself. This interaction is generally called request for information (RFI). The information sought might include the strength of the vendor's organization, educational background of employees, skill set and experience level of employees, past projects done, current and past customers or references, computing infrastructure, or information about processes used for executing projects.

Based on the information, the customer might short-list some vendors and possibly visit them. These organizations are the vendors with which the customer is willing to do business. Until the short-listing is done, no business transaction or commitment for business has taken place. After the customer has short-listed some vendors, the interaction becomes more specific. Depending on the customer's needs and the vendor organization, different models are used. The following briefly discusses some of the commonly used models at Infosys.

If a single project is the goal, the customer typically sends a request for proposal (RFP), along with a sample contract illustrating the type of clauses to be included in the contract. The RFP specifies the scope of the project. The customer might send the RFP to multiple vendors.

In response to an RFP, the vendor prepares and sends a proposal. Here, there are multiple models. First is the fixed-price model, in which the vendor analyzes the RFP, roughly estimates the effort and schedule, and—based on the estimate—gives the price (using some manpower rate) for executing the project. This price is fixed in the sense that, unless the requirements change, the customer will give only the agreed price to the vendor. If the effort estimates are lower than the actual effort, the vendor has to bear the cost of the extra effort; if the effort estimate is higher (which is rarer), the vendor effectively gets a higher profit margin.

The fixed-price model is used for making a proposal only if the requirements have a sufficient amount of detail and are precisely stated. (This situation might be the case if the customer has already completed a requirements analysis.) If the details are not sufficient to make a reasonably accurate proposal, the project is viewed as consisting of two parts—the first one for doing the detailed requirements analysis, and the second one for developing the software. In the first part of the proposal, the time and materials (T&M) model is used, in which the vendor agrees to provide one or more analysts at some agreed-on per person-month cost to the customer, without any hard estimate of how much effort it will take to do the analysis. That is, the customer agrees to pay the vendor for the first part of the project on the basis of actual effort spent by the analysts. This part ends with the analysts delivering to the customer the requirements specification document.

The proposal for the second part, which includes the detailed cost estimate, is given after the first part is over. A general rate for manpower might be agreed on at the start. When the first part is over and detailed requirements are available, a fixed-price bid is given for the development part. The vendors for the first and second parts might be different.

Besides these two models, there is a third model, which is doing the whole project on a T&M basis. In other words, the customer agrees to rates for payment and then pays based on the actual effort expended. This model is usually adopted when the customer is not very clear on the requirements or expects a continuous stream of projects, many of them small. In this context, it makes little sense to go through the RFP–proposal cycle, so a full T&M model is adopted. This model is also used for maintenance projects where a stream of requests—bug fixes or enhancements—keep coming and have to be serviced. A variation is to agree on a rate for per-unit work (for example, the rate per line of code in a reengineering or Year 2000 project). In this case, the actual payment by the customer is determined by the rate and the size of the work request.

A customer that is interested in a long-term relationship, getting many projects done in the future, might enter into a general service agreement. This agreement, besides containing various contract clauses, specifies the rate for payment. In other words, it specifies what the customer will pay to the vendor for each person-month of effort put by the vendor on the customer's projects. After this rate is agreed on, a work request is sent, usually informally, the purpose of which is similar to the RFP. Based on this work request, effort estimates are done and sent to the customer. After accepting the estimates, the client sends a *work order* or *purchase order,* essentially accepting the estimates and agreeing to pay for this work. The work then commences.

The various models are shown in the event sequence diagram shown in Figure 2.1. They are simplified event traces for the various approaches. In reality, depending on the situation, some activities might be done in parallel or some extra steps might be added. For example, it is common to conduct the contract preparation in parallel with the project work to avoid delaying the work. Similarly, the multiple-project approach shows work orders coming sequentially, although in reality many of them might come together and be serviced in parallel. Also, there might be protracted negotiations for the terms of the proposal and the contract; these scenarios are not shown here. The diagram represents project-oriented interaction with the customer. The off-shore development center (OSDC) model, mentioned in the Chapter 1, is not modeled here.

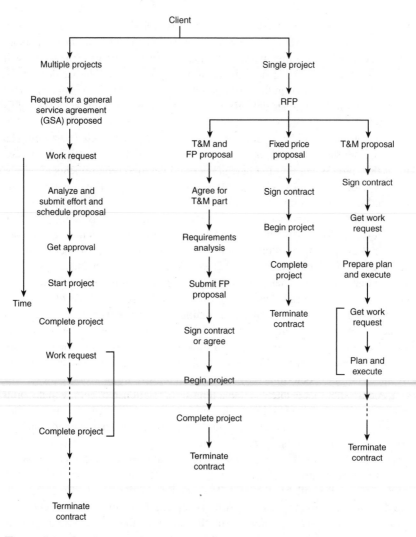

Figure 2.1   Customer and vendor interaction

2.2 The Proposal

As we have seen, the vendor might need to give a proposal to a potential customer. This section briefly discusses the main contents of a proposal. A proposal has two parts: technical and commercial, with the technical part basically
describing issues relating to project execution. Its main sections follow.

Technical description: Describes the requirements of the projects or refers to an RFP or requirements document. Also describes the methodology and tools that might be used and the vendor's experience with the methodology, tools, problem domain, technology, and so on.

Assumptions: All assumptions made while making the technical proposal are enumerated here. These assumptions frequently form the basis of contention between the customer and the vendor, and hence it is better to specify them explicitly. It is possible to eliminate some assumptions by resolving them and then placing the agreement in the relevant sections of the proposal.

Proposed solution: Specifies an approach for the solution. Can discuss an approach for planning, the strategy for carrying out the project, architecture, team structure, and so on.

Effort estimate: The effort estimate uses the methodologies described later in the book. An effort estimate is for the requirements that have been supplied. Any change in requirements that might come later does not form a part of this estimate.

Project schedule: The overall schedule of the project and the schedule for milestones. Scheduling guidelines are discussed later in the book.

Customer responsibility: It is well known that for the vendor to meet its schedule and other commitments, the customer has to play its role properly. All inputs to be given by the customer are specified in this section, including inputs regarding data, manuals, access to personnel, hardware/software (for development or installation), access to their sites, responsibilities of the customer contact person, and so on.

Penalty/reward for timely delivery: If there are to be any penalties for slippage or rewards for meeting the criteria or deadlines, they are specified here.

Risk management: Gives the risks to the project, which of those are assignable to the customer and which to the vendor, and how the vendor proposes to mitigate risks assignable to it.

Requirement changes: This clause specifies that if any changes are requested by the customer, the vendor will determine the effect of the change and bill the customer for any extra effort that might be required. This important clause also affects the technical project because requirement changes always take place. Frequently, some buffer is built for requirement changes in the proposal and this clause is used only if changes exceed the buffer.

Other requirements and issues: Country-specific or miscellaneous requirements that can include escalation mechanisms for problem resolution, security issues, project management issues, and so on.

The commercial part of the proposal basically deals with all of the monetary aspects. It gives the pricing details: rates for manpower for various seniority levels, travel costs, special hardware costs, data communication costs, consultancy costs. It also specifies the payment schedule: of the total cost, how much is to be paid when. Typically, some payment is released at each milestone. Alternatively, payments might be made monthly. A part of the payment is withheld even after delivery and installation and is paid only after the warranty period is over.

The proposal is generally prepared by the project leader, in consultation with the salesperson who is in direct contact with the customer. Although the project leader prepares the technical part, inputs are taken from the salesperson regarding the commercial part. There might be negotiations on effort estimate, schedule, or rate before the proposal is accepted finally.

2.3 The Contract

A contract is a legal document and generally covers areas not directly related to software development. Although a contract is usually desired before the work, sometimes there is a protracted negotiation on the terms of the contract. In such a situation, a "letter of intent" might be given to start the project work, with contract preparation done in parallel. If the contract agreement is taking a long time, the vendor might require a purchase order (or a work order) from the customer. A purchase order implies that the work can start and, if an agreement cannot be reached on the terms of the contract, the customer will pay for the amount of work done. Generally, a contract has the following types of clauses.

Scope of services: Essentially specifies that the contract is for providing software services and the general scope of work. The details of the work are not a part of the contract.

Estimates: Specifies what estimates imply for the T&M and the fixed-price models. In T&M, if effort estimates are done, they are only a guideline; if they are exceeded, the customer has to pay for the extra effort. In the fixed-price situation, the price remains fixed unless the requirements change.

Rates and payment: The agreed-on rates, based on which actual costs are derived, are specified here, along with the duration for which the rates are valid and any increases that might be there after the duration.

Hardware and software: Specifies in general terms what the vendor will provide and what the customer will provide. For example, it might say that generic hardware and software will be provided by the vendor, but any special software or hardware needed for executing the project will be supplied by the customer.

Confidentiality: Specifies that all business, personnel, and technical information provided by the customer to the vendor will be treated as confidential and care taken to properly handle such information.

Security: Indicates that security measures will be taken to ensure that security of the customer's computer systems and network is not breached.

Rights on data: Assures that the vendor has no rights to specific data or information provided by the customer; however, the vendor has rights to use, for future projects, the general knowledge or know-how it acquired by executing this project. This section also specifies that all programs, documents, and such for the project belong to the customer.

Nonsolicitation: Both parties agree not to try to recruit people connected to the project for up to some period after the project expires. This clause is to prevent the customer from recruiting the vendor's personnel during or soon after the project.

Warranty: The vendor gives a limited term warranty for the software it supplies. Generally, the warranty implies that the defects found during the warranty period will be fixed by the vendor free of cost.

Limitation of liability: This clause limits the vendor's liability due to malfunction of software or any similar reason. This liability for damages that might be related to the software is generally limited to the total cost of the software provided.

Indemnity: Essentially says that neither the client nor the vendor is responsible for any improper or illegal acts by the other party, in case a third party is affected by it and seeks damages.

Service-level agreements: Sometimes, particularly in production support systems, service-level agreements might be agreed on in terms of response time, for example. The customer might set up some reward or penalty clauses, depending on whether the service levels are met.

Besides these options, there are clauses on jurisdiction (which laws apply), arbitration (what to do in case of disputes), termination of contract, payment defaults, and more. The clauses might need negotiations between the client and the vendor, or between the lawyers of the two organizations. The clauses that tend to be contentious are the ones in which the interests of the customer and vendor differ. They include such clauses as limitation of liability, rate, nonsolicitation, penalty, and warranty.

2.4 Summary

Whenever a customer wants to obtain some services from a software services vendor, a clear understanding is needed between the customer and the vendor. The formalization of the understanding between the two parties is usually done in the form of contracts and proposals. A contract typically has clauses that cover scope, rates and payments, estimates, liability, security, rights of the vendor and customer, warranty, and so on. The proposal generally contains more precise clauses relating to the particular service transaction being negotiated. It gives the problem definition, assumptions, effort and schedule estimates, responsibilities, strategy for managing the project, approach for handling changes, and so on.

The contract and proposal together form the complete formal understanding between the customer and the vendor. Underlying many of the clauses are the models of interaction the vendor has set up for clients. Some of the models commonly used by Infosys for providing services to its customers have also been briefly discussed. They include the fixed-price model, the time and materials approach, and hybrids of the two.

Although proposals and contracts are not software engineering activities, a brief introduction to these has been included here because they do influence the processes used for providing services and form the basis for conducting the business of providing software development services.

3

Requirements Specification and Management

Good requirements are essential for successfully executing projects. Improperly understood or documented requirements, or insufficiently controlled requirement changes, inevitably lead to cost escalations, late delivery, and poor quality—in short, dissatisfied customers.

The two major activities relating to requirements are requirements analysis and specification and requirements change management. Whereas the requirements specification activity is done at the start of the project, change management is done throughout the project. Requirements traceability management is another activity related to requirements and aims to ensure that all requirements can be traced to elements in the outputs produced in later stages of the project and to the origins of the requirements. It is an important activity in ensuring that the major goal of the project—that the final software satisfies the customer's requirements—is met. Requirements traceability management also helps in evaluating the effects of requirements change requests. This chapter discusses all three aspects of requirements: analysis and specification, change management, and traceability management.

As seen in Chapter 2, the models of interaction between a vendor and customer are such that requirements are frequently compiled before the start of the formal project and before the final and formal estimates are made. With this approach, the whole project is essentially split into two somewhat independent projects—one for doing requirements analysis and the other for developing the software to satisfy the requirements. After the requirements analysis is complete, formal estimates for the second part (the development project) are done, based on the analysis. In some projects, requirements analysis is done by one organization, and development is done by a different organization.

With this approach, the actual software planning and project execution occur after the requirements are compiled. Hence, this chapter is under the

"Project Initiation" part of the book, before the part on "Project Planning." Although the specification activity is done during project initiation, change management and traceability management tasks are done throughout the project. A process for requirements analysis and specification is a requirement of the Software Product Engineering KPA at CMM level 3, and proper change management is the focus of the Requirements Management KPA at CMM level 2. This chapter also gives the high-level requirements document of our case study: the WAR project.

3.1 Requirements Analysis and Specification

The main objective of the requirements analysis is to produce a document that properly specifies all requirements of the customer. That is, the software requirement specification (SRS) document is the primary output of this phase. Proper requirements analysis and specification are critical for having a successful project. Many of the defects found in system and acceptance testing originate in requirements [7]. Removing an error injected during requirements can cost as much as 100 times more during acceptance than if it is removed during the requirements phase itself [2, 4]. The need for executing this phase properly to produce an SRS with the least defects should be evident.

Requirements analysis and specification constitute a large area, and various approaches have been proposed in literature to tackle this phase. The main tasks under this area are requirements elicitation and analysis, requirements documentation, and requirements review. For requirements analysis and elicitation, various methodologies can be used, with different situations requiring different models. We do not intend to give a tutorial on different approaches to analysis; the reader is instead referred to Davis [7]. Here we mention the steps involved in the requirements analysis and specification process of Infosys, and the template used for requirements specification.

3.1.1 Overall Process

The activities performed during the requirements phase largely focus on two areas: problem analysis and product description [7]. In the overall process shown in Figure 3.1, the problem analysis activities are grouped into the three phases of preparing, gathering requirements, and analysis. The product description activities are also grouped into three phases: preparing the SRS, reviewing it, and obtaining the final sign-off from the customer. After the sign-off, the initial baseline for requirements is established.

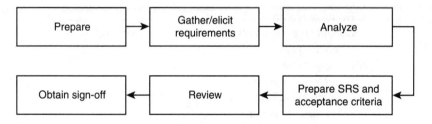

Figure 3.1　Process for requirements analysis and specification

Although the phases are shown as linearly arranged in Figure 3.1, clearly there is a need for backtracking, particularly between the requirements gathering, analysis, and SRS preparation stages. Still, conceptually, there is precedence among them—before analysis is done, the requirements must be gathered, and before they can be specified, they must be analyzed. Hence, in the process specification, these phases are linearly organized. The activities in the requirements phase are listed here. Most of these activities are self-explanatory; however, a brief description of the main activities is given later.

    Prepare for requirements gathering and analysis
        Do background reading on technical/business concepts and
            undergo training
        Become familiar with customer's methodology and tools to be
            used
        Identify methods for information gathering
        Prepare questionnaires for eliciting information
        Identify user groups and interviewees
        Plan prototyping
        Define requirement specification standards
        Develop interview plan and review with customer
    Gather requirements
        Establish objectives and scope of the system
        Gather functional requirements
            Identify business events
            Identify inputs and outputs for each business event
            Determine relationship between inputs and outputs
            Determine precedence relationships among events
        Gather information on external interfaces
        Gather operating environment requirements
        Gather performance requirements
        Gather standards requirements
        Gather special user requirements
        Prepare prototypes

Evaluate prototypes
Conduct feedback sessions (on current understanding of
   requirements)
Analyze requirements
   Develop process model
   Develop logical data model
   Set up data dictionary
Prepare software-requirements specification document
Prepare acceptance criteria
Review requirements specifications and acceptance criteria
Obtain customer sign-off for the requirements

To better understand the requirements of the customer, background reading is required in the domain of the business system as well as in technical concepts relating to hardware and software platforms, language, and such relevant to the system being developed. If the customer follows a particular methodology or uses certain tools, familiarization with them is required. When standard information and answers to closed-ended questions are to be gathered from many users, questionnaires become very useful; hence, the analyst should prepare questionnaires relating to the customer's business and operating environment. The analyst should also identify the user groups and other people that need to be interviewed. The organization structure can help in identifying the interviewees. Usually, the time the users can devote to giving information and requirements is limited, so a plan for interviewing should be developed to make effective use of the time available for requirements gathering, keeping in mind the order of information gathering and the availability of people.

A prototype is a limited simulation of the application to be developed and is usually created to give the user a feel for what the developed application would look like. If prototyping is needed in the project, prototyping objectives have to be established in advance and development and feedback collection planned.

Gathering requirements involves obtaining all relevant information that will help in understanding the customer's requirements. The customer's requirements can be classified as business, functional, interface, operating environment, performance, standards, and special requirements. Business requirements establish the goals and scope of the system. Functional requirements are the end-users' view of required business functionality, and implementing them is the basic purpose of the project. The business system responds to and processes a set of events; hence, understanding the business functions, for the most part, involves understanding the various events that take place and the business processing that happens in response to these events. Events can be of two types: external events triggered by external entities or temporal events triggered by time. Besides identifying the events, it is necessary to identify inputs and outputs for all events. The relationship between inputs and outputs of an event is really the processing that needs to be performed by the system in response to a business event.

The application being developed might have to interact with many other existing automated and nonautomated systems. These external interfaces must be identified to make sure the application will pass and receive data compatible with the external interfaces. The hardware and software environment in which the application is expected to operate needs to be clearly understood, because it will affect the design and implementation. The performance requirements are constraints the business places on response time, throughput, and so on. These requirements might be different for peak and normal conditions.

If some standards must be followed in the project, they need to be identified, including standards for user interfaces, coding, and documentation. Special user requirements encompass all supporting requirements. They include safety, security, reliability, backup, transaction, and legal requirements and can have a major influence on the system and the effort required to build it. Hence, they must be clearly understood.

Prototypes give the users a feel of the system and are a helpful technique in gathering requirements. If prototyping is to be used, the prototypes should be demonstrated to as many users as possible, and feedback collected. A prototype might be evolutionary or throwaway [6, 7]—that is, the prototype might be converted into the final system or it might be thrown away after the feedback has been collected.

The goal of analysis is to identify the requirements in a complete, accurate, consistent, and unambiguous fashion from the information collected. Analysis accomplishes this goal by constructing models of the system. The models concentrate on describing what a system does rather than how it does it. The process model of a system is a representation of the processes that transform the data in the system. Process modeling can be done by either of two approaches: the classical approach or the event-based approach. The classical approach is to draw the top-level data-flow diagram for the system by treating the system as a black box with inputs and outputs and then exploding this top-level diagram into lower-level data-flow diagrams [10, 11]. The latter approach lists the external business events to which the system will respond and then develops a model for each event [14].

The data model gives a logical structure to the user's view of the data in the system. Usually the data model is depicted in the form of an entity relationship diagram (a description of these diagrams can be found in any database textbook—for example, C. J. Date [5]). The entity relationship diagram shows the business entities in the system and the relationships between these entities. Entities can be thought of as the data groups that participate in the business processes. The physical database is later derived from the data model. A data dictionary is the central repository of all objects in the process model and data model. It describes the data stores, processes, and external entities in data-flow diagrams.

After the analysis, the SRS can be prepared. This task involves documenting the objectives and scope of the system and consolidating the process model, data model, data dictionary, and so on into a document. Unresolved issues should also be included in this document. Acceptance criteria are the conditions under which the customer will accept the delivered software. Preparing the acceptance criteria explicitly promotes a clear understanding with the customer about what the customer considers acceptable software. It also helps in quantifying the customer's expectations from the software. A review of the requirements specification document and the acceptance criteria should be done, after which a sign-off can be obtained from the customer.

The process described above is for traditional function-oriented analysis. For projects that will follow an object-oriented approach, a separate process has been defined. For requirements, the process for an object-oriented approach is similar except for the "analyze requirements" activity in the requirements process. In an object-oriented analysis, this activity involves *use cases,* one of the standard ways of doing object-oriented analysis [13]. In this approach, a use case is written for each business event (instead of drawing a process diagram), generally in the form of narrative text. For the use cases, various *actors* (users) are identified, along with the interaction of the actors with the system. These interactions or dialogs form the use cases. From the use cases and other analysis, classes are identified along with some methods, and a *class dictionary* is formed. Details of the process are omitted here and the reader is referred to Jacobson [13] for further details on this approach of doing object-oriented analysis.

3.1.2   Requirements Specifications

The planning, elicitation, and analysis activities culminate in requirements specification. The SRS document is the main output of the requirements stage. To ensure that all necessary requirements are specified, one simple approach is to specify a template for the SRS. The basic contents of the template used at Infosys are described here. The various items in the template also form a checklist to ensure completeness. The template is somewhat different if an object-oriented analysis is done.

Requirements elicitation, analysis, and specification is almost fully a human activity—trying to convert into a formal document concepts and goals people have in their minds. Clearly, in this process mistakes are likely to be made, and it is well known that a requirement defect, if caught during system testing, can cost as much as 100 times more to fix than if it were caught and fixed during requirements [4]. Besides, problems in requirements that might be caused due to communication gaps between the customer and the supplier have great

Template for SRS

1 OVERVIEW
Introduction to the system to be built.

1.1 Current System
Brief description of the current system, if a system exists.

1.2 Limitations of the Current System
List of limitations of the current system.

1.3 Proposed System
Overview of the proposed system.

1.3.1 Objectives of the Proposed System
List of the business objectives/expected benefits of the proposed system.

2 FUNCTIONAL REQUIREMENTS
List of requirements related to the customer's business.

2.1 System Requirements

2.1.1 Scope and Boundary

2.1.2 Context Diagram

2.2 Business Events

2.2.1 External Events
List of external events. External events are triggered by external entities, such as a client calling to place an order or a user entering a command.

2.2.2 Temporal Events
List of temporal events. Temporal events are triggered by time, such as producing a summary report every day at 9 P.M.

2.3 Inputs and Outputs
Give inputs and outputs for each business event.

2.4 Relationships
Specify relationship between inputs and outputs.

2.5 Precedence Relationships
Specify any precedence relationship between events.

2.6 Screens
Reports

3 EXTERNAL INTERFACE REQUIREMENTS
The application that is being developed might interact with many other existing automated and nonautomated systems. These external interfaces must be identified to make sure the application will pass and receive data compatible with the external interfaces. They are specified here.

4   OPERATING ENVIRONMENT REQUIREMENTS

4.1   Hardware

4.2   Software

4.3   Network

4.4   Communication

5   PERFORMANCE REQUIREMENTS

All performance requirements are specified here. Examples include online response time, number of transactions per second, number of customers to be serviced per hour, and constraints on the batch job window.

6   STANDARDS REQUIREMENTS

All standards that the customer requires to be followed during the project should be listed here. The actual standards themselves can be defined in a separate document.

6.1   User Interface

6.2   Detailed Design

6.3   Coding

6.4   Document

7   SPECIAL USER REQUIREMENTS

7.1   Security

7.2   Audit Trail

7.3   Reliability

7.4   Transaction Volume and Data Volume

7.5   Backup and Recovery

7.6   Legal

7.7   Data Migration

7.8   Data Retention

7.9   Installation

7.10   User Training

7.11   User Manual and Help

7.12   Automated and Manual Functions

7.13   Features Not Required

8   CONSTRAINTS

9   PROTOTYPE
If a prototype exists or is to be built, reference should be given to it.

10   GLOSSARY OF TERMS

potential to subvert customer satisfaction. Hence it is critical to carefully verify requirements to make sure that what is specified is indeed what is desired.

For requirements validation, as shown in the overall process, requirement reviews are done and usually involve the customer. As with any review, the effectiveness is increased if there is a checklist specifying what the reviewers should be looking for. The checklist is derived from the template and the nature of errors that have been found in the past. Special attention is given to errors falling in the categories of omission, incorrect fact, inconsistency, and ambiguity—the most common requirement errors [1, 9]. The review process itself is defined in a later chapter.

3.2 Requirements Change Management

Requirements change. This is a universal truth, and there are many reasons for it. One important reason for changing requirements is that the world around the system changes, requiring any system to adapt to the changes. A system employing software requires changes in the software to adapt to the changes. In addition, when users get some capability from a system that utilizes the power of computing, knowledge about what is possible makes the users desire better capability from their systems, requiring the systems to change. Another key reason for change is that sometimes the users or customers do not know fully what they want in the software, so they start with some requirements. As time passes and they become clearer on what is desired, their requirements change; hence, their requirements for software change.

Changes in requirements can come at any time during the life of a project, or after that. Instead of wishing that changes will not come, or hoping that somehow the initial requirements will be "so good" that no changes will be required, it is better to prepare the project to handle changes as and when they come. No amount of preparation or planning can avoid changes, and it is a myth that a project cannot start until requirements have been frozen [12].

The requirements change management process defines the set of activities that needs to be performed when there are some new requirements or changes to existing requirements (we will call both changes in the requirements). Requirement changes can occur at any point during the project execution stage. A change in the requirements might alter the schedule of the project—it might even affect the work products that have already been produced. The further down in the life cycle the requirements change, the more severe the impact on the project. Uncontrolled changes to requirements also have a high potential for seriously jeopardizing the chances of a project's success by having a very adverse effect on the cost, schedule, and quality of the project. Requirement changes can account for as much as 40% of the total cost [3].

The basic goal of the requirements change management process is to control requirement changes and minimize their effect on the project. This goal necessitates understanding the full implications of a requirements change request, as well as the cumulative impact of changes. It also requires making the customer fully aware of the effects of the changes on the project so that changes in the negotiated terms can be done amicably. The requirements change management process, in a sense, tries to ensure that a project succeeds despite requirement changes.

3.2.1 The Process

Requirements change management has two aspects: agreement with the customer about how to deal with the changes and the process of actually making the changes. The overall approach for handling changes has to be agreed to by the customer and is frequently a part of the proposal as well as the project management plan. Generally, it specifies how the change requests will be made, when formal approvals are needed, building a buffer in the estimates for handling changes, and so on. In the context of the overall approach, when a request for a requirement change comes in, the requirements change management process must be executed.

The project leader is primarily responsible for executing the process to incorporate the change in the project. The customer, the business manager to whom the project leader reports, and the development team also participate in this process. The entry criterion for this process is that a change request has been received, and the inputs are the change request and the work products that have already been produced in the project. The main outputs are the impact analysis report for the change request, the revised project plan, and the changed work products. The exit criterion is that the change has been incorporated. Following are the major steps in the process.

Log the changes
Perform impact analysis on the work products
Estimate effort needed for the change requests
Reestimate delivery schedule
Perform cumulative cost impact analysis
Review the impact with senior management, if thresholds are exceeded
Obtain customer sign-off
Rework work products

A change request log is maintained to keep track of the change requests. Each entry in the log contains a change request number, a brief description of the change, the effect of the change, the status of the change request, and key dates. The effect of a change request is assessed by performing impact analysis. Impact analysis involves identifying work products that need to be changed and evaluating the quantum of change to each; reassessing the project's risks by revisiting the risk management plan; and evaluating the overall implications of the changes for the effort and schedule estimates. The outcome of the analysis is reviewed and approved by the project leader and the customer. The change request itself is incorporated in the requirements specification document, usually as appendices. Sometimes the relevant portions of the document might also be modified to reflect the changes. Monitoring of approved change requests and ensuring their proper implementation are handled by the configuration management process, which is discussed in Chapter 10.

A change might be classified as minor if the total effort involved in implementing it does not exceed a predetermined value, say two person-days. Changes that are minor typically become part of the project effort, and the planned estimates must contain a buffer for such changes (typically a small percentage of the total project effort), with proper provisions made in the proposal and contract. If the actual cumulative effort on minor changes exceeds this threshold, the effort estimates might have to be renegotiated, perhaps by adding another buffer to absorb further changes. The delivery schedule might also be revisited and renegotiated, if necessary. Major changes usually have a larger financial cost and are formally approved by the client. Visibility in the changes being made is provided to senior management through status and milestone reporting, which are discussed in Chapter 13.

3.2.2 Examples

To specify the changes and the output of the change management process, a simple template has been defined, containing summaries of various attributes. Each change is assigned a unique number for reference that is specified by the *request number* field. The *change specification* gives a brief description of the requested change. The category of change (for example, design change, contract change, functionality change, performance change) might also be specified, and the nature of the change specified as *change category.* The summary of the *impact analysis* is recorded, with brief information being given regarding work products that will be affected, the effort involved, and the implications for the schedule. The state of the change request—what is being done with this request—is recorded in the *status* field. The date of the change request might also be recorded, along with the date the change was approved, if approval is needed.

Two examples of change requests are given in Tables 3.1 and 3.2, which use a customized version of the change request template. In these examples, the detailed contents of the impact analysis are not important for the purposes of understanding requirements change management. Although the change request is specified by using the template, the actual tracking of implementation of a change request is handled by the configuration management process, which is discussed later.

One danger of requirements changes is that, even though each change is not large in itself, over the life of the project the cumulative impact of the changes is large. For example, in a project that receives change requests frequently, even if each change request is small, the changes can have serious adverse effects on the project. Hence, besides studying the impact of individual changes and tracking them, the cumulative impact of changes must also be monitored. For cumulative changes, a table or a spreadsheet can be used that lists all changes, the ramificiations on effort and schedule of each change, and the overall effect of all changes on effort and schedule. The example in Table 3.3 illustrates how cumulative changes are maintained. For details of each request, the relevant change request can be accessed by using the change request number and date.

Table 3.1   A Change Request Example

Project XYZ	
Req. No.	10 Date: 23 Feb 1998
Change Spec.	PFNETCONFIG—Packed format netconfig support
Impact Analysis	CDMA needs to parse three new tables—CDMACONF, CDMACELL, and SBSINV. Two new modules need to be added: Dumptab parser module Cdmapfnetconfig module: Uses dumptab parsers to extract table objects and then uses resource objects to save configuration data.
On Schedule	Nil
On Effort	10 person-days
Status	Will be incorporated in the new CDMA package.

Table 3.2 Another Change Request Example

Project XYZ	
Req. No.	11 Date: 23 Feb 1998
Change Spec.	IS-41 Analyzer—IS-41 Analyzer support for CDMA
Impact Analysis	No particular change in configuration module and analyzers for CDMA. The TDMA code can be reused as is. Scripts can also be reused. Netconfig and analyzer classes can be reused. The impacted modules are as follows: cgaapp module: Has to trigger analysis for IS-41 also, separately. cdmaroi module: (a) TRIS41ROI has to be copied as TRCDMAIS 41ROI; (b) There is a pure virtual method in TRCDMAROI for setting the ActualCallModelManager. It needs to be redefined. silver06guiapp++ module: IS-41 has to be added in the resource list.
On Schedule	Nil
On Effort	5
Status	Will be incorporated in the new CDMA package.

Table 3.3 Example of Tracking Cumulative Effect of Changes

Chg. Req. No.	Date of Change Req.	Change Specs	Effort (person-days)	Status
1	18 Feb	Specify usage statistics	3	Closed, Feb 22
2	During demo	Blocking of users	2	Open
3	During demo	Force logout of users	2	Open
4	18 Feb	Archival of knowledge users	5	Closed, Feb 27
5	During demo	Cloning of window	1	Open
6	During demo	Saving off an expanded tree and retrieving the same on demand	10	Open
7	During demo	Ability to start from a specific node	2	Open
8	During demo	Listing of all nodes while deleting	1	Open
9	18 Feb	Annotations (creating/deleting/ approving/modifying/and so on)	10	Open
10	23 Feb	PFNETCONFIG—Packed format netconfig support	10	Open
11	23 Feb	IS-41 Analyzer—IS-41 Analyzer support for CDMA	5	Closed, March 1
		TOTAL	**51**	

From a spreadsheet of this type, the total cost of the requirement changes made so far in the project can be immediately seen. As mentioned earlier, projects frequently plan for some "buffer" for handling change requests. As long as the cumulative effort for all change requests is less than this buffer, nothing special needs to be done, because the changes fall within the planned limit. If the cumulative effort of all changes crosses this buffer, however, further changes can have an adverse effect on total cost and scheduling of the project. In this situation, the estimates might need to be revised.

3.3 Traceability Management

The basic goal of a project is to build a software system that will satisfy the requirements. This objective implies that some way exists for checking that the software meets all requirements. To aid this validation, traceability of requirements is important, meaning that it is possible to trace each requirement to design and code that implement that requirement and test cases that test the implementation. Through this tracing, it can be validated that the software has met all requirements and that the software has been tested for all requirements. Other types of analysis are also possible if traceability information exists.

Two types of traceability exist: forward and backward. Forward traceability implies that it is possible to trace a requirement to elements in the outputs of later phases (design, coding) in the life cycle. Backward traceability is the reverse; it implies that it is possible to trace elements in the output of various stages back to requirements. Backward traceability also frequently implies the ability to trace the requirements back to their origin. Forward traceability is essential to ensure that the software meets the requirements. Backward traceability is more useful during change, regression testing, and so on.

3.3.1 Traceability Matrix

Perhaps the simplest way to support traceability is to have a mapping from requirement elements to design elements, from design elements to code elements, and from code elements to test cases. At Infosys, this mapping is maintained in a traceability matrix. Table 3.4 gives the basic format of the traceability matrix, with some entries from a project. The format can be tailored to meet the demands of various types of projects. The matrix itself can be supported through a spreadsheet or a database.

In this matrix, *reqmt #* is a reference to the requirement specification. Use of this matrix requires a proper numbering scheme to be used in the requirements specification document, such that individual requirements have unique

Table 3.4 A Traceability Matrix

Reqmt #	Description	HLD doc. Ref #	Design (functional/ architectural, database) equivalent	Implementation (program, class, inherited class) equivalent	Unit test case	Integration/ system test case	Acceptance test case
1.1.2	Real-time integration of highlighter with data collection	5.3.2	Interface between data collection and highlighter	PB405 Data collection	# 12	# 46	# 11
				CICS203 Highlighter kickoff	# 1	# 47	# 11

numbers or labels. The *description* should be obtained from the requirement specification; it could be keywords, bullets, or a couple of sentences. This description might seem cumbersome or redundant, but having short descriptions makes the matrix more readable and stand-alone. The *HLD Ref #* is a reference to the functional specification that satisfies the corresponding requirement. The *design* is the section number from the corresponding design document that contains the part of the design that satisfies the specific requirement. The reference could be to functional, architectural, or database design. On most occasions, a requirement would result in a program. The *implementation* refers to the corresponding program that implements the requirement. It is sufficient to mention the name of the program (or any other programming unit) for this. Note that after the first two entries that specify the requirement, the matrix could include multiple entries for the same requirement. In such a case, they should be listed in different rows. The matrix can therefore capture the one-to-many mappings that might exist.

The described columns of the matrix aim to map the requirements to different units as the software evolves. This effort helps to ensure that the requirements have been incorporated in the software being built. In addition to verifying that all requirements have been implemented, a key objective is to make sure a test has been done for the requirements. This is particularly important for nonfunctional requirements, particularly performance requirements, for which many of the columns mentioned above might be empty in the traceability matrix. As a result, the traceability matrix also contains references to test plans and test cases. The *unit test case* represents the test case number in the unit test plan for the program that implements the requirement. Those requirements that do not have a program-level implementation might have no entry in this column. All requirements should have a test case at the integration or system level. The integration test plan typically has the business and technical test cases clearly identified. The *integration/system test case* refers to the test case for the particular requirement being traced.

Eventually all important requirements must tie back to the acceptance test plan. The corresponding acceptance test for the particular requirement is mentioned in *acceptance test case.*

The traceability matrix in Table 3.4 shows the traceability of one requirement: requirement number 1.1.2. This matrix says that this requirement (which is about integration of highlighter with data collection) is implemented by section 5.3.2 of the high-level design document, and at a detail level is implemented by the interface between the two modules. Two programs implement this particular requirement, and both are listed here on different rows of the matrix. For each of the two programs, Table 3.4 also gives the unit test case number in their respective unit test plans, the integration test case number in their integration test plans, and the acceptance test case number in their acceptance test plans.

3.3.2   Matrix Maintenance and Usage

The traceability matrix helps track/trace all requirements through the various life-cycle phases to ensure that all requirements have been incorporated, which also reduces rework due to missing requirements. The matrix aids reviews by providing a mechanism for reviewers to easily check that all requirements have been handled. The matrix contains the information that can be used for impact analysis when requirements change. It also helps in demonstrating to the customer that the software has been developed to meet all requirements and that it has been tested adequately.

A traceability matrix, unless maintained properly, is of limited use. Because of its design, it will not remain static and needs to be updated at many points in the life cycle. At the start, the matrix contains data in the first two columns only. As the development proceeds, data for other fields are added. The easiest way to update the matrix is to enhance it at the end of reviews of the relevant stages. For maintenance of a traceability matrix for a project, numbering schemes must be used in all documents for work products.

After the matrix is built and is being maintained, some completeness checks can be performed. Some of these checks and the steps to be followed for them are given here. Other checks can be easily devised, depending on the needs of the project or the client.

- Go through the requirement numbers in the matrix and the requirements in the requirements document and ensure that all requirements are listed in the matrix and none has been missed. This goal can be achieved easily by sorting the matrix by requirement number and then checking the numbers against the numbers in the requirements document.
- To ensure that all programs listed in the matrix are needed in the final software and no unnecessary code appears, every program, class, and other element must be mentioned in this matrix.
- One can check implementation of requirements by ensuring that functional requirements have no blank columns. For other requirements, if the design and program fields are blank, be sure you carefully check and verify that these requirements have no direct effect on programs.
- For each performance requirement, there should be some test cases. Using the matrix, you can easily check whether the test cases are suitable for checking the performance requirement.
- The integration and system test plan can be cross-checked with the matrix to ensure that all conditions in the requirements are included in the system test plan.

Maintaining the integrity of the matrix under requirement changes is not easy. Requirement changes are generally incorporated in the requirements document in two ways: by changing some existing requirement in the document or by appending the change request. The approach followed in updating the requirements specification document can also be followed in updating the traceability matrix. If the requirements change request is appended to the document, it is treated as an additional requirement and an entry is made for it in the matrix. If some existing requirement changes, you need to see if the entry in the matrix needs to change; if it does, the corresponding entry is modified. The former approach is used most commonly.

3.4 Example: The WAR System

We will use the Weekly Activity Report (WAR) system project as a case study for illustrating the execution of various processes employed in a project. This small project (final code size is about 14,000 LOC) was done for in-house use—that is, the client of the project is a group internal to Infosys. An internal project was chosen because it allows any aspect of the project to be shown without violating any confidentiality requirements of an external client. A small project was selected as a case study to succinctly illustrate the use of processes.

All Infosys employees fill out an activity report at the end of each week, in which they give a breakdown of their time. After a project is created (in a different corporate database) and its Microsoft™ project plan (MSP) is submitted, all people mentioned in the project are assigned to it. Each week, then, they have to submit their WAR for the project, listing the time spent each day on different activities. Codes are used to specify the activities.

The activities themselves are classified as either "planned" or "unplanned." Planned activities have been assigned to the person in the MSP of the project, and codes for them are automatically entered from the MSP into the person's WAR. Unplanned activities are the other activities; for these, the person filing the WAR has to explicitly specify activity codes. Codes used in the WAR system are discussed in Chapter 13.

The existing WAR system has a PC-based front end and a database server as a back end. This system does not allow people without a PC or without direct access to the server to submit the WAR. Currently, such personnel submit a WAR either on a hard copy (which is then entered in the system) or through some other means. With the arrival of the World Wide Web, it was felt that WAR should become Web-based to allow people with different front ends (UNIX, Apple, Windows) to submit their WARs easily through a browser. That was the origin of this project.

The requirements for the WAR system are specified in the requirements document. This document customizes the standard template to suit the project. Section 1 gives an overview that includes the existing system and the objectives of the proposed system. Section 2 specifies the high-level business requirements, grouped in terms of system requirements, business events, screens, and reports and forming the high-level functional requirements for the system.

The document also specifies the external interface requirements, operating system requirements, performance requirements, and standards requirements. The section on special user requirements specifies design constraints such as security and authentication, audit trail, transaction volume, and online help. Plans for building an evolutionary prototype are also part of the requirements.

Overall, this relatively succinct requirements document specifies all requirements at a high level. However, it does not provide all details regarding user interfaces and processing requirements—information a designer will need to build the system. This information was provided as appendices to this requirements document (they have been omitted here).

Based on the prototype, another document—called *functional specifications*—was developed. This document specifies all major modules needed for the system, all functions supported by each module, and detailed information about each function (including inputs, outputs, processing, and business rules). This much larger document, having about 50 pages, has been omitted here. This book gives only the high-level requirements of the WAR system.

Requirements Specification Document for WAR 2.0

1.   OVERVIEW
This document describes the requirements for the Weekly Activity Report system, version 2.0. Hereafter this system will be referred as WAR 2.0.

1.1   Current System
The current system used at Infosys for entering effort data on weekly activities is a GUI-based 16-bit application that can be installed on different operating systems, such as Windows 3.X, Windows 95, and Windows NT. The system has the following limitations:

1. No entries in MS Project can be deleted, because this deletion leads to loss of data.
2. The MS Project file cannot be changed during the course of the project.
3. People not on the local network cannot enter WAR.
4. Overwriting of MS Project data is not allowed.
5. Tasks cannot be marked 100% complete before the WAR is authorized. (Doing so leads to the disappearance of activity from the user's WAR if it is opened by the user before authorization.)
6. The MS Project data upload application is not robust.

(continued)

1.2   Objectives of the Proposed System

The aim of the proposed system is to address the limitations of the current system. The requirements for the system have been gathered from feedback obtained from a cross-section of the users and are also based on the requests and defects recorded in the past. Following are the objectives of the proposed system:

1. **Global accessibility.** WAR 2.0 should be made available on the Web (Internet/intranet/extranet).
2. **Location independence.** It should accommodate a wide variety of clients in different geographical areas.
3. **Flexible deployment.** As a consequence of location independence, users should have easy accessibility to data through local databases that are replicated in the respective locations.
4. **Reusability.** The system should be built so as to make the components reusable for future developments.
5. **Work flow.** The system should allow routing of WARs (forward/approve) with comments.

2.   FUNCTIONAL REQUIREMENTS

2.1   System Requirements

1. For each project, the system should allow users to specify a set of activity codes from the standard set and a set of module codes.
2. Project leaders should be allowed to purge project data from the MSP without having any effect on the WAR system.
3. Tasks can be marked 100% complete at any time.
4. MS Project will be the only project planning tool for WAR 2.0.
5. The system will purge and archive data automatically.

2.2   Business Events

External events

1. Entry of WAR
2. Review and authorization of WAR
3. Project-specific setup
4. Project closure
5. MS Project upload

Temporal Events

1. Periodic generation of reports and forwarding the same to the registered users

2.3   Screens

1. Login screen
2. WAR-entry screen

3. WAR review/authorization screen
4. Master maintenance for activity codes
5. Master maintenance for module codes
6. Reporting screen
7. User-registration screen for reports

2.4 Reports

1. Individual WAR reports for users who have submitted them
2. WAR report of users who have submitted to a particular authorizer
3. Automated report generation and notification to the users who have registered for the report

3. EXTERNAL INTERFACE REQUIREMENTS

1. The user IDs will be validated against the list of employee numbers (available from the corporate database).
2. Only projects that are defined in the corporate database can be used in WAR 2.0.
3. The current WAR system has an interface with the LEAVE system.

4. OPERATING ENVIRONMENT REQUIREMENTS

Requirements of hardware and software will be redefined after the HLD design is over.

4.1 Hardware

Pentium-based server with 64MB RAM and 4GB of disk space

4.2 Software

1. Netscape Web Server (FastTrack/Enterprise) running on Windows NT 4.0
2. SQL Server 6.5

4.3 Network

At least 10 mbps network for the desired response time

4.4 Communication

TCP/IP, IPX/SPX

5. PERFORMANCE REQUIREMENTS
- Time to open up WAR for a week should be 5 s or less.
- Time to save WAR details should be 5 s or less.

6. ACCEPTANCE CRITERIA

All requirements related to entry, review, and report should be available for acceptance of this system.

(continued)

7.   STANDARDS REQUIREMENTS

Infosys standards should be used where available. Otherwise, standards should be developed for a task before performing the task.

8.   SPECIAL USER REQUIREMENTS

8.1   Security and Authentication

There will be three classes of users: corporate administrator, project administrator, and user. Following are the security constraints:

1. Corporate administrator will have rights to maintain the entire list of activity codes used across the company.
2. Project administrator will have rights to define the group of activity codes or module codes for the project.
3. User is a valid user for whom the ID and password must be checked.

8.2   Audit Trail

Audit trail will be maintained to record only additions, modifications, and deletions done to corporate- and project-level activity or module codes. WAR entry and authorization will not have any audit trail entries.

8.3   Reliability

1. Deletion of an item in the MSP should not affect the WAR data. If data were entered for a deleted task, the task should continue to show until it is not needed.
2. Reports should pick up data from both the live and the offline tables.
3. The automatic generation of reports should be reliable and robust, and in case of any failure, the system should inform the person concerned in the MIS department.

8.4   Transaction Volume and Data Volume

The volume of data in the database can reach 100,000 records per table. If the limit is exceeded, data will be purged from the live tables and archived onto the offline tables automatically.

8.5   Backup and Recovery

No special requirement; backup policies of the organization suffice.

8.6   Distributed Databases

Every Infosys site should have a local database server/Web server, so that performance/uptime of the system can be improved.

8.7   Data Migration

All existing data (from both live and offline tables) shall be migrated to the respective tables of the new system as per the design changes made.

8.8   Data Retention

All data must be retained either in the live tables or in the offline tables.

8.9 User Training

User training will be provided for the pilot release of the application.

8.10 User Manual and Help

Online help will be provided and will be available as a part of the system. No user manuals will be provided for this system.

8.11 Automated and Manual Functions

Creating the corporate administrator account and migrating data from the existing system to the new system will have to be done manually.

9. CONSTRAINTS

Not applicable

10. PROTOTYPE

As detailed requirements will be driven by the user interface, a prototype will be developed for the user interfaces and navigation. The objectives of this prototype are as follows:

1. Validate the refined requirements by showing the screens (by showing screens for customization, details of the concept can be validated).
2. Get approval for limitations in the implementation imposed by the Web (running totals cannot be done, as in a spreadsheet, and a refresh button has to be clicked).
3. Get approval for the user interface and navigation options.
4. Get approval for details and data elements to be captured or displayed (details of input/output).
5. Add minor features.

3.5 Summary

Proper requirements are essential for successfully executing projects. The three important activities relating to requirements are analysis and specifications, change management, and traceability management. This chapter discussed the methods used at Infosys for performing these three tasks.

The process for requirements analysis and specification consists of preparing for analysis, gathering requirements, analyzing them, and then preparing the SRS and getting it reviewed. Each of these tasks involves several activities, which have been briefly discussed in the chapter. The template used for specifying requirements was also given.

Requirements generally do not remain "frozen" but change during the course of the project. Hence, proper methods for handling requirement changes are essential. In the method used at Infosys, a change request is first logged. Its effect on the project, including on effort and schedule estimates, is estimated and documented. In addition, a spreadsheet is maintained of all change requests received so far and their overall implications. This record is used to see the cumulative effect of all change requests received so far.

To ensure that all requirements are met and to perform impact analysis of change requests easily, it is desirable to have the ability to trace different requirements to different work products produced during the rest of the project. If traceability of requirements to design and code can be established, checking whether the project has implemented all requirements is easy. If traceability from requirements to test cases also exists, one can also check whether the testing has validated all requirements. At Infosys, a traceability matrix is recommended for these purposes. The matrix is essentially a table that lists all requirements, and then, for each requirement, lists the code that implements it, the test case that tests for it, and so on. Many validations can easily be done by using this matrix.

References

[1] V. R. Basili and D. M. Weiss. Evaluation of a software requirements document by analysis of change data. *Proceedings of the 5th International Conference on Software Engineering,* pp. 314–323, 1981.

[2] B. Boehm. Software engineering. *IEEE Transactions on Computers,* 25(12), 1976.

[3] B. Boehm. Improving software productivity. *IEEE Computer,* pp. 43–57, Sept. 1987.

[4] B. Boehm. *Software Engineering Economics.* Prentice Hall, 1981.

[5] C. J. Date. *An Introduction to Database Systems.* Addison-Wesley, 1986.

[6] A. M. Davis. Operational prototyping: A new development approach. *IEEE Software,* pp. 70–78, Sept. 1992.

[7] A. M. Davis. *Software Requirements: Objects, Functions, and States.* Prentice Hall, 1993.

[8] A. M. Davis. Software prototyping. In *Advances in Computers,* vol. 40, pp. 39–63. Academic Press, 1995.

[9] J. S. Davis. Identification of errors in software requirements through use of automated requirements tools. *Information and Software Technology,* 31(9): 472–476, 1989.

[10] T. DeMarco. *Structured Analysis and System Specification.* Yourdon Press, 1979.

[11] C. Gane and T. Sarson. *Structured Systems Analysis: Tools and Techniques.* Prentice Hall, 1979.

[12] W. S. Humphrey. *Managing the Software Process.* Addison-Wesley, 1989.

[13] I. Jacobson. *Object-Oriented Software Engineering—A Use-Case Driven Approach.* Addison-Wesley, 1992.

[14] E. Yourdon. *Modern Structured Analysis.* Yourdon Press, 1989.

PART II

Project Planning

4

Process Definition
and Tailoring

A process description is a sequence of steps that a project can follow for performing some task, along with guidelines for undertaking those steps. An organization-wide process essentially describes the manner in which the task for which the process is defined may be done. Having a standard process reduces variations in the performance of different projects. Without a standard process, projects may follow different processes, resulting in different outcomes along various dimensions like quality and productivity. In such a situation, the process becomes less predictable in that past performance has only a weak correlation with performance of future projects. Consequently, past data and experience cannot be used for estimation, and a new project cannot effectively learn from past projects (and learning from the past is essential for improving). Hence, for any organization that executes projects regularly, standardized processes are essential for having predictability, good estimation capability, and good learning.

It is usually not possible to have a standard process for all projects, as different projects have different needs. One way to handle this situation is to have a general process that describes a sequence of activities for a task, but allows for tailoring to suit a particular project. For this approach, tailoring guidelines need to be provided. With these guidelines, the types of processes that can be used are restricted to those that are allowable variations of the standard process. Process tailoring is an important project planning activity, although process definition is not. As tailoring is intricately tied to the process definition, however, both are discussed in this chapter.

As discussed in Chapter 1, Infosys has defined processes for the life cycle of different types of projects and for various management activities. As the selection of a proper process for executing the technical tasks is a key success parameter for a project, tailoring guidelines have been provided for the life-cycle processes. Here we discuss the development process and the tailoring guidelines for it.

Standard processes and tailoring guidelines are important requirements in the Organization Process Definition KPA of level 3 of the CMM, and use of the standard process and tailoring guidelines for determining the process for a project is an important requirement for Integrated Software Management KPA of level 3. Use of processes is also important for the Software Product Engineering KPA of level 3, which requires that the engineering activities be performed according to defined processes.

4.1 Development Process

The development process is the process by which the user requirements are elicited and software satisfying these requirements is designed, built, tested, and delivered to the customer. The development process is used when a new application is being developed or a major enhancement is planned for an existing application. Several process models for software development exist. The most common ones include the waterfall model (a description of this model and its limitations can be found in [2]), iterative enhancement [1], prototyping [5], and spiral [3]. The most widely used model is the waterfall model, which organizes the phases in a linear sequence, although most implementations of this model adapt it to minimize its shortcomings.

The development process used at Infosys resembles the waterfall model, except that the traditional phases have been broken into "smaller" phases or stages to allow parallel execution of some phases. For example, the system test planning is defined as a separate phase from the system testing phase. If necessary, the system test planning phase can then be done in parallel with coding, although system testing takes place only after coding is finished. The phases in the process include requirements analysis, high-level design, detailed design, build, unit testing, integration planning, integration, system test planning, system testing, documentation, acceptance and installation, and warranty support. The phases, although defined in some order in the process definition, do not impose an order by their placement. The dependence between phases is specified through the entry criteria. Figure 4.1 depicts the different phases and the dependencies between them. This overall process remains the same even for a project using an object-oriented approach, although the way in which some of the phases are done is different in a project that employs an object-oriented project. The difference in activities is mostly in the analysis and design phases, though the guidelines and standards for some of the later phases are also different.

The process is specified using the architecture described in Chapter 1. As per the architecture, entry and exit criteria, inputs and outputs, participants, activities, and other information are specified for each phase (stage). Generally, the process descriptions are brief, with the description of each phase taking one

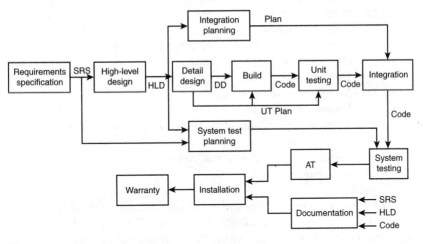

Figure 4.1   Development process

to two pages. Further details about the process take the form of guidelines and notes. The steps in the requirements analysis phase were discussed in Chapter 3. Here, we briefly describe the remainder of the phases and give the major activities in each phase along with the entry/exit criteria, inputs/outputs, participants, and so on.

4.1.1   High-Level Design

High-level design is the phase of the life cycle when a logical view of the computer implementation of the solution to the customer requirements is developed. It gives the solution at a high level of abstraction. This solution contains two main components: the functional architecture of the application (assuming that a function-oriented approach is used) and the database design. During design, a parallel activity of defining the standards also goes on.

The participants in this phase are the design team, the review team, and the customer. The entry criterion is that the requirement specification document has been reviewed and authorized. The main input is the requirements specification document, and the outputs are high-level design documents, project standards, the functional design document, the database design document, and high-level design review records. The exit criterion is that the high-level design documents have been reviewed and authorized. The measurements made in this phase focus on the high-level design effort, high-level design defects, review effort, and rework effort. The sequence of steps in the process is as follows:

Define standards (coding, documentation, user interface, and so on)
Determine/design details of operating environment

Do functional design
    Determine functions
    Create cross-reference between events and functions
    Determine processing details of each function
    Document the functional architecture
Develop physical database design
    Update data model
    Translate entities and relationships into tables/record types
    Perform sizing
    Perform controlled denormalization
    Determine indexes

Standards are essential to ensure uniformity in tasks managed by multiple people. They are required for all life-cycle stages in a project. Standards for requirements specification and user interfaces are finalized during the requirements analysis stage. Almost all other standards needed in the project should be developed during the design phase, including the detailed design standards, coding standards, document standards, and user interface standards.

The operating environment is the target platform on which the deployed application will finally run. Frequently, it is decided by the customer and is based on economic, technology, or other factors. As the operating environment may affect the solution, its details must be understood before the design is established.

Functional design is the activity that transforms the process model developed during the requirements analysis stage into a set of software functions, each representing a packet of business logic. Functions that constitute the application are derived from the processing requirements for each business event. A complex event could break down into many functions or more than one small event could be combined to make a function. A cross-reference between the business events in the process models and the functions should be established to make sure that all customer requirements are satisfied. This information may also be used to populate the traceability matrix. Once the functions in the application are determined, the business logic is specified for each function. The final functional specification for the application is detailed in a document that describes the various functions that form the application and the relationships between functions.

For a project using object orientation, the activity "do functional design" is replaced by "define logical and physical object model," which includes tasks to identify classes, their attributes, their methods, relationships between classes, and the dynamic interaction between objects. In the development process, high-level design is the main stage where the process for object orientation differs from the standard process. In the rest of the stages, the differences are mostly in the standards, guidelines, and checklists used.

From the data model prepared during the requirements analysis, the physical database structure is derived during the design phase. Physical database design involves the identification of tables/record types, fields, and other components. During design, the data model developed earlier may need to be modified based on the more detailed information that may become available during functional design—during functional design, it may be found that some entities need more attributes or that some attributes are unnecessary. Once the database structure is fixed, the entities in the data model are translated to tables/record types after normalization. Once the tables and records are known, the size of the database/files can be estimated. This information is useful when allocating space for the database.

A normalized database is not necessarily the optimal design. If an application requires frequent access to a set of fields that reside on multiple normalized tables, it may be inefficient to create joins. In such a case, the associated fields are brought into one table to improve response time. This case is one example of controlled denormalization. For performance reasons, it is often necessary to create indexes to randomly accessed tables/record types, so all indexes needed should be determined.

4.1.2   Detailed Design

During the detailed design phase, the view of the application developed during the high-level design is broken down into modules and programs. Logic design is done for every program and then documented as program specifications. For every program, a unit test plan is created. Important activities in the detailed design stage include the identification of common routines and programs (for example, date validation routines), development of skeleton programs, and development of utilities and tools for productivity improvement.

The participants in this phase are the members of the design team. The entry criterion is that the high-level design documents are reviewed and authorized. The input is the high-level design document, and the outputs are the functional specification document and unit test plans. The exit criteria are that the program specifications and unit test plans have been reviewed and authorized. Measurements needed in this phase involve the detailed design effort, design defects, unit test plan defects, program skeleton defects, and review and rework effort. The sequence of steps in this phase is as follows:

> Break down functions into their components
> Develop data migration programs, if needed
> Design/develop code skeletons
> Develop utilities/tools
> Do program design
>> Identify the method of program invocation

        Identify inputs and outputs
        Design program logic
        Identify data structures
        Identify common routines to be used
        Write program specifications and get them reviewed
    Plan unit testing
        Identify the testing environment
        Identify unit test cases
        Identify test data
        Write a unit test plan and get it reviewed

Functions are packets of business logic. They could break down into one or more programs or modules. Hence, the first step in detailed design is to break functions into programs and modules and to identify the programs that will form the interfaces between functions. If data must be migrated from some existing applications, then data migration programs also need to be developed and tested. Without them, programs for the current application cannot be tested properly, so it is important to develop and test them early. For this reason, they are done during the detailed design phase.

Skeletons or templates may play a key role in a development project. Many programs in a typical application can be categorized into a few types, with programs of the same type doing very similar tasks. A skeleton can therefore be written for these types, which can then be used to code a majority of the programs in the application. The advantage of building skeletons is that it minimizes dependence on individual programming styles and reduces the chances of making errors. As these skeletons will be used to develop many programs, it is important to carefully review and test them.

Utilities and tools can improve productivity. In many situations in a project, use of utilities and tools can speed up the development process. To derive the maximum benefit from these utilities, they should be developed early, before the coding activity starts. Hence, they are created during the detailed design phase.

Providing details of the invocation methods, inputs, outputs, logic, data structure, and other features of a program or module is called program design. The method of program invocation indicates how a program starts executing— for example, whether it is called by another program or is directly invoked using a transaction identifier. The method of invocation decides the way in which input parameters are passed to the program.

Each program being developed must undergo unit testing. During detailed design, when the logic of the program becomes clear, a plan for unit testing of the programs should be finalized. Unit test cases are the conditions for which the program needs to be tested. The test data for every test case should be decided in advance to ensure that the data are available for all test cases during testing. Testing procedures identify the method of setting up the test environment for a program, and they describe the way to set up data for the test. Documented test plans should be reviewed.

4.1.3 Build and Unit Testing

During the build phase, the detailed design is used to produce the required programs in a programming language. This stage produces the source code, executables, and databases (if applicable) following the appropriate coding standards. The output of this phase is the subject of subsequent testing and validation.

The participants are members of the team and the team leader. The entry criterion is that the program specifications are reviewed and authorized. The inputs for this phase are the physical database design document, project standards, program specifications, unit test plan, program skeletons, and any utilities and tools and their associated documents. The exit criterion is that all test cases in the unit test plan are successfully executed. The outputs for this phase include the test data, source code, executables, code review report/review records, and independent unit test report/review records. The measurements made during this phase capture the build and unit testing effort, code review defects, independent unit test defects, and review and rework effort. The activities in this phase are as follows:

> Generate test database
> Generate code
>> Code programs
>> Do code review
>> Log and fix review defects
>> Conduct self-unit test
>>> Do self-unit test
>>> Do additional testing
>>> Fix defects
> Conduct independent unit test
>> Prepare for independent unit test
>> Do independent unit test
>> Log all defects
>> Close independent unit test

The test database may be generated depending on the requirement. Generating code is the major activity of the build phase. During coding, the detailed design of software is translated into the selected programming language. The coding process involves creating source code and executables, getting the code independently reviewed, and performing self-tests (that is, the developer does the testing). During the self-test, the programmer also tests the programs using the unit test plan prepared during the detailed design phase. The defects found in this testing need not be logged, although the programmer must remove them.

Once the programmer is satisfied with the code, it is made available for independent unit testing. An independent tester/team tests the self-tested unit against the unit test plan. The independent tester studies the unit test plan and then sets up the test environment. A copy of test data is obtained or created, and test drivers and stubs are created or obtained. The unit is then tested according to the unit test plan. Any defects found are logged. During independent testing, unlike in self-testing, the tester does not fix any bugs but passes the program on to the programmer for fixing defects. Once the defects are fixed, the unit may be independently unit-tested again.

4.1.4   Integration Planning and Testing

Integration is a systematic approach to building the complete software structure specified in the design from unit-tested modules. Integration can be done in many ways, and the integration plan must specify the order in which the modules will be integrated. During this phase, tests are also conducted to find defects associated with interfacing. Integration is performed in the order specified in the integration plan and corresponding test cases for each integration phase are executed. The integration plan describes the sequence of integration, overhead software (stubs and drivers), test environment, and resources required. Along with integration planning, integration testing planning is also usually done.

The participants in this phase are members of the integration team. The entry criterion is that the high-level design documents are reviewed and authorized. The input for this phase consists of the high-level design documents and programs, and the output for this phase is the integration plan. The exit criteria are that the integration plan and integration test plan have been reviewed and authorized. The sequence of steps in integration planning and testing is as follows:

> Identify environmental needs
> Determine integration procedure
> > Identify critical modules to be integrated
> > Identify order of integration
> > Identify interfaces to be tested
> Develop integration test plan
> > Identify test cases and procedures to execute them
> > Identify test data
> > Identify expected results
> > Resequence test cases

The first step in integration planning is to identify the environment needs for integration. The integration environment needs include the physical characteristics of the hardware, the communications and system software, the mode of usage (for example, stand-alone), and so on. Integration can be done in many ways. The software can be developed and tested in small segments, where errors are easier to isolate and correct and interfaces are more likely to be tested completely. Alternatively, the main program can be developed and tested first and then integration performed by moving downward through the control hierarchy. The selection of a particular integration strategy depends upon the software's characteristics. The integration procedure should identify the critical modules (the ones that are complex, used by many programs, and so on) so they can be tested early, the order in which the modules will be integrated, the interfaces that should be tested, the activities for tool integration, and the procedure for checking the results of testing.

Along with planning for system integration, planning for integration testing should be done. In this effort, test cases are designed based on the order of integration. These test cases focus primarily on testing the interfaces of the modules. The procedure to execute each test case is described along with the test case, the input and output data, and the results expected after executing each test case.

Based on the integration plan, actual integration is carried out. Integration planning and integration testing are separate phases in the process. The reason for separating planning from the testing activity is the same as in unit and system testing—to allow parallel execution with some phases. For example, although actual integration cannot be done until the build phase is complete, integration planning can take place before, or even in parallel with, the build phase.

The integration test plan is used to test the integration. All defects found during integration testing must be logged and fixed. After integration is finished, a complete software product is available.

4.1.5   System Test Planning and Testing

System testing is an activity to validate the software product against the requirement specification. This stage is intended to find defects that can be exposed only by testing the entire system. Attributes such as external interfaces, performance, security, configuration sensitivity, coexistence, recovery, and reliability are validated during this phase. A series of different tests, each test having a different purpose, are done such that together they verify that all system elements have been properly integrated and that the system performs all its functions and satisfies all its nonfunctional requirements. Before system testing begins, it must be carefully planned in the system test planning phase.

The participants in the planning phase are members of the system test team. The entry criteria are that the requirements specification document and the high-level design documents are reviewed and authorized. Note that the system test planning can occur before coding is completed. Indeed, it is often done in parallel with coding. The inputs for this phase are the high-level design documents and the requirements specification document, and the outputs are the system test plan and test results. The exit criterion is that the system test plan is reviewed and authorized. The main activities in this phase are as follows:

Determine environmental needs
Determine system test procedure
    Identify features to be tested
        Identify user interfaces
        Identify hardware interfaces
        Identify software interfaces
        Identify communication interfaces
        Identify major business processes performed by the system
    Identify significant features not to be tested and the reasons for their omission
    Identify critical tests
Develop test cases
    Identify each test case and a procedure to execute it
    Identify input and output data requirements
    Identify expected results

After identifying the environmental needs, features that should be tested and features that need not be tested are identified, along with any critical tests that might be needed. These form the basis for developing test cases. System test cases are designed to test each feature identified for testing and for each critical test. The procedure to execute each test case is described along with the test case. The input and output data are identified. The results expected after executing each test case are detailed, along with the method of checking results.

Once the test plan is ready, actual system testing can be performed. During this testing, the system tester studies the test plan and sets up the test environment. This effort includes setting up test regions, test databases, tools, and other resources required for the system test. A copy of test data is obtained or created. The system is then tested according to the test plan, by executing the test cases in the system test plan using the procedures specified, checking test results, updating the system test plan with new test cases, and executing the new test cases. The test results are checked and the defects are logged. If additional test cases are needed, they are added to the test plan and the new test cases are executed. The tester passes the system to the development team to fix any defects. Once the defects are corrected, the system is tested again.

The tester determines whether the system passed or failed in each test case based on the expected results specified for that test case in the system test plan and logs defects. He or she also decides whether to continue with system testing, if major defects are found. The design and implementation of the system are revisited based on the test results and defects identified. The development team analyzes each failed test case and decides on an approach to fix defects, then updates documents to reflect the changes and fixes.

4.1.6   Documentation

Documentation refers to operation manuals, user manuals, and other documents needed by the customer. These documents may be developed by the development team itself or by a documentation team with input from the development team. The major activities in this phase are as follows:

> Prepare user manuals
> Prepare operation manuals
> Prepare data conversion manuals
> Prepare online help
> Review documentation/manuals

This phase is generally performed toward the end of the development effort, as fewer people are involved in the direct software development activities in the later stages of a project. User manuals, which depend mostly on the requirements specification, may be prepared in the early stages of the project.

4.1.7   Acceptance and Installation

Acceptance and installation is the phase in the software life cycle during which a software product is integrated into its operational environment and tested in this environment to ensure that it performs as required. This phase includes two basic tasks: getting the software accepted and installing the software at the customer site. Acceptance consists of formal testing conducted by the customer according to the acceptance test plan prepared earlier and analysis of the test results to determine whether the system satisfies its acceptance criteria. When the results of the analysis satisfy the acceptance criteria, the user accepts the software. Installation involves placing the accepted software in the actual production environment.

The participants are the installation team, the customer, and the project leader. The entry criterion is that the system test has been successfully completed, and the main inputs are the tested software and the acceptance criteria document. The exit criterion is that the customer signs off on the acceptance letter, and the main output is the installed software. The primary measurements are the effort spent and the defects found. The main activities in this phase are as follows:

Perform acceptance
    Plan for acceptance
        Get details of acceptance environment from customer
        Prepare installation plan
        Prepare software release document
    Participate in acceptance
        Install software in the acceptance environment
        Conduct live run
        Help customer do acceptance testing
        Fix acceptance defects
        Update documents to reflect any changes made
        Obtain acceptance sign-off from customer
Perform installation
    Install software in the production environment
    Set up production environment
    Load data and software
    Conduct live run
    Get customer sign-off for each installation
    Fix installation defects
    Conduct customer training

As with most other activities, a plan has to be first prepared for acceptance. A software release note is prepared that contains stepwise instructions for the user on how to install the software. The instructions include information on creating the directory structures, installing source and executables, loading data needed for installation, and so on. The primary responsibility for acceptance testing is assigned to the customer. The development team merely helps in this effort. Acceptance testing requires that a testing environment be set up that mirrors the production environment as closely as possible. The software is installed and the acceptance test data are created in the acceptance environment according to the installation plan. Any problems encountered during the installation are documented, and the installation plan is updated accordingly. Defects found in acceptance testing are logged and fixed.

After acceptance is achieved, the software must be released for production use. The sequence of steps here are the same as those for acceptance, except that the software is loaded on the user's main machine. During installation, the basic goal is to place the system in the production environment such that it is ready for use by the end-users. In preparation for this step, the final application with any necessary database data, the operating documentation, and the installation plan are packaged onto their respective media and delivered. The software and any required data are installed in the production environment according to the installation plan.

Available data are loaded into the database and live runs are conducted. If the site conditions affect system performance, such effects are documented.

Any problems encountered during installation are documented and fixed. At the completion of installation, customer sign-off must be obtained. Any training necessary to operate the software is provided to the concerned groups.

4.1.8   Warranty Support

Warranty support is the phase during which the installed application is supported until it stabilizes in the production environment. The participants are the installation team. The entry criterion is that the application goes live in production. The inputs in this stage include the installed application, user documents, and software trouble reports. The exit criteria are that the warranty support period as stipulated in the contract has ended and the customer has signed off on the entire project. The outputs consist of the sign-off document from the customer and the installed application. The measurements needed during this stage assess the effort and warranty support defects. After the warranty period expires, the software is fully handed over to the customer.

4.2 Process Tailoring

An organization's standard process for a task defines a standard way of doing that task. Clearly, no "standard way" will apply to all situations and all projects. For various projects, different approaches may be the best option. Indeed, insistence on following a standard process might impose a suboptimal process for a project. At the same time, the process used for executing projects should be standardized to realize the benefits of the process-based approach. One way to provide flexibility while maintaining standard processes is to have a set of standard processes rather than one standard process. For a project, any process from the set can be used. For example, as discussed earlier, Infosys has developed different standard processes for reengineering projects, maintenance projects, development projects, and so on. A project, depending on the type of work involved, selects one of these processes.

   This approach permits some flexibility, but at a very high level. It essentially creates different classes of projects. Although projects of different classes can use different processes, projects within a class are not allowed to use different processes—they must use the standard process for that class. For a project, however, more flexibility is needed in deciding how to execute it. This flexibility is provided, within the context of a standard process, by permitting tailoring of the standard process.

   Tailoring is the process of adjusting the standard process of the organization to obtain a process that is suitable for the particular business or technical needs of a project [4]. We can view tailoring of a process as adding, deleting, or modifying the activities of a process, such that the resulting process is better suited for achieving the goals of the project. Uncontrolled tailoring effectively implies that no standard process exists, as any process can be defined and used. To control this deviation, guidelines are provided for tailoring a process. These guidelines define permissible rules for changing the standard process for a project. In essence, they define a set of "permitted deviations" of the standard process in the hope that the "optimal" process can be defined for a project. Process tailoring and tailoring guidelines are key requirements at CMM level 3, particularly the Integrated Software Management and the Software Product Engineering KPAs. Figure 4.2 illustrates the role of tailoring guidelines for a project.

For example, let's take an activity in the build phase of the development process—*do code review.* Code review adds a great deal of value in many cases, but sometimes its value addition is not commensurate with the effort required. Also, the review could be done by either a group following the group review procedure or one person. The standard development process does not specify how code review should be performed. Tailoring guidelines can help a project by advising that the activity *do code review* be performed only for certain types of programs (such as complex programs or external interfaces) and by suggesting the optimal form of the review (group review or one-person review).

Tailoring guidelines try to capture the experience and judgment of people regarding how tailoring can be done effectively. With such guidelines, the past experience of people who have used the process becomes available so that even a newer person, who may not have the necessary experience, can select the optimal process for a project.

The tailoring principles defined by Humphrey [6] suggest that unique aspects of the project should be identified first, and then these features should be used to make adjustments to the standard process. A common approach to employ this principle for tailoring is to "tailor by degree"—that is, to allow different "degrees" for some attributes. Attributes that have been suggested for tailoring include: formality, frequency, granularity, and scope [4]. For example, for the formality attribute, the tailoring guidelines may specify the use of different degrees of formality for different projects and provide advice for selecting the proper degree.

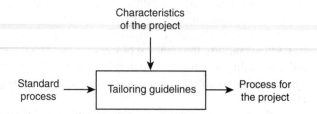

Figure 4.2   Role of tailoring guidelines

The approach for tailoring used at Infosys is similar to the table-based approach proposed by Ginsberg and Quinn [4], in which the process element, the tailorable attribute, the options for each attribute, and the reasons for selecting a particular option are specified. Tailoring occurs at two levels: summary and detailed. *Summary tailoring guidelines* suggest how some general activities should be performed in the project, based on some project characteristics. *Detailed tailoring guidelines* list all activities in a process for various life-cycle stages along with the information regarding tailoring for each activity.

4.2.1 Summary Tailoring Guidelines

Summary level tailoring, depending on the project characteristics, gives overall guidelines for detailed tailoring. That is, it provides some general rules regarding certain types of detailed activities. To perform this step, some characteristics for projects must be identified. For development projects, the following characteristics are used for tailoring:

- Skill level of the team
- Peak team size
- Application criticality

The skill level of the team is considered high if a majority of team members have more than two years of experience with the technology being deployed in the project; otherwise, it is considered low. Application criticality is considered high if the effect of the application on a customer's business or Infosys' business is significant; otherwise, it is low.

Summary tailoring guidelines are based on the values of these characteristics. For various combinations of values, different guidelines apply. The summary guidelines are primarily review-related, effort-related, or formality-related. Review-related guidelines specify when reviews should be done and what type of review should take place. The effort-related guidelines suggest steps to be taken for the project that may affect the effort. Formality-related guidelines recommend the degree of formality to be used for some activities. Summary guidelines for some types of projects are shown in Table 4.1.

Similar guidelines are provided for other combinations of values of characteristics. As we can see, these general guidelines concern only some activities and set the context for detailed tailoring. How they affect the activities that should be part of the process for the project will be decided by applying detailed tailoring guidelines.

4.2.2 Detailed Tailoring Guidelines

Once the summary-level tailoring is complete, the context for detailed tailoring is set. The detailed tailoring guidelines give options for various activities.

Table 4.1   Summary Guidelines for Tailoring

Size of Team ≥ 12, Skill Level—Low, Application Criticality—High	
Summary Guidelines	**Why?**
Review-related Guidelines	
• Conduct group reviews for all high-impact documents (for example, project plan, skeletons)	Identify problems very early, thus avoiding rework
• Identify reviewers from other groups for reviews	Leverage the expertise of other groups as not enough skilled reviewers are available in the project
• Group-review the first few outputs (code and documents) from each person	Because the skill level is low, initial guidance is necessary
Effort-related Guidelines	
• Divide the application into *independent* components	Reduce complexity
• Provide well-written and tested skeletons to developers	Improve quality
• Develop automated tools for similar type of output/activity (for example, generators for maintenance programs)	Reduce effort
• In schedule, budget for learning curve of new developers	
• Plan and conduct training in advance	
Formality-related Guidelines	
• Implement formal configuration management procedures; use CM tools	Because the team size is high, the absence of formal procedures may lead to confusion and loss of work
• Implement formal change management procedures	

Size of Team < 12, Skill Level—High, Application Criticality—Low	
Summary Guidelines	**Why?**
Review-related Guidelines	
• Conduct group reviews only for high-impact documents (for example, HLD, code for complex modules)	Because the skill level is high and criticality is low, group-review of all documents is not not necessary
• Number of reviews can be reduced	

Size of Team < 12, Skill Level—High, Application Criticality—Low (*continued*)

Effort-related Guidelines

• Provide skeletons only when usage is high	Because the skill level is high, skeletons will have a limited value unless used heavily

Formality-related Guidelines

• Change management procedures can be less formal	Because the team size is small and skill level is high

---

Summary tailoring guidelines provide the backdrop and reasons for making the selection. In contrast, detailed tailoring guidelines specify for each process step whether it is mandatory or tailorable and, if it is tailorable, what attributes of the activities can be tailored, the alternatives that are available, and guidelines for when to employ the different alternatives.

Examples of attributes for tailoring include execution, documentation, review, and level of detail. Alternatives when execution is the tailorable attribute are "perform this activity" or "do not perform this activity." Similarly, alternatives for documentation are "prepare document" or "do not prepare document." Alternatives for review are "group review," "do one-person review," or "do not review."

As examples, tailoring guidelines for two stages of the development process are shown in Tables 4.2 and 4.3. Only the tailorable activities are listed here; all other activities specified in the process are mandatory.

Table 4.2   Tailoring Guidelines for Requirements Analysis

Activity	Tailorable Attribute	Alternatives	Tailoring Guidelines
Prepare for Requirements Gathering and Analysis			
Identify methods of information gathering	Techniques	User interviews Observation	For new requirements For understanding the existing operations thoroughly
		Using any existing application	If an application already exists that covers at least some requirements of the users

(continued)

Table 4.2   Tailoring Guidelines for Requirements Analysis (*continued*)

Activity	Tailorable Attribute	Alternatives	Tailoring Guidelines
Prepare for Requirements Gathering and Analysis			
Undergo training	Execution	Do not perform this activity	If the analysts are experienced in application and techniques
		Perform this activity	For others
Plan prototyping	Execution	Perform this activity	When users are not clear about the proposed system or criticality of the requirement is high
		Do not perform this activity	When requirements are clear (for example, for batch functions, standard operations)
Define requirements specification standards	Execution	Perform this activity	If the customer's standards are not available, or if Infosys standards needs to be customized
		Do not perform this activity	If standards to be used are available
Develop interview plan	Documentation	Prepare a formal plan	Time availability of the users is limited
		Do not prepare formal plan	For others
Gather Requirements			
Prepare and demonstrate prototypes	Execution	Perform this activity	If a prototype is planned
		Do not perform this activity	For other cases
Analyze Requirements			
Develop process model	Level of detail	Detailed	For critical and complex business functions
		Overview	For other types of business functions
Develop logical data model	Level of detail	Detailed	For important entities
		Overview	For other entities

Table 4.3 Tailoring Guidelines for Build

Activity	Tailorable Attribute	Alternatives	Tailoring Guidelines for Development Project
Generate test database	Execution	Do not perform this activity	When test data are available from the existing system
		Perform this activity	If data needs to be generated
Do code review	Reviewer	Do group review	For all complex/critical/external interface programs; for all important server programs or first few programs of each type (online, batch, report) when skill level is low; or if specifically recommended by the high-level design group review team
		Do one-person review	For the first program of each type when skill level is high; for subsequent programs when skill level is low, until output is satisfactory; or for 30% to 100% of medium-complexity programs based on skill
		No review	For simple programs
Log and fix code review defects	Review records	Record comments	For all important comments
		Record only the number	For all cosmetic defects
Conduct independent unit test	Execution	Perform this activity	For all complex/critical/external interface programs; or for first few programs of each type (online, batch, report) when skill level is low
		Do not perform this activity	When skill level of the developer is high or when code is generated using a tool

Once the process is tailored for a project, the sequence of activities in the process for this project is defined. These definitions are then used to plan and schedule activities for the project and form the basis of process execution on the project. In some situations, the tailoring guidelines may not be sufficient and the project needs to modify the standard process further. In such a case, all "deviations" are to be highlighted in the project plan, thereby calling attention to such deviations and providing information for future enhancement of tailoring guidelines.

4.2.3   Example: Process Tailoring for WAR Project

We illustrate the use of tailoring guidelines by showing how they are deployed in the WAR project, our case study introduced in Chapter 3. The characteristics of this development project are summarized below:

Size of team	<12
Skill level of team	Low
Application criticality	Low

For this project, from the tailoring guidelines, the summary guidelines match those given in Table 4.4.

Table 4.4   Summary Guidelines for WAR Project

Review-related Guidelines

• Conduct group reviews for all high-impact documents
• Identify reviewers from other groups for reviews
• First few outputs from each person must be group-reviewed

Effort-related Guidelines

• Develop automated tools for similar types of outputs and activities
• Provide well-written and tested skeletons to developers
• In the schedule, budget for learning curve of new developers
• Plan and conduct training in advance

Formality-related Guidelines

• Implement formal change management procedures.

These summary guidelines serve as general guidelines for tailoring the development process for the WAR project. During detailed tailoring, options were chosen based on their suitability for the project and the summary guidelines. The options chosen and the reasons for choosing them for the requirements analysis and build phases are given in Table 4.5. The tailoring guidelines were discussed earlier in the chapter.

Table 4.5 Tailoring for WAR Project

Activity	Option Chosen	Reasons
Requirements Analysis		
Identify methods of information gathering	Using existing application	There is an existing WAR system and the new system has to be consistent with it
Undergo training	Perform this activity	Project persons may not always be familiar with the technology; also training is identified as a risk mitigation step
Plan prototyping	Perform this activity	Users were not comfortable with some restrictions that the Web interface would impose
Define requirement specification standards	Do not perform this activity	Infosys standards were used
Develop interview plan	Do not perform this activity	A user group was actively involved, and prototyping was planned
Prepare and demonstrate prototype	Perform this activity	Prototyping was planned
Develop process model	Overview	Business functions are not critical
Develop logical data model	Overview	Model for existing system exists
Build		
Generate test database	Perform this activity	From database of existing WAR system
Do code review	Group review	For complex modules
	One-person review	For medium modules
	No review	For simple modules
Log and fix code review defects	Record comments	
Conduct independent UT	Perform this activity	For all complex and medium programs

Similarly, choices were made for other stages. For this project, however, the tailoring guidelines were not sufficient to allow selecting the right process for the project. Hence, the process had to be modified beyond what was allowed by the tailoring guidelines. Two process deviations are described below:

- During design, a step was added to develop a proof-of-concept application. This change was made because the project was working with a new technology and had no experience with it.
- In the high-level design phase, a step was added to evaluate available options for the transaction server, so that a suitable product could be chosen and its facilities used in design.

The options chosen from the tailoring guidelines are either marked on the tailoring guidelines table or included appropriately in the MSP schedule of the project. Deviations in the process that are over and above what is permitted by tailoring guidelines represent potential risks and hence need to be highlighted. Such decisions are therefore mentioned in the project management plan, which is reviewed and approved.

4.3 Summary

This chapter examined the development process followed at Infosys, along with some of the tailoring guidelines. The development process is a standard waterfall-type process, with "smaller" phases that allow some parallelism. This process works well for a business where the clients are spread all over the world and a formal contract with the customer is important. In this kind of business, it is best to have clearly defined requirements, which are agreed to by the customer, and then base the development on these requirements. Having an explicit change management process allows for necessary changes. In this chapter, we also discussed the activities involved in the phases in the development process.

Process tailoring refers to the activity of taking a standard process and customizing it to suit the goals of a particular project. Tailoring of a standard process is necessary because different projects have different goals and needs. Tailoring guidelines provide the rules for "allowable tailoring" of the standard process. Some flexibility is provided to select an "optimal" process for a project while retaining a standard process for the organization. At Infosys, summary tailoring guidelines are used first to get some general rules regarding activities, based on some general project characteristics. These guidelines are then used to make decisions regarding the detailed activities in the development process.

References

[1] V. R. Basili and A. Turner. Iterative enhancement, a practical technique for software development. *IEEE Transactions on Software Engineering,* 1(4), 1975.

[2] B. W. Boehm. *Software Engineering Economics.* Prentice Hall, 1981.

[3] B. Boehm. A spiral model of software development and enhancement. *IEEE Computer,* pp. 61–72, May 1988.

[4] M. P. Ginsberg and L. H. Quinn. *Process Tailoring and the Software Capability Maturity Model.* Technical Report, Software Engineering Institute, CMU/ SEI-94-TR-024.

[5] H. Gomma and D. B. H. Scott. Prototyping as a tool in the specification of user requirements. *Proceedings of the 5th International Conference on Software Engineering,* pp. 333–341, 1981.

[6] W. Humphrey. *Managing the Software Process.* Addison-Wesley, 1989.

5

Process Database and Process Capability Baseline

In any organization, past experience plays a key role in improvement and management. Clearly, any good organization or manager will learn from the past experience of the organization or person. How effectively past experience can be used for improvement and process management depends on how well this experience is captured and organized to enable learning. In many aspects of project and organization management, learning can be enhanced and accelerated by systematically recording the history, deriving lessons from it, and then making the lessons available to others. For software projects, the process database (PDB) and process capability baseline (PCB) are two mechanisms for encapsulating past experience for use in project planning and management.

The PDB and PCB encapsulate the experience with previous projects, mostly in the form of software metrics data, and make it available to fresh projects. Information from PDB and PCB is used heavily during project planning. These two mechanisms are not part of the project planning phase. Instead, they provide the key inputs for planning and, in a sense, form the infrastructure for project planning. For this reason, they are described in this part of the book, before any discussion of other elements of planning it. This chapter considers how these two key planning support systems are implemented at Infosys.

The main source of data for these two components is the completed projects. The data collected in the projects is analyzed and then reported in closure reports (see Chapter 15), which form the main source for the PDB. The data in the PDB are then used to compute the PCB. The data used in the PDB and PCB primarily comes from projects. Thus projects provide data that is used by other projects. A project may use data from the PCB or from the PDB. The flow of data is shown in Figure 5.1. In addition to its direct use in projects, the PCB is employed to analyze the organization's overall process capability and its evolution over time.

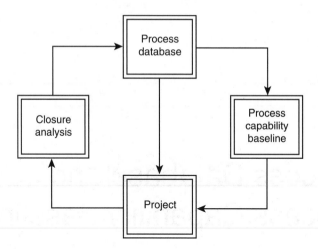

Figure 5.1   PDB and PCB

A process database is required at CMM level 3 in the Organization Process Focus and Organization Process Definition KPAs. At level 3, the database is largely used for collecting data, assets, and experience from different projects that then become available for use in project planning and management. At level 4, the PDB will likely be used for performing process analysis, computing the process capability, and quantitatively controlling a project. The PCB is of interest mostly at level 4—knowing the process capability in quantitative terms is essential for implementing level 4 (it is a goal for the Quantitative Process Management KPA, and the Software Quality Management KPA requires documentation of the capability of the process to satisfy quality goals). As both the PDB and the PCB focus on software metrics, which quantitatively characterize important features of the software or the process, let us examine the role of metrics in projects and processes before we discuss the PDB and PCB.

5.1 Software Metrics and Process Management

Software metrics can be used to quantitatively characterize different aspects of the software process or software products. *Process metrics* quantify attributes of the software process or the development environment, whereas *product metrics* are measures for the software products [3]. Product metrics remain independent of the process used to produce the product. Examples of process metrics include productivity, quality, resource metrics, defect injection rate, and defect and removal efficiency. Examples of product metrics include size, reliability, quality (quality can be viewed as a product metric as well as a process metric) complexity of the code, and functionality. Software metrics has been one of the most active areas of research. In this section we will discuss the use of metrics for managing the software process. For information about general metrics and models, the reader is referred to [3], [4], [10], and [14]. For further information regarding the use of metrics for process improvement and project management, the reader is referred to [6], [7], and [12].

5.1.1 Purpose of Collecting Metrics Data

The use of metrics necessarily requires that measurements be made to collect data. For any metrics program, we must clearly understand the reasons for collecting data as well as the models that will be used for making judgments based on the data. Otherwise, we may waste a great deal of energy in collecting data that has little value, which in turn dissuades people from collecting data. A corollary is that the use of data should be visible to the people collecting the data, and the analysis of data should likewise provide them with value. If the data are used only for analysis for some presentations and do not help the projects directly, then the motivation to collect data will decline over time. Hence, even though long-term trend analysis may be one objective of data collection, data should also be used to provide short-term benefits in project management and control. Although many reasons for collecting metrics data can be cited, the most important uses of metrics in a software organization are as follows:

- **Project planning.** Past data from completed projects are invaluable in developing reasonable plans for a new project and setting realistic goals for it.
- **Controlling a project's process.** Metrics can provide accurate information about the state of a project, which can then be used to take corrective actions in a timely manner.
- **Analyzing and improving the organization's processes.** Only through metrics can an organization know the quality and productivity capability of its processes and the change in quality and productivity with time. Identifying potential areas of improvement is also facilitated by the use of metrics.

These three uses generally provide the driving force for a metrics program in an organization. For using metrics for these purposes, a metrics infrastructure is needed. The PDB and PCB are components of this infrastructure and are very useful for planning and overall process analysis. The PCB, as its name suggests, focuses on process metrics. The main purposes of the metrics here are to understand the organization's process, which leads to the identification of areas for improvement and to help in planning the process of specific projects (that is, to help in prediction). The data in the PDB derives from projects and includes both process and product metrics.

If the goal of measurements is clear, then the next question is, What should be measured? Although the choice of which metrics to use, and how to use them, should be driven by the goals of the organization and the project (and an approach like the goal-question-metric paradigm can be used to identify the metrics that need to be measured [1, 2]), generally a few metrics will suffice for most purposes. Schedule, size, effort, and defects are the basic measurements for project and process management purposes [12] and form a good initial metrics set [6]. We will discuss data collection in detail in Chapter 13. In this chapter, we focus on how data are utilized in the PDB and PCB. Note, also, that the discussion here covers only the metrics used in the development process. For other processes, like the maintenance process, different metrics may be used (for example, in maintenance, a throughput metric of number of bug fixes per week is used to assess productivity).

5.1.2   Metrics and Statistical Process Control

Statistical process control (SPC) is a technique that has been used with great success in manufacturing. To apply SPC concepts to a software process, metrics are essential. Before we discuss how SPC may be used in controlling the software process, let us briefly consider some general SPC concepts. The reader is referred to any textbook on statistical quality control (for example, [11, 15, 16]) for further details.

A process is used to produce some output. The quality of the output produced can be defined in terms of some quality *characteristics.* The purpose of SPC is to control the process of production so as to reduce the variability in the values of the output's quality characteristics in order to improve the quality over time.

A number of factors affect the characteristics of the process output. These factors can be classified into two categories: *natural* or *inherent* causes for variability, and *assignable* causes for variability. Each of the many natural causes contributes to the variability, and controlling all of these causes is not practical, unless the process itself is changed. Assignable causes tend to have a larger influence over variability in the process performance and can be controlled. Figure 5.2 illustrates the relationship between causes and quality characteristics.

A process is said to be under *statistical control* if the variability in the quality characteristics is due to natural causes only. The goal of SPC is to keep the production process in statistical control.

For applying SPC, *control charts* are a favorite tool. For building a control chart, the output of a process is considered as a stream of numeric values, representing the values of the characteristic of interest for the outputs being produced

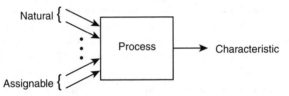

Figure 5.2 Natural and assignable causes

by the process. Subgroups of data are taken from this stream, and the mean values for the subgroups are plotted, giving the X-bar chart. A lower control limit (LCL) and upper control limit (UCL) are established. If a point fails outside the control limits, the large variability is considered to be due to assignable causes. Another chart, called the R-chart, plots the range (the difference between the minimum and maximum values) of the chosen subgroups. Control limits are established for the R-chart, and a point falling outside the control limits established for this chart is also considered as having assignable causes.

By convention, LCL and UCL are set at 3-sigma around the mean, where sigma is the standard deviation for data with only normal variability (that is, variability due to natural causes). With these limits, the probability of a "false alarm," in which a point with natural variability fails outside the limits, is only 0.27%. The *capability* of a process, which defines the range of expected outcomes when the process is under statistical control, is the range specified by the LCL and UCL.

In situations where the production process does not yield the same item repeatedly, as is the case with software processes, forming subgroups may not make sense; individual values are therefore considered. For such processes, XMR charts [11, 15, 16] may be used. In an XMR chart, a moving range of two consecutive values is considered as the range for the R-chart. For the X-bar chart, the individual values are plotted; the control limits are then determined using the average moving range. The upper (lower) limit is obtained by adding to (subtracting from) the mean of individual values 2.66 times the mean moving range [15, 16].

The control charts are used to continuously monitor the performance of the process and identify an out-of-control situation as soon as it occurs. Unfortunately, they only identify when the process goes out of statistical control. The action to be taken when a point representing some output falls outside the control limit is decided separately. Generally, two types of actions are performed:

- Rework this output, such that it has acceptable characteristics. That is, take corrective action.
- Do further analysis to identify the assignable causes and eliminate them from the process. That is, take preventive actions.

Next, we will consider how SPC and control charts can be applied to the software process using suitable metrics for characteristics. As mentioned earlier, for software processes, XMR charts may be best suited. For employing control charts, we will first identify the processes to which SPC can be applied. One choice is the overall process, whose output is the software product to be delivered. The characteristics that can be studied for the output of this process include productivity, defect density delivered, and defect injection rate, among others. The value of most of these characteristics for the output of the overall process can be obtained only after the project ends, so SPC for the overall process has limited value for project monitoring and control. Its value lies primarily in improving the overall process by taking suitable preventable measures.

To control a project, SPC can be deployed for "mini-processes" that execute during the course of the project, such as the review process or testing process. Under SPC, as soon as the process is completed in the project, its results can be analyzed. If required, control can be applied in the form of corrective or preventive actions for the project. Through corrective actions, the out-of-limit output is made acceptable; preventive actions help execute the remainder of the project better. We will discuss project-level control later in Chapters 12 and 13, when we discuss reviews and project monitoring.

In this chapter, we discuss the overall process metrics data only. For the overall process, data points are difficult to obtain, as one project generates only one data point. Furthermore, the performance variation in such data tends to be large [6, 8, 10]. One reason for the large performance variation is that, unlike in manufacturing, the next product (software) to be "produced" using the process may be vastly different in size, scope, and functionality from the previous one. Another possible explanation is that software processes are heavily people-dependent—people execute the various steps in the processes—so "specified process was not followed" is a major cause for performance variation.

Given the possibility of a large variation in performance, identifying points with only natural variability for determining the control limits is not an easy task. Hence, for computing the control limits from past performance data, judgment might have to be used to determine which data points should be excluded. Furthermore, past data should not be used blindly, and discerning management must always support its use. For example, just because the performance is out of the range computed from past data, a process failure is not always present [8, 10]. A more suitable approach is to use the performance range to "draw attention," after which the reasons for the deviation can be analyzed. Similarly, the data on past performance should not be used blindly during planning (for example, the effort estimate should not be obtained simply as a product of the size estimate and inverse of productivity).

5.2 Process Database

The process database is a permanent repository of process performance data from projects, which can be used for project planning, estimation, analysis of productivity and quality, and other purposes [8]. The PDB consists of data from completed projects, with each project providing one data record for the PDB. As can be imagined, to populate the PDB, data must be collected in projects, analyzed, and then organized for entry into the PDB. Data collection and analysis can be complex and time-consuming tasks, so it is important to state clearly which data are needed and why. There is no point in collecting vast amounts of data, unless the information can be used in some ways for attaining the project or the organization objectives. For this reason, the purpose of the PDB and the services it needs to provide to projects and the organization should be clearly delineated. The following are the key purposes of the PDB:

- To aid a new project in planning, particularly in the estimation of effort and defects
- To collect productivity and quality data on different types of projects
- To aid in creating process capability baselines
- To facilitate data analysis for identifying areas and scope of improvement

To satisfy these objectives, the process database contains metrics data, and some notes, about completed projects. It holds mostly data on the overall process, which describe the history of usage of the process on various projects. The data on reviews are not kept in this database (except at a summary level), but rather maintained separately. We will discuss the review data in Chapter 12.

5.2.1 Contents

Based on the services that the PDB should provide, the contents of the database can be decided. As one purpose of the PDB is to aid in project planning, particularly the estimation activities, it should contain all data about projects that may be useful for future projects in planning and estimation. The question then becomes, What information does a new project need about past projects that can be used in planning? Although some averages and general data can be extracted from past projects and made available to new projects, software projects tend to be different, so project managers might not feel very comfortable using "averages." One important way in which a new project can use information from past projects is to find a "similar" project, obtain data on various aspects of that project, and then use those data for planning. To allow for "similarity" checking, some general information about the project—such as languages used, platforms, databases used, tools used, size, and effort—should also be captured in the PDB. With this type of information, a project can search and find information on all projects that focused on a particular application domain, used a particular database management system (DBMS) or language, or targeted a specific platform, for example.

To achieve the other objectives of the PDB, data about productivity and quality must be captured. This effort requires that a summary of defects, effort, and size be captured. To aid in the creation of a process capability baseline, which gives the averages of various data and trends, data about the effort and defects also needs to be captured. In the PDB, each completed project forms one data point. In turn, each data point consists of many data elements about the project. The data about a project can be classified into the following categories:

- Project characteristics
- Project schedule
- Project effort
- Size
- Defects

The information on the project characteristics consists of the project name, the names of the project and module leaders (so they can be contacted for further information or clarifications about the project), the business unit to which the project belongs (to permit business-unit-wise analysis), the process being deployed in the project (that is, development, maintenance, reengineering, and so on, which allows analysis for different processes to be done separately), the application domain, the hardware platform, the languages used, the DBMS used, a brief statement of the project goals, information about project risks, the duration of the project, and team size. As can be seen, information on project characteristics is general information about the project that can be used to check for "similarity" with an upcoming project.

The information on schedule is primarily the expected start and end dates for the project, and the actual start and end dates.

The information on project effort includes data on the initial estimated effort and the total actual effort. The actual effort spent in the project includes the effort for project initiation, requirements management, design, build, unit testing, and other phases. Capturing the effort spent in the different phases makes it possible to analyze the distribution of effort—this analysis is required for the process capability baseline as well. How the effort data are actually captured in a project is discussed in Chapter 13.

The information on size includes the size of the software developed project. It may be stated in terms of LOC, the number of simple, medium, or complex programs, or a combination of these. (What units of size mean and how they are used in effort estimation is discussed in Chapter 6.) Even if function points are not used for estimation, a uniform metric for productivity may be obtained by representing the final size in function points. The final size in function points is usually obtained by converting the measured size of the software in LOC to function points, using published conversion tables [9]. The size of the final system in function points is also captured.

The information on defects includes the number of defects found in different defect detection activities. Hence, the number of defects found in requirements review, design review, code review, unit testing, and other phases is recorded. These data on distribution of total number of defects found in the project over the different detection stages are also used in the creation of the PCB. In addition, some notes are recorded in the PDB entry, including notes on estimation (for example, what criteria were used for classifying programs as simple, medium, or complex) and notes on risk management (for example, how risk perception changed through the project).

5.2.2 Data Entry and Access

The PDB contains data that are used by other projects and for computing the process capability. Hence it is essential that the data be properly controlled. Although the PDB is owned by the SEPG, all project leaders have read permission. Only the SEPG has the write access to the database. The data from completed projects comes in the form of a project closure analysis report (see Chapter 15), which is entered in the PDB.

The software engineering data may have errors and require validation [1, 7]. That is, the data must be checked before it is "accepted" and used as a basis for making judgments or decisions. For this reason, the project leader is not permitted to enter the data of a project directly in the PDB. Instead, the project leader and the quality advisor from the SEPG do the analysis together. The quality advisor examines the data and does some sanity checks on them and, when needed, seeks clarifications from the project staff. Finally, when the analysis is complete, the quality advisor submits the data to the PDB. The data analysis is also checked to see if the data is "fit" to be used for decision making. The manager SEPG performs this validation. Only when the SEPG manager "approves" the data does the information become visible to others and available for use in planning and PCB creation.

Besides validation, distribution and security issues arise with such a database [6]. These issues are addressed at Infosys by keeping the database on the intranet, accessible only from within the organization.

5.2.3 A Sample Entry

Data for a project are stored in four major tables containing the overall information, information about effort, information about defects, and information about size. A sample PDB entry for a project called NICE is given in this section. Data entry for the four major tables is shown (the example uses expressive names, but codes are used in the actual database for various phases and quality activities). In this example, the data are fairly complete; in other situations, however, the data may not be complete. Such data cannot be always discarded, as the information may still be useful [6]. Hence such data may also be captured in PDB.

Table 5.1 gives some overall information about the project including start and end dates (both estimated and actual), estimated effort (actual effort is not put in this table, as it could be computed from the effort table), peak team size, information about the risk, tools used, and other items. In addition, some other information—for example, about the client—is stored in this table.

Table 5.1   General Data about a Project

General Characteristics	
Field Name	**Value for NICE**
DeliveryCode	Development
DeliveryNotes	Retail market
ProcessTailoringNotes	Nil
PeakTeamSize	12
ToolsUsed	VSS5.0 for CM
	LOCCOUNTfor counting SLOC
EstimatedStart	01-Oct-96
EstimatedFinish	23-Apr-97
EstimatedEffortHrs	12410
EstimationNotes	Effort of prototypes developed at the beginning of the project was used as the basis for estimation. Size of prototypes was found to be 5,000 lines/module. The actual project had 10 modules, so total size was estimated as 50,000 lines and was later changed to 60,000 lines
ActualStart	01-Oct-96
ActualFinish	23-Apr-97
First Risk	New technology
Second Risk	Attrition of staff
Third Risk	Other
RiskNotes	Talks by team members helped spread knowledge and reduce the learning curve. Two onsite members did liaison with the client and helped freeze requirements faster. Team building exercises were done.

The second table captures the information about effort. For different stages in the process, it includes data on the effort spent in doing the activity and the effort spent in doing rework after the task. Rework effort is captured because it helps in calculating and understanding the cost of quality (or cost of defects). The effort data are obtained from the weekly activity report system, in which each project team member indicates where his or her effort was spent (more discussion is given in Chapter 13). The effort data for the NICE project are given in Table 5.2, in terms of person-hours. In this project, rework effort was separately entered only for the two main phases: design and coding.

Table 5.2   Effort Data

Effort by Stage		
Stage	**TaskEffort**	**ReviewEffort**
Requirements analysis	3,936	0
Design	784	471
Coding	4,728	537
Independent unit testing	637	0
Integration testing	700	0
Acceptance testing and installation	14	0
Project management	90	0
Configuration management	10	0
Project-specific training	1,200	0
Others	310	0

The third table contains information about defects. With defects, it is desirable to know not only when the defect was detected, but also when it was injected. Hence it is desirable to record the number of defects found for each injection stage and detection stage combination. The detection stages consist of various reviews and testing, whereas the injection stages involve requirements, design, and coding. If the defects detected by a stage can be separated by their injection stages, then removal efficiencies of the defect detection stages can be computed. This information can be very useful for identifying potential improvement areas. The defect data for the NICE project are shown in Table 5.3.

The last table contains information about the size. Different languages may be used in a project, so this table may have multiple entries. Besides the language, the table captures the unit of size, as multiple units are possible. Generally, if the size is given in LOC, then size in function points may also be computed by using conversion tables. This information is used to calculate productivity in terms of function points. The computation of function points can be carried out as and when needed. As size is a critical factor in determining productivity, other factors such as the operating system and hardware used are captured as well. The values for this table for NICE are shown in Table 5.4.

Table 5.3   Defect Data

Defects by Stage		
StageDetected	**StageInjected**	**DefectCount**
Design review	Requirements	18
Design review	Design	182
Code review	Requirements	7
Code review	Design	10
Code review	Coding	476
Unit testing	Requirements	0
Unit testing	Design	10
Unit testing	Coding	89
System testing	Requirements	2
System testing	Design	13
System testing	Coding	112
Acceptance testing	Requirements	0
Acceptance testing	Design	0
Acceptance testing	Coding	7

Table 5.4   Size Data

Size		
LangCode	C++	Visual C++
OSCode		MS Windows
DBMSCode		
HWCode	PC	PC
MeasureCode	LOC	LOC
ActualCodeSize	32,092	56,296

5.2.4 Process Assets

The process database itself contains mostly metrics data for the project. As discussed earlier, these data may be used by a future project for planning purposes. In addition, if a project finds that a past project was similar in some respects, the project might want to reuse some of its outputs. Reusing artifacts can save effort and increase productivity. To promote this goal, just like the metrics data of a project, some *process assets* are collected from projects when they terminate. The following assets are typically collected and made available through a separate system:

- Project management plan
- Configuration management plan
- Schedule
- Standards, checklists, guidelines, templates, and other aids
- Developed tools and related notes
- Training material
- Other documents that could be reused by future projects

Links to process assets are maintained in the process database. The process assets can therefore be viewed as a logical extension of the process database. They are maintained separately as a collection of files. (Their nature and the size of the files makes it difficult to accommodate them in a table-based database.) General-purpose checklists, templates, forms, standards, and other documents that are part of the quality system also form part of the process assets. They are available online to the projects as well.

A process asset system is used for managing these assets. This Web-based system has a search engine and online submission. The assets are organized based on the type of process used in the project (for example, development process, maintenance process). The process assets in the system are periodically reviewed for purging and for incorporating the suitable ones into the organization standards.

5.2.5 Body of Knowledge

Knowledge management has become very important in knowledge-based organizations such as solution providers and consulting companies. Many organizations have developed systems to effectively leverage the collective experience and knowledge of their employees. At Infosys, besides the process database (and process assets), another system called the Body of Knowledge (BOK) is used to encapsulate experience.

The Web-based BOK system has its own keyword- or author-based search facility. The knowledge in BOK, which is primarily in the form of articles, is organized by different topics. Key topics include the following:

Human resource development

Computer and communication services

Requirements specification

Build

Tools

Methodologies/techniques

Education and research

Other facilities

Design

Reviews/inspection and testing

Quality assurance and productivity

Project management

In the BOK system, articles relating to "lessons learned" and "best practices" are posted. The entries in the BOK system are more general and not tied
to any particular project. Any member of the organization can submit an entry
for inclusion in BOK, using a template set up for this purpose. Each submission
undergoes a review, which focuses on its usefulness, generality, changes
required, and other characteristics. Editorial control is maintained to ensure that
entries meet the quality standards. Financial incentives have been provided for
employees to submit information to BOK, and the department that manages
BOK actively pursues new articles. To further the cause, submission to BOK is
one factor considered during employees' yearly performance appraisal.

A quarterly target for BOK entries is set for the organization. Currently, the
system includes more than 350 articles on different topics, and every year about
75 new articles are added.

An awareness program has been conducted about BOK for Infosys
employees, and all new hires are given a demonstration of the system and its
capability. A project accesses the BOK system during its planning and other
phases to see if anything can be of help.

5.3 Process Capability Baseline

Whereas the PDB contains a data point for each project, the process capability
baseline represents the *capability* of the process in quantitative terms. The capability of a process is essentially the range of outcomes that can be expected if
the process is followed [12]. In other words, if a project follows a process, the
process capability can be used to determine the range of possible outcomes for
the project. Baselining involves the collection and analysis of data across proj-

ects such that a reference point can be derived [5]. The focus of a baseline is primarily on quality and productivity [9].

The first issue that must be resolved is what the PCB should contain—that is, what types of "outcomes" the PCB should include. The PCB at Infosys contains the process performance stated primarily in terms of productivity, quality, schedule, and effort and defect distributions. It specifies the following:

- Delivered quality
- Productivity
- Schedule
- Effort distribution
- Defect injection rate
- In-process defect removal efficiency
- Defect distribution

This information can be useful in project planning. Productivity, for example, can be used to predict the effort for the project from the estimated size, and the distribution of effort can be used to predict the effort for the various phases of the project and to make staffing plans. Similarly, the defect injection rate can be used to predict the total number of defects for a project, and the distribution of defects can be used to predict the defect levels for various defect detection activities. Overall defect removal efficiency or quality can be used to forecast the number of defects that may crop up after the software is delivered and to plan for maintenance.

The PCB serves an important role in overall process management in the organization. For example, process improvements can be measured easily by analyzing the trends in the PCB over time. Some such analysis of trends in quality and productivity is discussed later in this chapter. Planning of improvement initiatives can also be improved by using information on distribution of effort and defects, defect injection rates, removal efficiencies, and other measures. Process improvement planning, monitoring, and analysis are outside the PCB, although they represent an important SEPG task.

Because a baseline indicates the capability of a process, a separate baseline must be created for each process that an organization may have. At Infosys, separate processes are defined for maintenance, reengineering, and development projects; a separate baseline is therefore defined for each of these processes. Even these processes are too "broad" and provide only very general guidelines to projects. If projects of a certain type are executed frequently, then a PCB for that type of project is created. This "focused" baseline will likely give a much tighter range, in terms of expected results, for that type of project.

5.3.1   Baseline Creation

A process baseline represents the expected outcomes by following the trail of a process. The outcome of the project itself is called process performance (on that project). In SPC, the capability of a process is defined as the 6-sigma spread around the mean value [11], which signifies the range of values that are likely to occur due to natural variability in the process. As discussed earlier, in a software process, the performance variation tends to be large and separating natural causes from assignable causes tends to be difficult. As a consequence, statistical techniques must be used in a relaxed manner. Note, also, that the main purpose of control charts and limits is to identify points with assignable causes. Nevertheless, analysis of the points outside the limits must be performed to determine which actions to take. If "tighter" limits are used, then more points may fall outside the limits, thereby requiring the analysis of more points.

At Infosys, the capability of a process, which also specifies the control limits, is computed from the process's actual performance on past projects. The capability is computed as follows. Data for the past projects are plotted, and 3-sigma and 2-sigma bands are drawn. The points that lie outside these bands are examined and may be removed (a judgment call). The remaining points are plotted again. The process of removing outliers may be repeated. Finally, the mean and spread of the data for a characteristic are taken as the capability of the process for that characteristic. For some processes, the formulae for XMR charts are used to compute the control limits.

Before we give an example of the PCB, some definitions are in order. *Productivity* is defined in terms of function points per person month. *Quality* is defined as delivered defects per function point, where the number of defects delivered is approximated by the number of defects found through acceptance testing, during installation, and during the warranty period. The *defect injection rate* is the total number of defects injected during the life cycle of the project normalized with the size. The total number of defects in a project is the sum of the number of defects found by the different defect detection stages in the process and the number of defects found after delivery. *Overall defect removal efficiency* is the percentage of total defects that are detected inside the process by the various defect detection activities. In summary, if we have

F = Size of the software in function points
E = Total effort spent in the project
D_1 = Total number of defects found during development (before delivery)
D_2 = Total number of defects found after delivery
$D = D_1 + D_2$

for a project then we have the following definitions:

Productivity = E/F
Quality = D_2/F
Defect injection rate = D/F
Overall defect removal efficiency = D_1/D

The preceding discussion focused on size in function points. For completed projects, however, size in LOC is often easier to compute. In these situations, the size measured in LOC is converted to function points using published conversion tables. The defect injection rate is defined above as normalized with respect to size. Many times, the size in function points may not be known at the start of the project, but the defect injection rate may nevertheless be required for planning and estimating the defect levels. The curve of the defect rate is usually similar to the effort buildup curve—that is, defects can be considered as proportional to the effort [13]. The defect injection rate is also computed as normalized with respect to effort, and it can be used along with effort estimate to estimate the defect levels.

5.3.2   Development Process Baseline

As mentioned earlier, there are different PCBs for different process types. The PCB given in Table 5.5 is applicable for development projects and for projects done in a third-generation language (3GL). The PCB for maintenance projects, for example, differs somewhat not only in terms of actual figures in the PCB, but also in the information included (to suit the maintenance process). As mentioned in the Preface, the numbers used in this PCB are for illustration purposes only and may have been sanitized to protect the confidentiality of such data.

Table 5.5   Process Capability Baseline for 3GL Development Projects

SI #	Metric	Remarks	General Baseline, Development Projects
1	Delivered quality	Delivered defects/FP (delivered defects = acceptance defects + warranty defects)	0.04–0.09/defects/ FP (avg: 0.06 defects/FP)
2	Productivity	1 person-month = 8.5 person-hours × 22 days = 187 person-hours	4–18 FP/person = month (avg: 10 FP/ person-month)
3	Schedule		85% of projects delivered on time All projects should aim for delivery on time
4	Effort		
4.1	Effort ratios		Simple is ≤ 0.6 Medium is = 1.0 Complex is ≥ 2.0
4.2	Average build effort		Average build effort for medium should be 4–6 person-days

(continued)

Table 5.5 Process Capability Baseline for 3GL Development Projects *(continued)*

SI #	Metric	Remarks	General Baseline, Development Projects
4.3	Effort distribution		Min–Mid–Max
		RA = requirements analysis DE = design	RA + DE = 17%–20%–24%
		BD = build (code + CWT + unit testing)	BD = 34%–38%–42%
		TT = integration + system testing	TT = 7%–10%–13%
		AW = acceptance testing and warranty	AW = 2%–4%–6%
		PM = project management CM = configuration management	PM + CM = 7%–8%–10%
		TR = training	TR = 6%–8%–10%
		OT = other	OT = 9%–12%–15%
5	Defects		
5.1	Defect injection rate		0.8–1.2 defects/FP (avg: 0.95 defects/FP; around 0.05 defects/person-hour)
5.2	In-process defect removal efficiency		90%–95% (avg: 93%)
6	Defect distribution		Percentage of total defects
		Requirements specifications review + HLD review + detailed design review	15%–20%
		CWT + unit testing	50%–70%
		Integration testing + system testing	20%–28%
		Acceptance testing	5%–10%

Given the definitions of the various factors included in the PCB, the interpretation of this PCB should be obvious. The PCB states that for projects following the development process, the average productivity is around 10 function points per person-month, with the range being from 4 to 18 function points. Similarly, the quality figure says that the average quality of development projects is 0.06 defect per function point, with the range being between 0.05 and 0.09. For effort, the distribution of effort, the ratio of effort for the different types of programs, and the average build effort for the different program types are given. The utility of this information will become clearer when we discuss effort estimation. It was observed that, although the average effort varied considerably depending on the definitions used for classifying programs, the ratios of efforts were more stable. Hence these ratios were also captured in the PCB.

The data in PCB include the average and the range for some parameters that represent the capability of the process. For a process under statistical control, the actual performance of the process on projects will generally fall within this band around the mean. The control charts for two characteristics of the development process are shown in Figures 5.3 and 5.4. The outliers are also shown in these figures, although they may not have been considered in the final computation of capability. Similar charts are drawn for other characteristics such as delivered quality, defect injection rate with respect to size, and schedule variability.

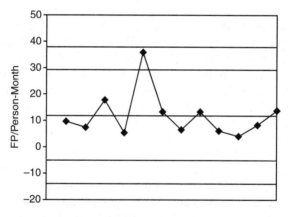

Figure 5.3   Productivity of Development Projects

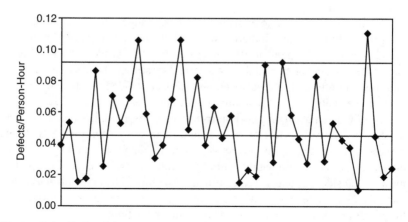

Figure 5.4   Defect injection rate with effort

This approach to defining the capability baseline results in a simple and succinct baseline that nevertheless requires a considerable amount of data to create and maintain. This simple baseline captures the current state of the process in quantitative terms. It is different from the one described in [9] in which goals, analysis, and other features are a part of the baseline. With this example PCB, these issues are outside the baseline and must be addressed separately.

5.3.3 Process Improvement and Analysis

As mentioned earlier, the PCB helps in project planning and process analysis and improvement. We will discuss the use of the PCB in project planning in later chapters. Here we focus on the use of the PCB for process improvement and analysis.

By computing the PCB at regular intervals and examining the trends in the values of the various parameters in the PCB, improvement can be quantitatively measured. At Infosys, a comparison of the PCB of the current year with the PCB for the previous year showed that the average quality of the software delivered for 3GL development projects had improved substantially, and the defect density delivered was reduced to 50%. No change in productivity was observed.

Because the variability in the performance of different projects is large, and because this improvement observation is based on only two PCBs, these improvement figures are being used with caution within the organization. In an attempt to understand the reasons for these improvements, analysis of other parameters was also done. The PCB data comparison showed that the defect injection rate had declined by about 40%, although the overall defect removal efficiency remained the same. This fact largely explains why the delivered defect density has decreased—reducing defect injection and maintaining the defect removal efficiency also reduced the number of defects found in acceptance testing and beyond.

No reason was found to explain why these changes took place, as no special process improvement initiative was undertaken. The organization had an overall improvement goal of 10% so different projects likely tried different approaches to meet or exceed this goal. And they seem to have succeeded! The improvement efforts in projects were also probably aided substantially by the quantitative visibility and quantitative control that the process provided.

The PCB can boost process improvement efforts as well. When the project finishes, its overall performance is evaluated in the closure analysis. If the process performance on the project is within the range specified by the PCB, then it can be considered within natural variability of the process. If the performance is outside the range, then causal analysis should be undertaken to determine the assignable cause, and the assignable cause should be removed from the process so that it cannot affect the outcome in the future.

Causal analysis for the overall process takes place during the closure analysis of the project (discussed in Chapter 15). For closure analysis, the ranges specified in the PCB are used in a relaxed manner. In general, if the performance differs dramatically from the average, then an attempt is made to identify the causes. The understanding of causes may also lead to process improvement suggestions (which might later be incorporated into the process by the SEPG).

The PCB also aids in process improvement planning. For example, by looking at the distribution of effort, it may be decided that one way to improve productivity is to reduce the effort in some phase that is consuming too many resources. An initiative may be planned to achieve this goal through the introduction of some tools. Similarly, analysis on defect injection rates can identify phases where initiatives might reduce the number of defects introduced. Analysis of defect removal rates can help identify defect removal activities that are candidates for improvement. Suitable quantitative targets can be set for such initiatives based on the PCB data, and the overall effects of the initiatives can also be measured by analyzing the trend.

5.4 Summary

This chapter discussed the concept and need for a process database (PDB) and a process capability baseline (PCB) and examined how both are defined at Infosys. The PDB is a repository of data about previously completed projects that can be used by future projects for project planning and monitoring. The data from the PDB are also used for creating a PCB and as part of various analyses. The contents of the PDB at Infosys were discussed, and a sample entry was provided. The PDB is augmented by a system that keeps the process assets and a Body of Knowledge (BOK) system that facilitates knowledge management.

A process capability baseline defines the range of expected results for a process, if the performance variation is solely due to natural variability. A PCB can be used by a project for setting its expectations during planning. It is also an invaluable tool for analyzing quality and productivity trends in the organization and for improving the process. Infosys's PCB contains data on productivity, quality, defect injection rate, defect removal efficiency, effort and defect distribution, and more. An example of the PCB for the development process was given. The derivation of a PCB from past data was also discussed, along with its relationship to statistical process control.

References

[1] V. R. Basili and D. M. Weiss. A methodology for collecting valid software engineering data. *IEEE Transactions on Software Engineering,* 10(6):728–738, 1984.

[2] V. R. Basili, G. Caldiera, and H. D. Rombach. Goal question metric paradigm. In *Encyclopedia of Software Engineering.* John Wiley and Sons, 1994.

[3] S. D. Conte, H. E. Dunsmore, and V. Y. Shen. *Software Engineering Metrics and Models.* Benjamin/Cummings, 1986.

[4] N. E. Fenton and S. L. Pfleeger. *Software Metrics, a Rigorous and Practical Approach,* second edition. International Thomson Computer Press, 1996.

[5] D. Garmus and D. Herron. *Measuring the Software Process, a Practical Guide to Functional Measurements.* Yourdon Press Computing Series, 1996.

[6] R. Grady and D. Caswell. *Software Metrics: Establishing a Company-wide Program.* Prentice Hall, 1987.

[7] R. Grady. *Practical Software Metrics for Project Management and Process Improvement.* Prentice Hall PTR, 1992.

[8] W. Humphrey. *Managing the Software Process.* Addison-Wesley, 1989.

[9] C. Jones. *Applied Software Measurement—Assuring Productivity and Quality,* second edition. McGraw Hill, 1996.

[10] S. H. Kan. *Metrics and Models in Software Quality Engineering.* Addison-Wesley, 1995.

[11] D. C. Montgomery. *Introduction to Statistical Quality Control,* third edition. John Wiley and Sons, 1996.

[12] M. Paulk, et al. *The Capability Maturity Model for Software, Guidelines for Improving the Software Process.* Addison-Wesley, 1995.

[13] L. H. Putnam and W. Myers. *Industrial Strength Software—Effective Management Using Measurement.* IEEE Computer Society Press, 1997.

[14] D. B. Simmons, N. C. Ellis, H. Fujihara, and W. Kuo. *Software Measurement—A Visualization Toolkit.* Prentice Hall PTR, 1998.

[15] J. A. Swift. *Introduction to Modern Statistical Quality Control and Management.* St. Lucie Press, 1995.

[16] D. J. Wheeler and D. S. Chambers. *Understanding Statistical Process Control,* second edition. SPS Press, 1992.

6

Effort Estimation
and Scheduling

Effort estimation is one of the most difficult, but most important, activities in managing any project. Although both effort and schedule estimates are needed for planning, schedule estimation becomes easier if effort estimates are known. Hence the focus in software projects is usually on effort estimation. Without an estimate of how much effort and time will be needed to execute a project, effective project planning and management are not possible. A fundamental requirement for effective planning is to be able to estimate the effort and schedule for the project and various tasks in the project—without these estimates, we cannot even ask the questions "Is the project late?" or "Are there cost overruns?"

Besides its use in project planning and management, estimation is essential for business reasons. As discussed in Chapter 2, contracts between the vendor and the customer rely on cost and schedule estimates. Without these estimates, a client has little basis for judging a proposal. Frequently, the terms of a contract incorporate the estimates of cost and schedule, and these terms are considered as fixed. As a result, the vendor needs accurate estimates, as any underestimation can hurt the supplier—that is, the customer will pay only the estimated cost on which the agreement was based but not any overruns. Thus good estimation is extremely important for any software organization, particularly those in the business of developing software for third parties.

Cost and schedule estimates must be developed for all projects. A basic goal of executing a project is to execute it within the proposed (estimated) cost and schedule. Theoretically, it is possible to execute a project without any estimates and to compute the cost (and schedule) at the end of the project. In practice, this approach is rarely taken because no one wants to jump into a project without having any sense of its potential cost. Some estimation is therefore always done to ascertain the cost and schedule before starting a project. The degree of formality of estimation may differ from project to project and from discipline to discipline, depending on the needs of the project and the prediction methods and tools available. In the construction industry, for example, tools are available to estimate the cost of constructing a house down to the last few dollars.

In a software project, the cost is usually proportional to the effort expended to build the software. When building software, manpower is the primary resource that is being consumed. Consequently, cost is frequently assessed in terms of person-months or person-days. The effort estimate is converted to actual cost by using standard rates for per-unit effort. These rates take into account other costs, such as the hardware and the infrastructure cost. Such estimates not only help in defining the cost, but also help in planning for the project's human resources needs. With an estimate of the effort, the task of estimating the schedule becomes easier, as the schedule can be modeled as a function of effort. It can be safely said that without good effort estimate, effective planning of a software project is not possible.

A proper effort estimation method is a requirement for the Software Project Planning KPA of CMM level 2. At level 4, the use of past data for estimation is expected to increase and the goals of the Quantitative Process Management KPA cannot be satisfied unless a good estimation procedure is in place. The Integrated Software Management KPA at level 3 also assumes that good estimation methods are available to projects for planning. This chapter focuses first on the general background of estimation and models for estimation, then discusses the approaches followed by Infosys.

6.1 Background

Effort estimation usually takes place in the early stages of a project, when the software to be built is being understood. It may be redone later in a project when more information about the project becomes available. Effort estimation can rely on a "gut feeling" or on previous experience; indeed, it is often done this way (which will put the organization at level 1 of the CMM). A more scientific and desired approach, however, is to use some estimation model for obtaining the effort estimates. Let us first discuss estimation models.

6.1.1   Effort Estimation Models

The basic activity of estimation is to get input in the form of the values of some characteristics of the software under development, and, using these input values, estimate the effort for the project. A software estimation model defines precisely which values it needs and how these values are used to compute the effort. In a sense, the effort estimation model is a function that takes some inputs (values of characteristics of the software) and outputs the effort estimate. This process is shown in Figure 6.1.

Note that an estimation model does not—and cannot—work in a vacuum; it needs some inputs to produce the effort estimate as output. At the start of a project, when the details of the software itself are not known, the hope is that the estimation model will require values of characteristics that can be measured at that stage.

It is generally agreed that the size of the software is the predominant factor in determining how much effort is needed to build it. But the size of the actual software is not known when the project is being conceived, and the software does not exist. Hence, if size is to be used for the effort estimation model, then when estimation is being done initially, size must be estimated. In other words, this approach reduces the effort estimation problem to a size estimation problem. With the estimate of the size, an estimate of the effort can be obtained, frequently by using some equations.

One approach for estimating size is to decompose the system into smaller parts and then estimate the size of the system based on the sizes of its parts. This approach is preferred, as estimating size for a smaller system is much easier than carrying out the same task for a large system. If function points are used for size, then the size in function points can be "counted" using the function point rules.

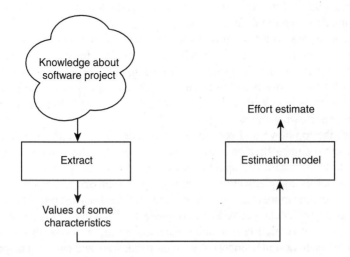

Figure 6.1   Estimation Model

6.1.2   Top-Down and Bottom-Up Approaches

With size estimates, a common approach is to use some simple equation to obtain an estimate of the overall effort from the size. Once the overall effort for the project is known, then the effort for different phases or activities are determined as percentages of the total effort. This approach is called the *top-down approach* to estimation. In this strategy, the overall effort is first estimated from size, then broken down for the activities and the phases in the project. Many top-down models have been proposed [2, 3], with the COCOMO model being the most famous [3, 4]. Models using function points (instead of LOC) as size units have also been built [8, 9].

A somewhat different approach to estimation is the *bottom-up approach* [3]. In this approach, the estimates are first obtained for parts of the project, then the overall estimate is obtained. That is, the overall estimate of the project derives from the estimates of its parts. One bottom-up method calls for using some type of activity-based estimation. In this strategy, the major activities in the project are first enumerated, then the effort for each activity is estimated. From these estimates, the effort for the overall project is obtained.

The bottom-up approach renders itself to direct estimation of effort—once the project is partitioned into smaller tasks, then directly estimating the effort required for them becomes possible. Although size does play a role in determining the effort for many activities in a project (for example, the activity "code module A"), this approach does not require explicit size estimates for the software; it does require a list of tasks in a project, however. Such an approach can work without past data if necessary, as experience can be used to predict the effort for the various activities. This approach is also effective when the project involves a mix of different software languages and technologies, making size estimation a much more difficult problem.

The main risk with bottom-up methods is that one may miss some important activities in the list of tasks, thereby not accounting for the effort required for that activity. Also, it may prove difficult to directly estimate the effort required for some "overhead" tasks such as project management that span the project and are not as clearly defined as "coding" or "testing." Bottom-up strategies can be somewhat tedious to apply, too.

Both the top-down and bottom-up approaches require information about the project to estimate their basic input data—size for top-down approaches and a list of tasks for bottom-up approaches. In many ways, the bottom-up estimation approach is complementary to the top-down approach [3]. Both types of estimates become more accurate if more information about the project is available or as the project proceeds. For example, estimating the size is much more difficult when very-high-level requirements are given, but becomes considerably easier when design is done and even more accurate and easy when code is developed. Thus the accuracy of estimates depends on the point at which effort is estimated, with the accuracy increasing as more information about the project becomes available [4].

6.1.3 Building Estimation Models

Size-based, top-down estimation models are generally built from data taken from completed projects. For the completed projects, the actual size of the software and the actual effort expended are known (assuming that the organization measures these characteristics). These values are then used to build a size-based effort model that "best fits" this data. Fitting a regression line or a regression curve is one way of accomplishing this goal [3, 6].

Many factors affect the effort required for a project. One study analyzed 68 factors that might potentially influence productivity, and found that 29 of them had a significant effect on productivity [13]. If a factor will be used in an effort estimation model, metrics are needed to quantify that factor and data analysis is needed to understand the factor's effect on effort. As the number of factors increases, the number of data points required to perform analysis to understand the effects of factors increases as well; a multivariate regression analysis is then needed [6]. Frequently, due to variations created by factors that cannot be controlled or modeled, clear patterns may not emerge from the data analysis. At best, one can hope that the estimation model will account for a few factors. The COCOMO model incorporates these factors by first estimating the effort based on size only, and then correcting the estimates based on the value of 15 different parameters (including complexity, database size, and performance requirements) [3].

Another approach to "accommodate" the various factors that affect effort required in a project is to adjust the size of the system based on these parameters. The original proposal of function points tries to accomplish this goal by starting with an unadjusted function point count and then adjusting it based on the values of 14 different system characteristics (although the adjustment function is such that the size changes by at most 35%) [1].

When using these models to estimate effort for a project, keep in mind that the size of the software must initially be estimated from whatever information is available at the time. If the requirements are known, then size must be estimated from them. This act is sometimes called "software sizing," and, unless it is done with some accuracy, the resulting estimates will not be useful. "Garbage in, garbage out" works for estimation models, too—if the size estimates are highly inaccurate, then even the best model cannot give a reasonable estimate of effort. One reason why estimation accuracy increases as the project progresses is that the size estimates become more accurate because more information about the project is available.

Because of the lack of accuracy in measuring size and productivity, the possibility of slack time available to programmers while they are participating in a project, and the "stretchability" of humans, very fine estimates are not necessary for a software project. Reasonable estimates in a software project tend to become a self-fulfilling prophecy—people work in a manner to ensure that the schedules are met (which are derived from effort estimates). In other words, estimates are often met not because they are very accurate, but rather because they are reasonable, and with the effort and schedule targets, human nature and the desire to succeed then ensure that the estimates are met. Indeed, in software projects, one cannot even precisely answer the question "Is this estimate accurate?" as the only way to ascertain the accuracy of an estimate is to compare it with the actual effort expended. Because of the reasons mentioned earlier, and because of the general human psychology that makes the maxim "work expands to fill the available time" hold true, one cannot say that just because the actual effort expended matches the estimated effort, the estimates are "accurate."

Let us illustrate this point with an example. Consider a project in which the effort estimate is 200 person-months, and the project finishes on time and takes 200 person-months. The estimate was good, that is clear. But was it the best estimate? How can we say that the work could not have been accomplished in 180 person-months? Perhaps it took 200 person-months, instead of 180 person-months, because the work "expanded" to fill the time, and people worked at a pace suitable to achieve the target set for the project. If the effort for the project was estimated as 220 person-months, we might have seen that the project took 220 person-months and team members worked at a more relaxed pace. If the estimate was 100 person-months, however, then these targets might not have been met and the actual effort might have exceeded the estimates. Hence, due to the ability of humans to work at a speed to finish the work in the available time, we must talk about "reasonable" estimates—where the goals are met and the project personnel are not "burned out." The range of reasonableness is not very wide, and depends on human factors, but it is probably wide enough to give sufficient leeway for estimation models.

6.2 Bottom-Up Estimation

At Infosys, estimation generally takes place after analysis. That is, when estimation is done, a fair amount of details are known about the work at hand and the requirements are well understood. The business processes are organized to support this approach (see Chapter 2). This organization permits the use of a bottom-up estimation method, if desired. For projects that are well defined and that may follow different types of processes (due to the nature of work) for which little past data may be available, a bottom-up approach is a better choice.

As the types of projects undertaken at Infosys vary substantially, the bottom-up approach is preferred and recommended. The company employs a "task unit approach" [3], although some of the limitations of this strategy have been overcome through the use of past data and the capability baseline.

6.2.1   Estimation Approach

In Infosys's bottom-up approach, the software under development is first divided into major programs (or units). This step occurs during the requirements analysis or high-level design of the system. Each program unit is then classified as simple, medium, or complex based on some criteria. For each classification unit, some "standard" effort for coding the unit and self-testing (together called the "build effort") is identified. This standard coding effort can be what is recommended, what some project used in the past, or some variation of these (depending on the nature of the project). Once the number of units in the three categories of complexity are known, and the estimated build effort for each program is selected, then the total effort for the build phase of the project is known. That is, this method estimates how much time it will take to code the programs.

Note that, although past data can be used to estimate the build time for each unit, the work is partitioned into small program units, so the build effort can also be directly estimated without past data. In other words, when the programming units are not too large, then designers and programmers can estimate the effort needed to code them directly. In fact, programmers and designers are frequently more comfortable estimating programming effort rather than estimating size, if the estimation units are not too large.

Many complexity measures have been proposed, with the most famous ones being cyclomatic complexity [10] and software science metrics [7]. Many of the proposed metrics require that either the logic of the programs or their interfaces be known. Such measures are useful only in later stages, when such information is more readily available. The purpose of complexity characterization here is primarily for estimation purposes, although it is used for quality planning as well. Furthermore, this measure can be employed at estimation time, when little is known about the programs' interfaces or logic, but considerable information is available on their functionality or specifications. Hence, instead of using an algorithmic definition of complexity to compute the complexity metric, a simple classification scheme for complexity is used.

Once the effort for coding is known, the effort required for the other phases and activities of the project is determined as a percentage of the coding effort. From the process capability baseline or the process database (discussed in Chapter 5), the distribution of effort in a project is known. This distribution is used to determine the effort for other phases and activities. From these estimates, the total effort for the project is obtained.

This approach renders itself to a judicious mixture of experience and data. If suitable data are not available (for a new type of project, for example), then the build effort can be estimated by experience, once the project has been analyzed and the various program units in the system are known. With this estimate available, the estimate for other activities can be obtained by working with the effort distribution data obtained from past projects. This strategy even accounts for activities that are sometimes not easy to enumerate early on but do consume effort—in the effort distribution for a project, the "other" category is frequently used to handle miscellaneous tasks.

The estimation is performed when the requirements are clear or at least approved. As mentioned earlier, the main data source for estimation is the process database and the process capability baselines, along with the estimate of the number of program units of different categories in the system. The procedure for estimation includes the following steps:

1. Identify programs in the system and classify them as simple, medium, or complex (S/M/C). As much as possible, use the definitions that are provided or definitions used in other projects.

2. If a project-specific baseline exists, get the average build effort for S/M/C programs from the baseline.

3. If a project-specific baseline does not exist, use project type, technology, language, and other attributes to look for similar projects in the process database. Use data from these projects to define the build effort of S/M/C programs.

4. If no similar project exists in the process database and no project-specific baseline exists, (that is, this project involves a new area or technology), use the average build effort for S/M/C programs from the general process capability baseline.

5. Use project-specific factors to further refine the build effort for S/M/C programs.

6. Get the total build effort using the build effort of S/M/C programs and the counts for them.

7. Use the effort distribution data in the capability baseline or similar projects in the process database to estimate the effort for other tasks and the total effort.

8. Refine the estimates based on project-specific factors.

As discussed earlier, many factors can affect the effort required for a project. To obtain a better estimation, it is essential that estimation account for project-specific factors. Instead of classifying parameters into different levels and then determining the effect on the effort requirement for the project, the approach outlined earlier leaves the impact of project-specific factors to the project. The effects will be decided based on the experience of the project leader and team members as well as data from projects found in the process database.

When using the process database to seek out information about related projects, either averages of many similar projects or data about a similar project can be used. In general, the estimates obtained via the process database or process capability baseline should not be used blindly. Instead, they should be refined to suit project-specific needs, as projects have unique characteristics that must be taken into account.

This method of classifying programs into a few categories and using an average build effort for each category is followed for overall estimation. In detailed scheduling, however, where each program unit must be scheduled and assigned to some programmer, characteristics of a unit may be taken into account to give more or less time than the average for its development.

6.2.2 Some Criteria for Classification of Program Units

Table 6.1 gives some of the criteria used by Infosys for classification. Given the diverse nature of projects executed, which utilize different software and hardware technologies, a single classification is not feasible. The basic scheme of classifying units as simple, medium, or complex is therefore preserved, but the programming unit and the definition for each category differ for various types of projects. Some of the classifications definitions are given in Table 6.1. This type of "loose" classification also simplifies the task of classifying a module, as only a rough estimate is needed for the size or other characteristics employed for classification purposes.

Table 6.1 Module Classification Criteria

Language/ DBMS/ Platform	Unit	Simple (S)	Medium (M)	Complex (C)
Ingres ABF on UNIX	Program	Less than 500 LOC	500–1,000 LOC	Other cases
Cobol, CICS with IMS for Y2K	Program	Less than 700 LOC; JCLs (for which a standard effort of two hours is estimated)	700–1,000 LOC	Other cases
C on Oracle/ UNIX	Program	Less than 100 LOC or up to 5 SQL statements	100–500 LOC or 5–20 SQL statements	Other cases

(continued)

Table 6.1   Module Classification Criteria (*continued*)

Language/ DBMS/ Platform	Unit	Simple (S)	Medium (M)	Complex (C)
GUI development environment	Screen- or form-based user interface programs	List display or search-criteria screens with not more than two to three criteria; form calls no other forms and is called from one place only; less than 10 data entry fields using simple controls	Involved display-data logic having interfaces with two to three screens or functions; multiple modes of operation; 10–20 fields using simple controls; up to one grid with not too many features	General-purpose screen called from multiple places for maintaining multiple tables; more-involved display-data logic and multilevel screens; multiple editable grids; "live" calculated fields; context-sensitive screens
Cobol/Oracle; Cobol/IDMS on mainframe	Report or related programs	Less than 16 fields to print; less than 5 tables to refer; up to 1 summary field to print	16–35 fields to print; 5–8 tables to refer; 2–4 summary fields to print	More than 35 fields to print; more than 8 tables to which to refer; more than 4 summary fields to print
C++	Class or its member functions	No complex user interaction; base class (with no inheritance); easy portability; up to 10 LOC per member function	Use of data structures such as queues and lists; use of serial communication; two-level inheritance; 10–30 LOC per member function	Multithreading libraries; IPC/ networking class libraries; complex inheritance; porting, persistence, and synchronization issues; DLL problems; more than 30 LOC per member function

6.2.3 Examples

Example 1. This project employs different languages and technologies. As a result, criteria for classifications for each language and technology must be decided first; for each criterion, an estimate for the build has to be fixed. The project also involves converting some existing Visual Basic (VB) programs to 32-bit programs, and adapting some AS/400 programs for the new SQL server. In addition, it requires some modules for adaptation to the WinRunner testing tool. For the conversion and adaptation, it was felt that no classification was needed. The classification criteria and the corresponding build effort are given in Table 6.2.

Table 6.2 Classification Criteria and Estimated Build Effort for Example 1

Program/Function	Criteria	Estimated Effort
Simple VB programs	• No data access • Only one file accessed • Only four prebuilt combos/trees	3
Medium VB programs	• Up to four files accessed • One grid • Fresh building of combos/trees required • Complex but can use the template of a complex program • Has screen-level menus that invoke up to two forms	5
Complex VB programs	• More than four files accessed • More than one grid • Invokes graphs • Has screen-level menus that invoke more than two forms	7
Simple AS/400 programs	• Only one file accessed • Medium but can use the template of a medium program • Minor modifications of up to two existing programs	3
Medium AS/400 programs	• Up to four files accessed • Minor modifications of up to five existing programs	6
Complex AS/400 programs	• Involves research and development of new concepts/features • Minor modifications of more than five existing programs • Involves data access plus calculations with NECOM	9

Table 6.2   Classification Criteria and Estimated Build Effort for Example 1
(*continued*)

Program/Function	Criteria	Estimated Effort
Conversion to 32-bit programs	• Migrate 16-bit DLL declarations/ calls to 32-bit	1
	• Migrate Microsoft and custom controls from 16-bit VBX to 32-bit OCX	
	• Redesign user interface to suit Windows 95 standards	
Oracle-SQL adaptation— VB programs	• Adapt screens	0.2
Oracle-SQL server adaptation	• Create Oracle database and population with data	1
	• Test NEFORSQL client on Oracle	
	• Port COBOL server programs to PROCOBOL on UNIX	
WinRunner adaptation	• Automate NEFOR GUI testing using WinRunner	10

From the analysis of the project, the number of programs within different categories was obtained. This number, along with the build effort required (obtained by multiplying the build effort for a program of a category with the number of programs in that category) is given in Table 6.3.

Table 6.3   Program Category Counts and Total Build Effort for Example 1

Category	Number of Programs	Total Build Effort
Simple VB programs	28	84
Medium VB programs	20	100
Complex VB programs	30	210
Simple AS/400 programs	2	6
Medium AS/400 programs	6	36
Complex AS/400 programs	4	36
32-bit conversion	48	48
VB programs—SQL server-compatible	50	10
AS/400 programs—SQL server-compatible	30	30
WinRunner adaptation	5	50

The total build effort for this project is 610 person-days. From the build effort and the percentage distribution of effort, the effort for each phase and overall effort is obtained (Table 6.4).

Table 6.4 Estimated Effort for Example 1

Activity	Estimated Effort (Person-Days)	Estimated Effort (%)
Requirements analysis	61	4
Design	273	18
Build	610	40
Integration and system testing	125	8
Acceptance testing (including installation and warranty)	45	3
Project management	105	7
Project-specific training	90	6
Other (including leave)	210	14
Total effort	**1,519**	**100**

Example 2: The WAR Project. In this example, we give the estimates for the WAR project. First the criteria for simple, medium, and complex are given, along with the build effort for each type (Table 6.5). For estimating the build effort based on data from past projects and experience, the average build effort for a medium-complexity module was set as 6 person-days. Using the build effort ratio for simple, medium, and complex as 0.6:1.0:2.0, we find the build effort for the different module categories to be 3.6, 6, and 12, respectively. Using experience and project-related factors, the build effort for simple, medium, and complex modules was set as 4, 6, and 12 person-days, respectively. Then each of the major modules in the system is listed, along with its classification (Table 6.6).

Table 6.5 Basis for Estimation for the WAR Project

Classification/ Type	Classification Criteria	Build Effort (Person-Days)
Simple	Programs with minimum business logic and not more than 2–3 table access and very little data display	4
Medium	Programs with moderate business logic and 2–4 table access with moderate data display	6
Complex	Programs with complex business logic and more than 4 table access and much data display	12

Table 6.6 Module Details for the WAR Project

Program/Function	Complexity
Entry of WAR	Medium—planned/unplanned section
Activity list filter	Complex—filter criteria for tasks
Submission of WAR	Simple—workflow function
Review of WAR	Medium (which has one more screen for the submission list than the entry of WAR function)
Project-level setup	Medium—project-level activity codes/module codes
Activity code setup	Simple—corporate-level activity codes maintenance
Mail interface	Medium—formatting data and sending mail
WAR remainder	Simple
Onsite WAR entry	Complex—Needs to be handled for various modes; should support 4 platforms and 2 layers (user interface and data storage)
WAR Data entry program	Medium (for entry of WAR for users who have filled in a sheet that needs to be entered manually—VB program)
Other systems interface	Medium—Interface to other systems like leave, HRIS, and INMASS
Project plan upload	Medium
Reporting module	Complex—Includes automatic generation of reports (scheduler) on specific intervals other than those for standard reports (assuming 10 reports)
Middle layer	Complex—Consists of the processing logic/database layer/ system layer
Architecture	Complex—three phases (design/build/implement—includes distributed databases, Web servers, and so on)
Help	Simple
User preferences	Medium—users' default settings
Batch process	Medium—static HTML generation in Web server for activities code, module, and so on (to enhance performance)
Other system modification	Modify existing tables to new

Table 6.7 Build Effort for the WAR Project

Complexity	Number of Units	Build Effort/Unit (Person-Days)	Total Build Effort (Person-Days)
Simple	4	4	16
Medium	10	6	60
Complex	5	12	60
Total	**16**	—	**136**

Now we know that the build effort is 136 person-days (Table 6.7), we can use the distribution of effort in different stages, as given in the PCB, to determine the effort for other stages as well as the total effort for the project. This information is given in Table 6.8.

Table 6.8   Estimated Effort for the WAR Project

Stage	Percentage of Effort (%)	Effort
Requirement analysis	4	14
Design	20	68
Build	40	136
Testing	10	34
Acceptance	4	14
Project management	8	27
Training	5	17
Other	9	30
Total	**100**	**340**

We can use this effort estimate to derive an estimate of the size in function points as well. As this project is to be done in Visual Basic 5, the expected productivity is between 20 and 40 FP per person-month (as specified in PCB for fourth-generation languages). As this project involves a new technology, the productivity expected will be toward the lower end of the spectrum. We expect to achieve a productivity of 22 FP/person-month. Taking 22 working days in a month, we obtain a size in FP of $340/22 \times 22 = 340$ FP.

6.2.4   Effectiveness of the Approach

The common way to analyze the "effectiveness" of an estimation approach is to see how the estimated effort compares with the actual effort. As discussed earlier, this comparison gives only a general idea about the accuracy of the estimates—it does not indicate how "optimal" the estimates are. That information requires actually studying the effects of estimates on programmers (for example, whether they were "stretched" or were "underutilized"). Nevertheless, a comparison of actual effort expended and estimated effort does give an idea of the reasonableness of the estimation method. Use of a bottom-up method requires, in addition to an estimation method, a way to capture accurate effort data from projects. If the effort data captured from projects are not accurate, then this analysis will have little meaning. We discuss later how effort (and other) data are obtained from projects.

For completed projects, the process database includes information on the estimated effort as well as the actual effort. The scatter plot of estimated effort and actual effort for the recently completed development projects is shown in Figure 6.2.

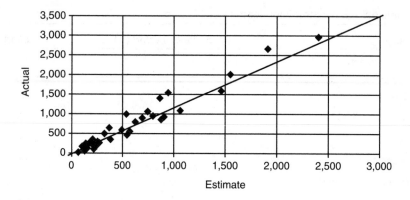

Figure 6.2   Actual versus estimated effort

As the plot shows, the estimation approach works quite well—most of the data points are close to the 45-degree line in the graph (if all estimates match the actual effort, then all points will fall on the 45-degree line). The data also show that more than 50% of the projects are within 25% of the estimated effort. Nevertheless, the data indicate that the estimates are usually lower than the actual effort; note that most of the points are above the 45-degree line rather than below it. That is, people tend to underestimate more often—something that afflicts the software industry in general. On average, the actual effort was 25% higher than the estimate. Overall, although there is room for improvement, the bottom-up estimation approach is reasonably effective.

6.3 Top-Down Estimation

Although many projects use the bottom-up estimation method, a project can also use a top-down approach for estimation. This approach is frequently used for conversion or reengineering projects in which the size of the existing system to be converted is known quite precisely. It is also recommended where doubts exist about the estimates obtained. In such cases, this method may be used for validating the estimates.

Like any top-down approach, the approach discussed here starts with an estimate of the size of the software. The size is expected to be cited in function points. The function points for the project may be counted using standard function point counting rules. Alternatively, if the size estimate is known in terms of LOC, then it can be converted into function points.

Besides the size estimate, a top-down approach needs to fix a productivity level for the project. With the size and productivity in hand, an effort estimate can be easily derived. Using productivity directly to create the estimate assumes that productivity is independent of size. It is generally believed that productivity decreases as size increases. That is, the productivity is lower for larger systems than for smaller systems. For smaller systems, however, a linear equation for effort with respect to size (constant productivity) works well [2]. Even in the COCOMO model, the estimation equation for the organic systems (which represent applications such as management information systems) is almost linear—the exponent is 1.05 (instead of 1.00, which is the case if productivity is constant) [3]. Note that the results may actually vary from project to project for project-specific reasons such as complexity and technology.

Thus the basic approach is to start with standard productivity levels, which are available for projects in the process database or the process capability baseline, and then change those levels, if needed, to suit the project. An estimate of the productivity level is obtained in this way for the project, then used to calculate the overall effort estimate. From the overall effort estimate, estimates for the different phases are derived by using the percentage distributions. (These distributions, as in the bottom-up approach, are obtained from the process database or the capability baseline.)

To summarize, the overall approach for top-down estimation involves the following steps:

1. Get the estimate of the total size of the software in function points.

2. Use the productivity data in the process capability baseline for a similar process type or the productivity data in the process database for similar projects to fix the productivity level for the project.

3. Obtain the overall effort estimate from productivity and size estimates.

4. Use effort distribution data from the process capability baseline (or similar projects) to estimate the effort for different phases.

5. Refine the estimates, taking project-specific factors into consideration.

Like the bottom-up estimation, the top-down approach allows the estimates to be refined using "project-specific factors." This allowance, without actually defining these factors, acknowledges that each project is unique and may have some characteristics that do not exist in other projects. It may not be possible to enumerate these characteristics or formally model their effects on productivity. Hence, it is left to the project to decide which factors should be considered and how they will affect the project.

6.4 Scheduling

The scheduling activity can be broken into two subactivities: determining the overall schedule (the project duration) with major milestones, and deciding the detailed schedule of the various tasks.

6.4.1   Overall Scheduling

Developing guidelines for overall scheduling is, in some sense, a more difficult task than building guidelines for effort estimation. Once the effort is known or fixed, various schedules (or project duration) are possible, depending on the number of resources (people) put on the project. For example, for a project whose effort estimate is 56 person-months, a total schedule of 8 months is possible with 7 people. A schedule of 7 months with 8 people is also possible, as is a schedule of approximately 9 months with 6 people. As is well known, however, manpower and months are not fully interchangeable in a software project [5]. For instance, in the example here, a schedule of 1 month with 56 people is not possible, even though the effort matches the requirement. Similarly, no one would execute the project in 28 months with two people. In other words, some flexibility in deciding the schedule is possible once the effort is fixed by appropriately staffing the project, but this flexibility is not unlimited. This limited flexibility has been corroborated by data [12].

Due to this possible flexibility, building strict guidelines for scheduling may not be desirable. Furthermore, the overall schedule for the project is often driven more by the business requirements of the customer than by any other factor. As a result, scheduling guidelines are more useful for checking whether the schedule is within the "flexibility range"—that is, that the schedule is feasible—than for deciding the schedule itself.

If the schedule is set based on the effort estimates of the project, one method for determining it is to use some function to derive the schedule from the estimated effort. As is the situation in building top-down effort estimation models, this function is built by studying the patterns that arise in data from completed projects. For example, one might obtain a scatter plot of effort and schedule for completed projects and then fit a regression curve through this scatter plot. This curve will generally be nonlinear, as the schedule does not grow linearly with effort. The equation for the curve can then be used to determine the schedule for a project whose effort has been estimated. Many models follow this approach (a summary of the various models is given in [3]). The scatter plot of the schedule and effort for previously completed development projects, plus a nonlinear regression curve fit for the scatter plot, is shown in Figure 6.3.

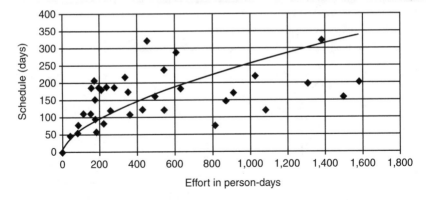

Figure 6.3   Schedule as a function of effort

The equation of the curve in Figure 6.3 is "schedule = 23.46 (effort)$^{0.313}$." (As the relationship between effort and schedule is nonlinear, this equation can also be obtained by fitting a regression line in a log-log curve.) From the distribution of the points, it is evident that schedule is not just a function of effort. Thus, the equation for this curve cannot be used directly for schedule estimation. It can, however, be used as a guideline or a check of the reasonableness of a schedule, which might be decided based on other factors. Likewise, the schedule and effort data from similar projects can be used to check the reasonableness of any proposed schedule.

Once the overall duration of the project is fixed, then the schedule for the major milestones must be decided. To determine the milestones, we must first understand the manpower ramp-up that usually takes place in a project. The number of people in a software project tends to follow the Rayleigh curve [11, 12]. That is, in the beginning and the end, few people work on the project; the peak team size is reached somewhere around the middle of the project. This behavior occurs because only a few people are needed in the initial phases of requirements analysis and design. The human resources requirement peaks during coding and unit testing. Again, during system testing and integration, fewer people are required. Frequently, the staffing level in a project does not change very often, but approximations of the Rayleigh curve are used—assigning a few people in the start, having the peak team during the build phase, and then leaving a few people for integration and system testing. If we consider design, build, and test as three major phases, the manpower buildup in projects will typically resemble the function shown in Figure 6.4.

In other words, generally there are fewer people in the starting and ending phases, with maximum people during the build phase. During the build phase, the peak team size (PTS) for the project is usually achieved. Actually, for ease of scheduling, all required people may be assigned together around the start of a

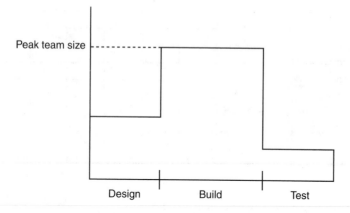

Figure 6.4   Manpower buildup

small project. This approach can lead to people being unoccupied, as the work in a project does tend to follow the Rayleigh curve. Nevertheless, projects frequently require training in the technology being used, and this training consumes a fair amount of effort (as can be been seen in the effort distribution given in the PCB). In such a case, the "slack" time available to the staff members who are assigned early can be gainfully utilized by providing them with the necessary training. Similarly, the slack time available in the end can be utilized for documentation and other closure tasks.

From this general pattern, it should be clear that the schedule distribution will differ from the effort distribution. For these three major phases, the percentage of the schedule consumed in the build phase will be smaller than the percentage of the effort consumed, because this phase involves more people. Similarly, the percentage of the schedule consumed in the design and testing phases exceeds their effort percentages. The exact schedule depends on the availability of resources or the manpower ramp-up that is planned. Generally speaking, the schedule is divided into three roughly equal parts, one for each major phase. This type of guideline is only a check for the milestones, which may be set based on other constraints.

6.4.2   Effectiveness of the Approach

As with effort estimates, one way of checking the schedule estimates is to plot the actual schedule against the estimated schedule and see how close the points are to the 45-degree line. If they all fall very close to the 45-degree line, then the scheduling approach can be considered to be "effective." This plot for previously completed development projects is shown in Figure 6.5.

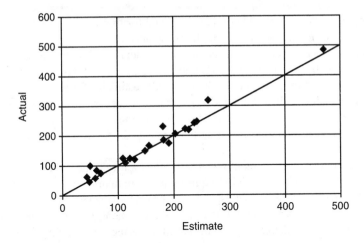

Figure 6.5   Actual versus estimated schedule

As we can see, the scheduling approach results in schedules that match reasonably well with the actual schedule. Keep in mind, however, that other factors may determine whether the estimated schedule is met. Some of these factors were discussed earlier in the section on effort estimation.

6.4.3   Detailed Scheduling

Once the high-level schedule is fixed, then the overall project duration and the major milestones are known. As the effort required for the various phases (and the build phases of various modules) is also known, the resource requirements for the various phases can be determined easily. In other words, once the effort is estimated and a reasonable schedule is fixed, then the value of the remaining variable—manpower—is fixed so as to meet the schedule and be consistent with the effort estimates. Some negotiation may be necessary to adjust the schedule and milestones (with effort as fixed) depending on the availability of manpower.

Once the milestones and the resources are fixed, then the detailed scheduling is set. In setting the detailed schedule, the tasks in the overall schedule are broken down into small schedulable activities in a hierarchical manner. For example, the overall detailed design task is first broken into detailed design tasks for the major modules in the system. These tasks are then further broken down into detailed design activities for components in the modules. The same type of decomposition is done for the build and other tasks.

Generally, at each level of refinement, a check is made for the earlier estimate and the schedule (including the milestones) is adjusted, if necessary. For example, suppose eight resources are assigned for four modules in the detailed design phase. Each module then might be assigned two resources who are asked to come up with a detailed schedule for the detailed design activity of that module. Next, the schedules for detailed design for the different modules are checked against the overall effort and schedule estimates for this phase. If discrepancies appear, then the detailed estimates are reevaluated and the overall estimates or detailed estimates changed so that they become consistent. Thus scheduling is an iterative process. This process is followed for each of the phases.

Generally, the refinement is carried out to a level where the lowest-level activity is a schedulable activity requiring no more than a few days from a single resource. General activities, such as project management, coordination, database management, and configuration management, are also added. These activities have less direct effect on the schedule, as they are ongoing tasks rather than schedulable activities. Nevertheless, they consume resources and effort and hence are included in the project schedule.

For detailed scheduling, features of Microsoft Project (MSP) can be used. For each activity listed in MSP, the effort, duration, start date, end date, and resources are mentioned. The project leader usually enters only a few fields; the dependent fields are then fixed by MSP. For each activity, the activity code (a code describing the activity, examined further in Chapter 13), the program code, and the module code are also specified. Dependencies between activities, either due to inherent dependency in them (for example, a unit test plan for a program can be done only after it has been coded) or due to resource-related dependency (same resource is assigned two tasks), can be specified in MSP as well.

After these inputs are entered, the "resource leveling" or "resource loading" analysis of MSP may be used. Essentially, MSP analyzes the schedule and gives the loading of resources. If some resources are overloaded and some are underloaded, then either the schedule of activities can be changed or the resource assignment can be altered so that resources become evenly loaded. This attempt to properly utilize resources also makes scheduling an iterative exercise.

Finally, the schedule includes all schedulable activities. For each activity, its start date, its finish date, personnel assigned, and so on are given. This information provides the basis for executing the project. Of course, this project schedule is not static. Changes may be needed because the actual progress in the project may be different than planned, newer tasks are added through change requests, or unforeseen situations crop up. Changes are done as and when the need arises.

The final schedule, as recorded in MSP, is perhaps the most "live" project plan document. As changes occur, MSP is always kept "current" to reflect the actual situation in the project. The schedule is also a key input in project monitoring. We discuss project monitoring in Chapter 13.

6.4.4 Example: Schedule of WAR

Let us consider the example of the WAR project. The effort estimates for WAR were discussed earlier. The customer gave approximately 7.5 months to finish the project. As the effort estimate was 340 person-days, this duration was found acceptable, and 4 resources were assigned (most working part-time). The customer, in consultation with the project leader, also fixed milestones.

To create the schedule for WAR, first the overall schedule is decided for the major phases in the project. With the effort for each phase estimated and the number of resources known, the actual schedule for these phases can be determined. During detailed scheduling, each top-level activity is further broken down into schedulable activities. In this way, the schedule also becomes a checklist of tasks to be done in the project. Frequently, this "exploding" of a top-level activity is not done fully at the start but rather takes place many times during the course of the project. For example, only the design activity may be detailed out in the initial schedule. Later, when the design phase ends, the build task might be detailed. Part of the top-level schedule of the WAR project is shown in Table 6.9 (in this table, predecessors for activities are not specified).

Table 6.9 Top-Level Schedule for WAR Project

Task Name	Duration	Start	Finish	Resource Names	Effort (Hours)
Weekly Activity Report 2.0	**159d**	**10/21/97**	**6/10/98**		**2975.2h**
Requirements stage	26.5d	10/21/97	12/1/97		208.8h
Requirements specification	10d	10/21/97	11/6/97	PL[.6]	48h
Review and rework of SRS	1d	11/5/97	11/5/97	PL[.4],BM[.3]	5.6h
Prototyping	16d	11/6/97	11/27/97	DV1[.6],DV2[.6]	134.4h
Prototype review and rework	1d	11/28/97	11/28/97	PL[.6],MIS	12.8h
Review with users	0.5d	12/1/97	12/1/97	PL,Users	8h
Functional specification	8d	1/5/98	1/15/98	PL[.4],DV1[.8], DV2[.8],DV3[.8]	163.2h
System test plan	2d	1/16/98	1/19/98	PL[.4]	12.8h

Table 6.9   Top-Level Schedule for WAR Project (*continued*)

Task Name	Duration	Start	Finish	Resource Names	Effort (Hours)
Weekly Activity Report 2.0	159d	10/21/97	6/10/98		2975.2h
Database design	5d	1/20/98	1/27/98	PL[.5],DV1[.6]	40h
Detailed design	12d	1/28/98	2/12/98	PL[.2],DV1[.8], DV2[.8],DV3[.8]	249.6h
Unit and integration test plan	3d	2/13/98	2/17/98	DV1[.8],DV2 [.8],DV3[.8]	57.6h
Build (client and server)	40d	2/18/98	4/14/98	DV1[.8],DV2 [.8],DV3[.8]	768h
UT and IT	5d	4/15/98	4/21/98	DV1[.8],DV2 [.8],DV3[.8]	96h
System testing	5d	4/22/98	4/28/98	DV1[.8],DV2[.8], DV3[.8],PL[.1]	100h
Acceptance testing	5d	4/29/98	5/6/98	User Group	40h
Implementation plan	5d	5/7/98	5/13/98	PL[.6], DV1[.8]	56h
Pilot run and bug fixes	20d	5/14/98	6/10/98	PL[.4],DV1[.6], DV2[.6],DV3[.6]	352h

Besides the life-cycle phases, the top-level schedule includes management-related tasks such as project management, training, configuration activities, management, and database administering. The detailed schedule for the project is fairly long, with more than 110 line items in its MSP. The build phase, for example, expands into about 10 items, and design includes more than 50 items. Each line item is the lowest level of task that is scheduled, assigned to one person, and tracked. Most items have a duration of 1 to 2 days, though the range is one-half day to about 9 days.

It is clear that scheduling—particularly detailed scheduling—is an iterative process. The project leader must try different schedules to ensure that the milestones can be met and that resources are properly loaded. Although this chapter discussed the top-down approach for scheduling, a bottom-up approach may also be followed during the detailed scheduling. In this case, a schedule for a phase as a large task may be developed independently by first enumerating all activities, estimating their effort, and scheduling them, keeping the resource constraints in mind. Next, MSP can give the overall schedule and effort for the higher-level tasks. This output may or may not match with the effort and schedule decided earlier. The detailed schedule may then need to be reviewed to see if it can be "optimized."

6.5 Summary

This chapter discussed effort estimation and scheduling. The basic goal for estimation is not to create an "accurate" estimation, which is not easy to define, but rather to have "reasonable" estimates, which will work most of the time. Estimation models are used; they take some characteristics of the project as input and give the effort estimate as output. The estimation approach can be either top-down or bottom-up. In a top-down approach, size is estimated first, and then the total effort is estimated. In a bottom-up approach, estimates for smaller tasks are developed first, and the overall estimate is built from them.

In the bottom-up approach employed at Infosys, the software to be built is initially broken into programming units. Each unit is classified as simple, medium, or complex. For each type of module, a standard effort for build is fixed. Using the count for each type of module and the standard build effort identified for each, the total build effort for the project is estimated. The total estimate for the project and estimates for other phases are then made using the effort estimate for the build phase as well as the effort distribution among various phases. The data from past projects show that this estimation approach does, indeed, produce reasonable estimates.

Scheduling is a two-level activity. First, the overall schedule (the project duration) is fixed along with the major milestones. Next, the detailed schedule is decided.

Some degree of flexibility exists when deciding the overall schedule. Once it is fixed, the number of resources needed for the project—to match the effort estimate—can be determined. Using resources and other factors, the overall schedule and milestones are fixed, along with the resources needed for each phase.

The detailed schedule is determined by refining each task in the top-level schedule. Each activity under a top-level activity is scheduled in a manner such that the schedule for the top-level activity can be met. Detailed scheduling is highly iterative. The final schedule enumerates all tasks to be done in the project, along with the start date, end date, assigned personnel, and other information for each task. In many senses, the detailed schedule of the project is the final representation of all planning activities, as all activities planned are incorporated into this schedule.

References

[1] A. J. Albrecht and J. R. Gaffney. Software function, source lines of code, and development effort prediction: a software science validation. *IEEE Transactions on Software Engineering,* 9(6): 639–648, 1983.

[2] V. R. Basili. *Tutorial on Models and Metrics for Software Management and Engineering.* IEEE Press, 1980.

[3] B. Boehm. *Software Engineering Economics.* Prentice Hall, 1981.

[4] B. Boehm. Software Engineering Economics. *IEEE Transactions on Software Engineering,* 10(1):135–152, 1984.

[5] F. Brooks, Jr. *The Mythical Man Month.* Addison-Wesley, 1975.

[6] S. D. Conte, H. E. Sunsmore, and V. Y. Shen. *Software Engineering Metrics and Models.* Benjamin/Cummings, 1986.

[7] M. Halstead. *Elements of Software Science.* Elsevier North-Holland, 1977.

[8] C. F. Kemerer. An empirical validation of software cost estimation models. *Communications of the ACM,* 30(5): 416–429, 1987.

[9] J. E. Matson, B. E. Barrett, and J. M. Mellicham. Software development cost estimation using function points. *IEEE Transactions on Software Engineering,* 20(4):275–287, 1994.

[10] T. J. McCabe. A complexity measure. *IEEE Transactions on Software,* 2(4): 308–320, 1976.

[11] L. H. Putnam. A general empirical solution to the macro software sizing and estimating problem. *IEEE Transactions on Software Engineering,* 4(4): 345–361, 1978.

[12] L. H. Putnam and W. Myers. *Industrial Strength Software—Effective Management Using Measurement.* IEEE Computer Society Press, 1997.

[13] C. E. Walston and C. P. Felix. A method of programming measurement and estimation. *IBM Systems Journal,* 16(1):54–73, 1977.

7

Quality Planning and Defect Estimation

Quality, along with cost and schedule, is a major factor in determining the success of a project. The concept of software quality is not easily definable. Software has many possible quality characteristics, and an international standard for quality even exists [5]. In practice, however, quality management often revolves around defects. Hence we use *delivered defect density*—that is, the number of defects per unit size in the delivered software—as the definition of quality. This definition is currently the de facto industry standard [2]. Using it signals that the aim of a software project is to deliver the software with as few defects as possible. But what is a defect? Again, there can be no precise definition of a defect that will be general and widely applicable (is a software that misspells some word considered to have a defect?). In general, we can say a defect in software is something that causes the software to behave in a manner that is inconsistent with the requirements or the needs of the customer.

For high-quality software, the final product should have as few defects as possible. As discussed earlier, software development is a human activity, so it is not possible to prevent injection of all defects (although one can reduce the level of injection). Hence, for delivery of high-quality software, active removal of defects is necessary; this removal takes place through the quality control activities of reviews and testing. Quality control is different from quality assurance. Whereas quality control focuses on finding and removing defects, the main purpose of quality assurance is to verify that applicable procedures and standards are being followed.

This chapter discusses how quality control activities are planned and managed. Software quality control is clearly very important for any project. The Software Product Engineering KPA of CMM level 3 includes some key practices that target testing. The focus is on ensuring that quality control activities are planned and properly executed. We call this strategy "the procedural approach to quality control." Quantitatively planning and controlling the quality in a project are the focus of the Software Quality Management KPA at level 4. In this chapter, we first discuss some concepts and approaches for quality management and then describe the quality planning method employed at Infosys.

7.1 Quality Management

7.1.1 Software Quality and Defects

Before considering techniques to manage quality, we must first understand the defect injection and removal cycle. Software development is a highly people-oriented activity—and hence error-prone. Defects can be injected in software at any stage during its evolution. That is, during the transformation from user needs to software to satisfy those needs, defects can be injected in all transformation activities undertaken. These stages are primarily the requirements specification, high-level design, detailed design, and coding.

If we accept that defects will be introduced and that the objective is to deliver software with few defects, it is clearly imperative to remove defects before delivery. A project's process includes many activities for defect identification, which then leads to their removal. Although identification and removal are two distinct activities, we will use removal to refer to them collectively. The larger the latency of a defect, the more it costs to remove it [1]. Thus any mature process will include quality control activities after each phase in which defects may potentially be injected. The activities for defect removal include requirements reviews, design reviews, code reviews, unit testing (UT), integration testing (IT), system testing (ST), and acceptance testing (AT) (we do not include reviews that are done for plan documents, although they also help in improving quality of the software). This process of defect injection and removal is shown in Figure 7.1.

The task of quality management is to plan suitable quality control activities and then properly execute and control these activities such that most defects are detected "in-process"—that is, before the software is delivered.

7.1.2 Procedural Approach to Quality Management

As noted earlier, defects are detected by performing reviews or testing. Whereas reviews are structured, human-oriented processes, testing is the process of executing software (or parts of it) in an attempt to identify defects. In the procedural approach for quality management, procedures and guidelines for the review and testing activities are established. In a project, these activities are

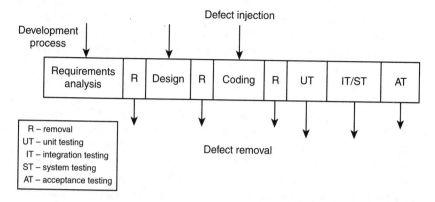

Figure 7.1   Defect injection and removal

planned (that is, it is established which activity will be performed and when); during execution, they are carried out according to the defined procedures. The execution of the activities identifies defects, which are later removed. For example, the system testing procedure generally involves making a test plan that lists all test cases that should be executed during testing, getting the plan reviewed, and then executing the plan. We refer to this defect identification approach as the procedural approach—executing some processes at defined points to detect defects. At level 3 of the CMM, a proper procedural approach to quality management is expected.

The procedural approach to defect removal does not allow claims to be made about the percentage of defects removed or the quality of the software following the procedure's completion. In other words, merely executing a set of procedures does not provide a basis for judging the effectiveness of the defect removal procedures or assessing the quality of the final code. Furthermore, such an approach is highly dependent on the quality of the procedure and the quality of the procedure execution. For example, if the test planning is done carefully and the plan is thoroughly reviewed, the quality of the software after performing the testing will be better than if testing was done but the test plan was not carefully thought out and the review was done perfunctorily. A key drawback in this procedural approach is the lack of quantitative means for a project manager to assess the quality of the software produced—the only factor visible to the manager is whether the quality control tasks are executed.

7.1.3   Quantitative Approach to Quality Management

To better assess the effectiveness of the defect detection processes, some method needs to be applied that goes beyond asking, "Has the method been executed?", and looks at some defect data for evaluation. Based on this analysis of the data, a judgment can then be made about the quality of the software produced and a decision can be taken about whether more testing or reviews are needed. If the quality of the software is controlled quantitatively (that is, if controls are applied during the software project based on quantitative data to achieve a quantitative quality goal), then the analysis of the metrics data must be refined further to provide these controls.

Quantitative quality management has two key aspects: setting a quantitative quality goal and then managing the software development process quantitatively so that this quality goal is met (with a high degree of confidence). Managing the process quantitatively requires that intermediate goals be set for different stages in the project; if these intermediate goals are met during the actual project execution, the quality goal will be met. These intermediate goals can then be used for quantitatively monitoring the execution of the project. Proper quantitative quality management is expected at level 4 of the CMM.

One approach to quantitatively controlling the quality of the software is to work with software reliability models. Most software reliability models use the failure data during the final stages of testing to estimate the reliability of the software. These models can indicate whether the reliability is acceptable or more testing is needed. They can also be used to assess how much more testing needs to be done to achieve a desired reliability goal. Unfortunately, the reliability models do not provide intermediate goals for the early phases of the project. They also impose some restrictions on the type of test cases used during testing and are generally applicable only to large systems. Overall, such models are helpful in estimating the reliability of a software product, but have a limited value for quality management. (For more information on reliability models, the reader is referred to [4, 6, 7].)

A good quality management approach should provide warning signs early in the project and not just toward the end, when the options available are limited. Early warnings allow for timely intervention. To achieve this goal, it is essential to predict the values of some parameters at different stages in the project such that controlling these parameters during the project execution will ensure that the final product has the desired quality. If such predictions can be made, then the actual data garnered during the execution of the process can be used to judge whether the process has been applied effectively. With this approach, a defect detection process does not terminate with the declaration that the process has been executed—instead, the data from process execution are used to ensure that the process has been performed in a manner that exploited its full potential.

This approach makes the management of quality closely resemble the management of effort and schedule—the two other major success parameters of a project. A target is first set for the quality of the delivered software. From this target, the values of chosen parameters at various stages in the project are estimated; that is, milestones are established. These milestones are chosen such that, if the estimates are met, the quality of the final software is likely to meet the desired level. During the project execution, the actual values of the parameters are measured and compared with the estimated levels to determine whether the project is going along the "desired" path or if some actions need to be taken to ensure that the final software has the desired quality.

Another well-known quality concept in software is defect removal efficiency. This parameter provides a good measure of the effectiveness of quality control activities in a process. Although various definitions are possible for this concept [6], most are similar to the one we use here. For a quality control (QC) activity, we define the defect removal efficiency (DRE) as the percentage of total defects that exist at that time that are detected by the QC activity. That is, for a quality control activity,

$$DRE = \frac{\text{Defects found by the QC activity}}{\text{Total errors in the product before the QC activity}}$$

The DRE for the full life cycle of the project—that is, for all activities performed before the software is delivered—represents the in-process efficiency of the process. If the overall defect injection rate is known for the project, then DRE for the full life cycle also defines the quality (defect density delivered) of the software.

Defect removal efficiency, although a useful metric for evaluating a process and identifying areas of improvement, is not suitable by itself for quality management. The main reason is that the DRE for a QC activity or the overall process can be computed only at the end of the project, when all defects and their origins are known. Hence it provides no way to control quality during project execution.

7.1.4 Quantitative Quality Management Through Defect Prediction

One approach to quantitative quality management is through defect prediction. In this approach, the quality goal is set in terms of delivered defect density. The other aspect of quality management—managing the development process—requires that the process be controlled (quantitatively) in a manner such that the desired defect density goal is met. This aim is achieved by estimating the defects that may be identified by various defect detection activities and then comparing the actual number of defects with the estimated defect levels. In other words, once the quality goal has been set, the defect levels at different stages are estimated such that meeting the estimates will ensure that the target quality is achieved. For process management, the predicted defect levels become the benchmark against which actual defect levels are compared to evaluate whether the development process is moving in the direction of achieving the quality goal.

The effectiveness of this approach depends on one key factor: how well we can predict the defect levels at different stages of the project. One approach to making this prediction is to use the concepts of defect removal efficiency and defect injection rate. If the defect injection rate of each phase is known (or can be estimated), and the DRE for each of the QC activities is known (or can be estimated), then the expected defect level at each QC activity can be predicted by using the size estimate of the system. In other words, if we know the defect injection rates for requirements, design, and coding, and we know the defect removal efficiencies of reviews, unit testing, system testing, and other phases, then we can estimate the number of defects that the project should expect to catch for each of these QC activities. These predictions can then be used for quantitative quality management purposes.

Yet another approach is to use the observed defect pattern in projects to forecast defect levels. It is known that the defect rate follows the same pattern as the effort rate, with both following the Rayleigh curve [6, 8, 9]. In other words, the number of defects found at the start of the project is small, but keeps increasing until it reaches a peak (around unit testing time), before it begins to decline again. As the defect identification in a project occurs at defined points, the defect rate curve in a project is not smooth, but rather a step curve with the steps first climbing and then descending. If we plot the number of defects found in each phase, the nature of this curve will be something like that shown in Figure 7.2.

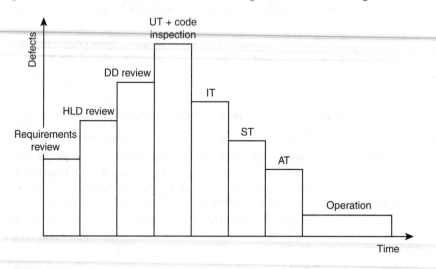

Figure 7.2   Defect detection in a project

As there are defined points for defect detection in a process, this curve can also be specified in terms of percentages of total defects detected by the different detection stages. That is, the defect rates for different quality control activities can be replaced by the percentage of total defects detected by that activity. If the total number of defects introduced into a project can be estimated, then the percentage distribution can be used to estimate the number of defects expected to be identified at different stages. The total number of defects in a project increases with the size of the software [3, 9]; its normalized value can be represented as defect injection rate, which is the number of defects per unit size. With this defect injection rate and a size estimate, the total number of defects can be estimated. This approach for defect level prediction is similar to both the base defect model and the STEER approach of IBM FSD [6].

A major assumption in this approach is that defect injection rates can be predicted for a project. As we saw in Chapter 5, the defect injection rate is fairly stable across projects. Hence past data on injection rates can be used to estimate the injection rate in current projects. As with any other metric, however, large variations are possible. As a result, when the actual number of defects is less than the "target," one cannot say whether the injection rate is low or the removal process was not executed properly. To resolve this issue, the project must look at other indicators [6]. We will discuss this problem in Chapter 12 (for reviews) and Chapter 13 (for testing). Keeping this uncertainty in mind, if the actual data are "out of range," this fact is used to draw the attention of the project management, which will look at other indicators to decide what the actual situation is and what action, if any, is needed. As effort spent on tasks is an excellent indicator to help resolve the issue, monitoring tends to report actual and estimated effort as well as actual and estimated defect levels.

7.2 Quantitative Quality Management Planning

We now consider how Infosys handles quantitative quality management by using the defect prediction approach. As discussed earlier, when planning for quantitatively managing quality for a project, the key issues are setting the quality goal and predicting defect levels at intermediate milestones that can be used for quantitatively monitoring the progress of the project toward that quality goal. For both issues, data on past projects from the process database (PDB) or the process capability baseline (PCB) are used.

In the PCB, defect data are normalized with respect to size or effort. If information normalized with respect to size will be used for predicting defect levels, a size estimate in FP will be needed. As discussed in Chapter 6, during the initial stages of a project, Infosys frequently estimates size in terms of the number of programs of different complexity levels. If a size estimate in FP is not directly available, then effort estimates can be used to predict the size by using the expected productivity level for the project. The effort estimate can also be directly used by taking advantage of the effort-normalized injection rate of the process.

7.2.1   Setting the Quality Goal

The quality goal for a project is the number of defects that the project aims to deliver. That is, the quality goal is the expected number of defects during acceptance testing. The quality goal can be "set" to be what is "computed" using past data; in this case, it is implied that the standard process will be used without modifications, and hence "standard" results will be expected for quality. Alternatively, a quality goal different from the "standard" can be set. In this case, the process must be modified according to the quality goal. Two primary sources may be used for setting the quality goal: past data on similar projects and data from the PCB.

   If data on similar projects are used, then the number of defects found during acceptance testing of the current project can be estimated as the product of the number of defects found during acceptance testing of the similar projects and the ratio of the estimated effort for this project and the total effort of the similar projects. If the set of similar projects is SP and the current project is P, then the estimate for defects in acceptance testing of P is

$$\text{Estimate for AT defects (P)} = \frac{\text{AT defects (SP)} \times \text{effort estimate (P)}}{\text{actual effort (SP)}}$$

This equation gives the number of defects that can be expected if the same process is used as in the similar projects. If data from the PCB are used, then several methods can be used to compute this value. The parameters whose values are needed for defect estimation and their current values in the PCB are given in Table 7.1.

Table 7.1   Parameters for Defect Estimation

Productivity	4–18 FP/person-month (avg: 10 FP/person-month)
Delivered quality	0.04–0.09 defect/FP; (avg: 0.06 defects/FP)
In-process defect removal efficiency	90%—95% (avg: 93%)
Defect injection rate	0.8–1.2 defects/FP (avg: 0.95 defects/FP or around 0.05 defects/person-hour)

   If the quality target is set as the number of defects per function point, then size in function points is estimated as discussed earlier and the expected number of defects is the product of the quality figure and the estimated size. The following sequence of steps is used:

1. Set the quality goal in terms of defects per FP (from the PCB).
2. Estimate the expected productivity level for the project.
3. Estimate the size in FP as (expected productivity × estimated effort).
4. Estimate the number of AT defects as (quality goal × estimated size).

Instead of setting the quality goal in terms of defects per function point, it sometimes is more useful to set the target in terms of the process's defect removal efficiency. In this situation, the number of defects to be expected during acceptance testing can be determined from the defect injection rate, the target in-process removal efficiency, and the estimated size. The sequence of steps is as follows:

1. Set the quality goal in terms of defect removal efficiency.
2. Estimate the size (as described earlier).
3. Estimate the total number of defects (defect injection rate × estimated size).
4. Estimate the number of AT defects from total number of defects and quality goal.

Yet another approach is to use the quality data from the PCB that is normalized with respect to effort. In this case, the goal is obtained from the estimated effort and this figure.

One of these approaches can be used to set the quality goal (or different approaches can be used and an average value can be taken). A project can set a quality goal that is better (or worse) than the quality level of a similar project or that matches the results of the standard process. The expected number of defects for the higher goal can then be determined by using the quality goal set for the project. Alternatively, after determining the expected number of AT defects, the quality goal can be set by choosing a different number of AT defects as the target. In either case, the process used by the similar project or the standard process must be modified for use in the current project to ensure that the quality target is met. How we accomplish this task is discussed next.

7.2.2 Quality Process Planning

If the quality goal has been set based on the data from some similar projects, and the quality goal is higher than that of the similar projects, it is unreasonable to expect that following the same process as used in the earlier projects will achieve the higher quality goal. If the same process is followed, the reasonable expectation is that similar quality levels will be achieved. Hence, if a higher quality level is desired, the process must be suitably "upgraded." Similarly, if the quality goal is set higher than the quality levels given in the PCB, then it is unreasonable to expect that following the standard process will lead to the higher quality level. Hence a new strategy will be needed—generally a combination of training, prototyping, testing, and reviews. This strategy is explicitly stated in the project management plan for the project. Here we focus on testing and reviews—the two main quality processes.

Different levels of testing are deployed in a project. The overall testing can be modified by adding or deleting some testing steps from the process (these steps will show up as process deviations in the project management plan). In addition, the approach to testing may be enhanced, for example, by performing a group review of the test plans and test results.

The choice of work products to be reviewed in a project is generally made by the project leader. The set of documents reviewed may, in fact, change from project to project. It can be adjusted according to the quality goal. If a higher quality level is set, then it is likely to be achieved by having a larger number of programs group reviewed, by including a group review of the test plans, by having a more critical review of detailed designs, and so on. If this approach is selected, then it will be mentioned as the strategy for meeting the quality goal. To further elaborate on the implications of this type of strategy for the project, all documents that will be reviewed and the nature of those reviews are specified in the project plan.

The data in the process capability baseline can be used to estimate the effects of the process changes on the effort and schedule planned for the project. Once the process is set, the defect levels at the various stages of the process can be estimated as well. Using data on effort per defect, which can be obtained from the effort distribution data and the defect distribution data, the implications on the effort needed for different activities in the process can be outlined. Although it is possible to estimate the effects of changes on the effort and schedule by using past data, more likely, once the process changes are identified, their effects will be predicted based on past experience. This tactic is usually acceptable, as the changes are generally minor.

7.2.3   Estimating Defects for Other Stages

Once the process has been designed to meet the project's quality goal, defect levels for the various quality control activities should be estimated to enable quantitatively controlling the quality. The approach for estimating defect levels for some defect detection activity is similar to the approach for estimating the defects in acceptance testing. From the estimate of the total number of defects that will be introduced during the course of the project, the defect levels for different testing stages are forecast by using the percentage distribution of defects as given in the PCB (or as reported for similar projects in the PDB). The percentage distributions given in Infosys's PCB appear in Table 7.2.

In a project, estimation should be done, at a minimum, for system and integration testing. System testing is singled out because it is the major testing activity and the final quality control activity performed before the software is submitted for acceptance by the customer. Estimating defects for system testing

Table 7.2   Defect Distribution in Infosys's PCB

Process Stage	Percentage of Total Defects
Requirements specification review + HLD review + detailed design review	15%–20%
Code reviews + unit testing	50%–70%
Integration testing + system testing	20%–28%
Acceptance testing	5%–10%

and then monitoring the actual number of defects found with respect to the estimate help to determine whether the system testing has been sufficient and the software is ready for release. For reviews, instead of making an explicit prediction of the defect levels, norms given in the review baseline can be used to evaluate the effectiveness of a review immediately after it has been executed. Quantitatively managing reviews is discussed in more detail in Chapter 12. Similarly, the results of each unit testing can be evaluated based on past data, as is discussed in Chapter 13.

7.2.4   Examples

This section presents two examples to show how quality management might be performed. The first uses data from two similar projects along with data from the PCB to set its quality goal and estimate defects for system testing. The second consists of the quality plan for the WAR project, which used data from the PCB.

Example 1.   ABC 2.0 is a project that includes two parts developed earlier, each done as an independent project. As these three projects are all similar in many respects (for example, in terms of client, language, domain, and nature of application), the past data from the two completed phases will be the best source of information for planning. Hence data from the earlier ABC projects is used. The acceptance test defects and the total effort for the previous two projects appear in Table 7.3.

Table 7.3   Past Projects Data for Example 1

Earlier Project	Effort (Person-Days)	Acceptance Defects	Integration/System Testing Defects
ABC 1.2	628	27	64
ABC 1.2A	182	6	15
Total	**810**	**33**	**79**

The estimated effort for the current project, ABC 2.0, is 1,519 person-days. Using the effort as the basic predictor for defect levels, we obtain the estimated number of defects in acceptance testing for ABC 2.0:

$33 \times 1,519/810 = 62$ defects

If we estimate the acceptance test defects by using the data from the PCB (with an acceptance defect rate of 0.0035 defect per person-hour), then we obtain an estimate of the number of acceptance defects:

$0.0035 \times 1,519 \times 8.5 = 45$ defects

This value is lower than what is predicted by the past data on similar projects. The quality goal of this project is then set as a range rather than a fixed number (remember that a target number is also just an expected value). The quality goal is *45 to 60 acceptance defects.* As this rate is similar to the past project quality level and along the lines of quality levels suggested by the PCB, no special process change is needed to achieve this target.

For estimating defects at other stages, it was decided to estimate defects only for integration and system testing—the minimal requirement for quantitatively controlling the quality. Once again, defect levels are estimated based on data from the past two projects as well as data from the PCB. The estimated number of integration and system test defects found by using data from past projects is

$79 \times 1,519/810 = 148$ defects

When using the PCB, the total number of defects injected must be estimated first. By using the data from the PCB, we obtained 45 as the number of acceptance test defects. If 6% of the total defects are found during acceptance testing, and 24% of the total defects are found during integration testing, then the estimated number of defects for integration and system testing is

$45 \times 24/6 = 180$ defects

Again, instead of setting one number as the target, both numbers are used to set a range. If the actual number of defects found during integration testing falls within this range, then the data will seem to suggest that integration and system testing (and previous defect detection activities) have performed satisfactorily. Otherwise, some action might need to be taken to ensure that the quality goal is not violated.

Armed with these data, the overall project quality goals can be set. They are given in Table 7.4.

Example 2: Quality Plan of WAR.   The WAR project is our primary case study. Because it used new technology and tools, this project had few similar projects. From past data on new technology projects, it was estimated that, due to lack of

Table 7.4 Project Quality Goals for Example 1

Goal	Based on Data from ABC Projects	Based on Organization-wide Norms (PCB)	ABC 2.0 Goal
Acceptance defect density	62 defects	45 defects	45–60 defects
System/integration testing	148 defects	180 defects	148–180 defects

experience, the defect injection rate will be approximately 1 defect per person-day (0.012 defect per person-hour) or about 1 defect per function point. Hence the total number of defects introduced in this project is estimated at 340 defects.

As prototyping will occur during the requirements stage and as the design will be group-reviewed, it is expected that 30% of the defects will be detected during requirements and design, compared with the organization-wide norms of 15% to 20%. During code reviews and unit testing, 50% of the defects will likely be detected (the organization-wide norms are 50% to 70%). System testing will then detect lesser defects, as many design and requirements defects would have been identified previously during the requirements and design phases. The estimate for system testing is therefore 12%. The defects found during acceptance testing are expected to be 8% of the total (that is, the total in-process defect removal efficiency is 92%). With this information, the quality goal of the project can be set, as shown in Table 7.5.

Table 7.5 Project Quality Goals of the WAR Project

Goals	Value	Organization-wide Norms
Acceptance defects	27 (8%)	0.05–0.09/FP
System/integration testing	41 (12%)	0.07–0.13/FP; 20%–28% of defects
Requirements/prototypes and design	102 (30%)	15%–20% of defects
Code reviews and unit testing	170 (50%)	50%–70% of defects

7.3 Summary

This chapter described two approaches for managing the quality in a project. In the procedural approach, quality control procedures are planned and then properly executed. The procedural approach to quality management is expected at levels 2 and 3 of the CMM. In the quantitative quality management approach, a quantitative quality goal is set for the project; to achieve this goal, the actual execution of the process is monitored quantitatively. Any quantitative monitoring of a process's performance will require some baseline or estimates against which the actual performance can be compared.

The chapter discussed the implementation of quantitative quality management through defect prediction. In this approach, quality is defined as the defect density delivered (or the number of defects delivered for a project). To achieve the quality goal, the defect levels for the various defect detection stages in the process are estimated. During the execution of the project, the actual defect numbers are compared with the estimates to see whether the project is progressing satisfactorily toward achieving the goal or whether some correction is needed.

The approach of quantitative quality management through defect prediction taken at Infosys was then described. The quality goal is the number of defects found during acceptance testing. For monitoring and control, the number of defects expected at specific defect detection activities is predicted. Defects can be forecast by using the effort estimate and the defect rates normalized with respect to effort. With a size estimate in hand, the defect injection rate can be used to estimate total defects. Defect distribution percentages are then applied to estimate defects at different stages. The use of the final quality plan for project monitoring and control is discussed in Chapter 13.

References

[1] B. Boehm. *Software Engineering Economics.* Prentice Hall, 1981.

[2] N. E. Fenton and S. L. Pfleeger. *Software Metrics, a Rigorous and Practical Approach,* second edition. International Thomson Computer Press, 1996.

[3] D. Garmus and D. Herron. *Measuring the Software Process, a Practical Guide to Functional Measurements.* Yourdon Press Computing Series, 1996.

[4] A. L. Goel. Software reliability models: Assumptions, limitations and applicability. *IEEE Transactions on Software Engineering,* 11:1411–1423, 1985.

[5] International Standards Organization. *Information Technology—Software Product Evaluation—Quality Characteristics and Guidelines for Their Use.* ISO/IEC IS 9126, Geneva, 1991.

[6] S. H. Kan. *Metrics and Models in Software Quality Engineering.* Addison-Wesley, 1995.

[7] J. D. Musa, A. Iannino, and K. Okumoto. *Software Reliability—Measurement, Prediction, Application.* McGraw Hill, 1987.

[8] L. H. Putnam and W. Myers. *Measures for Excellence—Reliable Software on Time, within Budget.* Yourdon Press, 1992.

[9] L. H. Putnam and W. Myers. *Industrial Strength Software—Effective Management Using Measurement.* IEEE Computer Society Press, 1997.

8

Risk Management

Any project can fail. The reasons for a project failure might include a lack of proper engineering, lack of proper management, occurrence of some unforeseen events, or other problem. The basic goal of all activities undertaken during a project is to ensure that the project succeeds. The engineering activities attack the project's technical aspects and try to ensure that the project does not fail on the engineering front (for example, making sure that it has proper performance, functionality, and quality). Project management activities focus on making sure that the project does not fail due to poor management. Risk management tries to minimize the chances of failure caused by unforeseen events.

In a project, a risk is any condition or event whose occurrence is not certain, but that can affect the outcome in an unfavorable manner if it occurs. In other words, a risk to a project is a condition or event that may occur and that may have undesirable consequences. The two key elements of risks are that (1) the occurrence of the risk condition is probabilistic and (2) if it does occur, it can cause damage to the project.

Risk management aims to identify these risks and then take actions such that their effect on the project is minimized. Risk management is a relatively new management area in software. It first came to the forefront with Boehm's tutorial on risk management [2]. Since then, several books have targeted risk management for software [5, 7]. Proper processes for risk management are a requirement for the Integrated Software Management KPA at CMM level 3. In this chapter, we first discuss the general concept of risks and risk management before turning to Infosys's approach for risk assessment and risk control—the two major steps in risk management.

8.1 Background

Risks are those events or conditions that *may* occur, and whose occurrence, if it does take place, has a harmful or negative effect on the project. Risks should not be confused with events and conditions that require management intervention or action. Project management must deal with and plan for those situations that are likely to occur, but whose exact nature is not known beforehand. Such situations are not risks, however. For example, it is almost certain that defects will be found during software testing, so a reasonable project must plan to fix these defects when they are found. Similarly, it is almost certain that some change requests will come, so project management must be prepared for some changes and plan accordingly to handle such "normal" events.

A risk, on the other hand, is a probabilistic event—it may or may not occur. In software projects, because the level of predictability is low, some premises of "normal" project management may not hold; hence risk management becomes essential [6]. As risks are probabilistic events, we frequently have an optimistic tendency to just "not see them" or "wish that they will not occur." Social and organizational factors also may consider risk to be a stigma and discourage clear identification of risks [6]. This kind of attitude gets the project in trouble if the risk events materialize, which is likely to happen in a large project. Not surprisingly, then, risk management is considered first among the best practices for managing large software projects [3]. Before we discuss risks in the software context, let us examine the concept a bit more with the aid of an example.

Consider a computer show for which an important goal is to provide uninterrupted computer services. For this goal, one clear risk is electric power failure. The power may fail or it may not. If it does fail, even for a second, the computer services will be affected substantially (the machines will have to reboot, data will be lost, and so on). If this case is unacceptable (that is, if the cost of the power failure is high), then a universal power supply (UPS) can be deployed to minimize its consequences. If it is suspected that the power may go out for a long period, a backup generator may be set up to minimize the problem. With these risk management systems in place, if the power does go out, even for a long period, the show-related goal will not be compromised.

The first thing to note from this example is that risk management entails *additional cost.* Here, the cost for the UPS and the generator set is extra, as these components would not be needed if the risk of power failure was not there (for example, if the electric supply company guaranteed continuous power). Hence risk management can be considered cost-effective only if the cost of risk management is considerably less than the loss incurred if the risk materializes [7]. (Actually, the cost of risk management should be less than the expected value of the loss.) For example, if the loss due to power failure is low, then the cost of a UPS is not justified—a situation that prevails in homes.

The second thing to understand is that it is not easy to measure the value of risk management, particularly when looking back in time. If the power fails for one-half hour during the show, then the value provided by the UPS and generator set might be calculated as the "savings" achieved by having the computers running while the power was out. Suppose, however, that the power supply did not fail even for a second for the duration of the computer show. The UPS and the generator set were therefore not used at all. Does that mean that the expenditure on these components was a waste? Clearly not, because it could not be guaranteed that the power would not fail. If the risk does not materialize, then the value of using risk management cannot be directly measured in terms of value or output produced. Because risks will likely be events that occur infrequently, the chances are high that risk management systems will not be utilized during the project. In such situations, the value provided by the risk management systems has to be defined in terms of the potential value provided, which can be estimated or modeled, but not directly measured.

From this example, it should be clear that the first step in risk management is to identify the possible risks (power failure in this example) and to assess the consequences (loss of face or clients). Once risk assessment is done, a risk management plan can be developed (for example, having a UPS). Overall, then, risk management has two key components: risk assessment and risk control. Each component involves a few different tasks, as shown in Figure 8.1 [2].

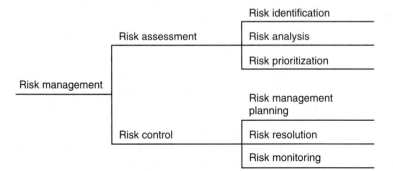

Figure 8.1 Risk management activities

The purpose of the risk assessment task is to identify the risks, analyze them, and then prioritize them. Prioritization is undertaken so as to identify the risks for which risk management should be done. In other words, prioritization determines where the extra effort for risk management should be spent to get the maximum benefit from the risk management efforts. For this effort, two factors are clearly important. First is the chance of a risk occurring—the risk that is more likely to occur will be a natural candidate for risk management. Second is the effect of the risk—a risk whose impact is very high is also a likely candidate. One way to prioritize risks, therefore, is to estimate the probability of the risk's occurrence and the consequences it has when it does occur. The product of these values, the "expected value" of the loss for the risk, can be used for prioritization purposes. This expected value is called risk-exposure. If Prob(R) is the probability of a risk R occurring, and Loss(R) is the total loss incurred if the risk materializes, then risk exposure, RE, for the risk is given by the following equation [2]:

$$RE\ (R) = Prob(R) \times Loss(R)$$

Once the risks have been prioritized, then we must decide what to do about them. Which ones will be managed is a management decision. Perhaps only the top few need to be handled in a project.

One possible approach is to take preventive or avoidance actions such that the perceived risk ceases to be a risk. For example, if new hardware is a risk, then it could be avoided by deciding to implement the project with proven hardware. Such actions are not always feasible, however (for example, if working with new hardware is a requirement from the customer). In such situations, the risks to the project must be handled properly.

For each risk that will be handled, risk management plans must be devised and then executed. Both the risk and the execution of the plans to minimize its consequences must be monitored, as risk perception changes with time. In a project, the risk perceptions may evolve naturally or the risk management plans put into action may reduce the risk. In either case, it is important to continually gauge the status of risks and their management plans. Overall, the different tasks in risk management can be combined into three key activities [6]:

1. Project risks are clearly and completely understood.
2. Risks are continuously and visibly monitored.
3. Project management actively controls risks.

Risk management can be integrated in the development process itself, as is done in the spiral model for software development [1]. If risk management is treated as a separate process, then its relationship with project execution has to be understood. This relationship is depicted in Figure 8.2. As shown in the figure, risk assessment and monitoring take information from project execution, along with other factors, so as to identify risks to be managed. The risk management activities, on the other hand, affect the project's process to minimize the consequences of the risk.

Even without a risk-driven process model, simple techniques can be applied for risk management. These techniques can prove very effective if risks are accepted as reality and something that is not to be feared but boldly handled. The remainder of this chapter discribes how risk management takes place at Infosys, which uses simple, but effective techniques. The activities for risk management are combined into two tasks: risk assessment and risk control. We discuss each separately.

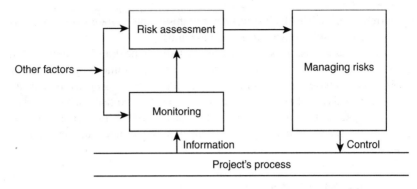

Figure 8.2   Risk management and project execution

8.2 Risk Assessment

At Infosys, risk assessment consists of the traditional two components: risk identification and risk prioritization. The risk identification activity focuses on enumerating possible risks to the project. The basic activity is to peer into the future and try to envision all situations that might make things in the project go wrong. The risk prioritization activity considers all aspects of all risks and then prioritizes them (for the purposes of risk management). Although the two are distinct activities, they are often carried out simultaneously. That is, risks may be identified and analyzed together.

8.2.1   Risk Identification

For a project, any condition, situation, or event that can occur and then can jeopardize the success of the project constitutes a risk. Identifying risks is therefore an exercise in envisioning what can go wrong. Though there are no general guidelines for performing this task of envisioning, keeping risk identification as an explicit activity and requiring the project leader to explicitly think about possible risks will help in identifying risks. Methods that can aid risk identification include the following [7]:

- Checklists of possible risks
- Interviews, meetings, and brainstorming
- Review of plans, processes, and work products
- Surveys

Checklists of frequently occurring risks are probably the most common technique for risk identification. SEI has provided a taxonomy of risks to aid in risk identification [4]. At Infosys, the commonly occurring risks for projects have been compiled. This list can help a project leader in identifying risks for the current project. This list is given later in this chapter, along with commonly used or recommended risk management methods.

In most situations, risks for a project are likely to be drawn from this list. If they are not, information about risk management on similar projects found in the process database can be studied to get an idea about risks faced by the current project. This act of evaluating previously encountered risks also helps identify other risks, as the process of evaluating risks and thinking about them will suggest other risks that may be more pertinent to this project but do not appear on the list.

8.2.2   Risk Prioritization

The identified risks for the project merely give the possible events that can hinder the project from meeting its goals. The consequences of different risks may be different, however. Before we proceed with managing risks, we must prioritize them, so management energies can be focused on the highest risks.

Prioritization requires analyzing the possible effects of the risk event, in case it actually occurs. That is, if the risk materializes, what will be the loss to the project? The loss could include a direct loss, loss due to lost business opportunity or future business, loss due to employee morale, and so on. Based on the possible consequences, and the probability of the risk event occurring, the risk exposure can be computed. This value represents the "expected loss" for a risk. Risk exposure can then be used for prioritizing risks.

This approach requires a quantitative assessment of the risk probability and the risk consequences. Usually, little historical data are available to help do a quantitative estimation of these parameters. As risks are probabilistic events, they occur infrequently, which makes gathering data about them more difficult. Furthermore, any data we have on risks and their impact must be interpreted properly, as the act of managing the risks affects them. This fact implies that risk prioritization activity will be based more on experience than on hard data from the past. In this situation, categorizing both the probabilities and consequences in a few categories can serve the purpose of separating "high-priority" risk items from lower-priority items [7]. Here, the probability of risk occurring is categorized in three categories for banding purposes: low, medium, and high. The probability range for each of these categories is given in Table 8.1.

Table 8.1   Risk Categories

Probability	Range
Low	0.0–0.3
Medium	0.3–0.7
High	0.7–1.0

For ranking the effects of a risk on a project, a unit of impact has to be selected. Sometimes, the consequences are measured in monetary terms. To keep risk management simple, however, the risk impact is viewed here as being on a scale of 1 to 10. Within this scale, the risk effects can be rated as low, medium, high, or very high. Table 8.2 gives the range for the consequences for each of these ratings.

Table 8.2 Impact Categories

Level of Consequences	Range
Low	0–3
Medium	3–7
High	7–9
Very high	9–10

With these ratings and ranges for each rating in hand, a simple method for risk prioritization can be specified. The basic steps in risk prioritization are as follows:

1. For each risk, rate the probability for the risk item happening as low, medium, or high. If necessary, assign probability values in the ranges given for each rating.

2. For each risk, assess its effects on the project as low, medium, high, or very high. If necessary, assign a weight on a scale of 1 to 10 for the consequences.

3. Rank the risks based on the probability and effects on the project—that is, a high-probability, high-risk item will have higher rank than a risk item with a medium probability and high risk. In case of conflict, judgment may be used (or numbers may be assigned to compute a numeric value of risk exposure).

4. Select the top few risk items for mitigation and tracking.

Note that this method allows the use of numbers for the probability and effects, thereby giving a number for risk exposure. Also note that a project may be analyzed just by classifying the risk probability and effects as low, medium, or high. This tactic is also acceptable even though it will make ordering of risks somewhat more difficult. Strict prioritization of risks is not so important, however. The main objective of risk management is to identify the top few risk items and then focus on them. For this purpose, working with a classification also works well. Clearly, a risk that has a high probability of occurring and that has high consequences is a risk with high risk exposure and, therefore, one with a high priority for risk management. When working with classifications, a problem in prioritization can arise if the risk probability and risk effects ratings are either (high, medium) or (medium, high). In this case, it is not clear which risk should be ranked higher. For a project, however, both can be considered important and should be viewed as serious enough to merit risk mitigation. If needed, differentiation between these types of risks can be done by using actual numbers.

As mentioned earlier, one of the best aids for risk identification is to list the set of risks commonly found in projects. This list can form the starting point for identifying risks for the current project. Frequently, the risks in the current project will appear on the list. To prepare this list, previous projects are surveyed. Based on the results of the survey, the top risks and the mitigation steps suggested by projects are then compiled.

This approach for prioritizing risks helps focus attention on high risks, but it does not help in doing a cost-benefit analysis of risk mitigation options. That is, by stating the consequences in terms of a scale, rather than in terms of money value, one cannot calculate the expected loss due to a risk in financial terms. Hence one cannot analyze whether a risk mitigation strategy, costing some amount, is worth employing. Such an analysis is generally not needed, as the focus of risk management is primarily on managing risks with the least cost and not on whether doing risk management is beneficial. On the other hand, if a decision is to be taken about whether a risk should be managed or whether it is financially smarter to leave it unmanaged, then the financial impact of the risk must be understood.

8.3 Risk Control

Once the risks have been identified and prioritized, the question becomes what to do about them. Knowing the risks is of value only if we can prepare such that their consequences are minimal—that is the basic goal of risk management. Minimizing the risk effects is done in the second phase of risk management—risk control. Essentially, this step involves planning of risk mitigation, followed by execution of the plan and monitoring of the risks.

8.3.1   Risk Management Planning

Once risks are identified and prioritized, it becomes clear which risks the project should handle. For managing the risks, proper planning is essential. The main task is to identify the actions needed to minimize the risk consequences. These steps are generally called "risk mitigation steps." As in risk identification, a list of commonly used risk mitigation steps for various risks is compiled to aid the project leader in selecting a suitable risk mitigation step. Infosys's list appears in Table 8.3. This table is a starting point not only for identifying risks, but also for selecting risk mitigation steps once the risks have been prioritized. As with identification, a project is not restricted to the steps mentioned in Table 8.3. The process database (refer to Chapter 5) can also be used to identify risks and risk mitigation steps.

Table 8.3 Top Ten Risks and Their Risk Mitigation Steps

Sequence Number	Risk Category	Risk Mitigation Steps
1	Shortage of technically trained manpower	• Make estimates with a little allowance for initial learning time • Maintain buffers of extra resources • Define a project-specific training program • Conduct cross-training sessions
2	Too many requirement changes	• Obtain sign-off for the initial requirements specification from the client • Convince the client that changes in requirements will affect the schedule • Define a procedure to handle requirements changes • Negotiate payment on actual effort
3	Unclear requirements	• Use experience and logic to make some assumptions and keep the client informed; obtain sign-off • Develop a prototype/get the requirements reviewed by the client
4	Manpower attrition	• Ensure that multiple resources are assigned on key project areas • Have team-building sessions • Rotate jobs among team members • Keep extra resources in the project as backup • Maintain proper documentation of individual's work • Follow the configuration management process and guidelines strictly

(continued)

Table 8.3   Top Ten Risks and Their Risk Mitigation Steps (*continued*)

Sequence Number	Risk Category	Risk Mitigation Steps
5	Externally driven decisions forced on the project	• Outline disadvantages with supporting facts/data and negotiate with the personnel responsible for forcing the decisions • If inevitable, identify the actual risk and follow its mitigation plan
6	Not meeting performance requirements	• Define the performance criteria clearly and get them reviewed by the client • Define standards to be followed to meet the performance criteria • Prepare the design to meet performance criteria and review it • Simulate/prototype performance of critical transactions • Test with a representative volume of data where possible • Conduct stress tests where possible
7	Unrealistic schedules	• Negotiate for a better schedule • Identify parallel tasks • Have resources ready early • Identify areas that can be automated • If the critical path is not within the schedule, negotiate with the client • Negotiate payment on actual effort
8	Working on new technology (hardware and software)	• Consider a phased delivery • Begin with the delivery of critical modules • Include time in the schedule for a learning curve • Provide training in the new technology • Develop proof-of-concept application
9	Insufficient business knowledge	• Increase interaction with the client and ensure adequate knowledge transfer

Table 8.3   Top Ten Risks and Their Risk Mitigation Steps (*continued*)

Sequence Number	Risk Category	Risk Mitigation Steps
10	Link failure/slow performance	• Organize domain knowledge training • Simulate/prototype the business transaction to the client and get it approved • Set proper expectations with the client • Plan ahead for the link load • Plan for optimal link usage

Most of the risks and their mitigation steps in Table 8.3 are self-explanatory. As can be seen, the top few risks are concerned with manpower and requirements. Many of the items here are similar to those in the top risk lists given in [2, 7]. It should be emphasized that selecting a risk mitigation step is not just an intellectual exercise. The risk mitigation step has to be executed (and monitored). To ensure that the actions needed for risk mitigation are executed properly, they must be incorporated into the project schedule. In other words, the schedule of the project, which lists the various activities to be done in the project and when they will occur, must be updated suitably to include the actions related to the chosen risk mitigation steps.

8.3.2   Risk Monitoring and Tracking

Risk prioritization and consequent planning are based on the risk perception at the time that the risk analysis is performed. The first risk analysis takes place at the time of project planning, and the initial risk management plan reflects the situation as viewed at that time. Because risks are probabilistic events, frequently depending on external factors, the "threat" due to risks may change with time as factors change. Clearly, then, the "risk perception" may also change with time. Furthermore, the risk mitigation steps undertaken may affect the risk perception.

This dynamism implies that risks in a project should not be treated as static and that reevaluation of risks needs to be done periodically. Hence, besides monitoring the progress of the risk mitigation steps that have been planned, the risk perception for the entire project needs to be revisited periodically. This review is done at milestones by reporting the risk status in the milestone analysis reports. The status of the risk mitigation steps is reported, along with the current "risk perception" and strategy. This revision is prepared by doing afresh the risk analysis to determine whether the priorities have changed. The milestone analysis is discussed in Chapter 13.

8.4 Examples

This section includes two risk management plans: one for the WAR project and one from another project. As we can see, the risk management plans tend to be small—usually a table that fits in a page. The activities mentioned in the mitigation plan become part of project activities that may even be explicitly scheduled.

Example 1: The War Project.   The WAR project chose to work with numbers for risk prioritization and analysis. As can be seen in Table 8.4, the top five risk items have consequences ratings that range from 7.2 to 2.5. The risk mitigation steps are also shown for each risk. For example, the third risk is working on a new technology. That is, the project incurs a risk because the technology for the project is new to the project personnel. The risk mitigation plan for this risk is the most obvious one—plan for training in the new technology. Training is also a suggested risk mitigation step in the table of common risks and common risk

Table 8.4   Risk Management Plan for the WAR Project

SI #	Risk	Prob-ability	Conse-quences	Risk Exposure	Mitigation Plan
01	Availability of functional/ technical group for reviews	0.80	9.0	7.2	• Decide on possible dates for review at least one month early, so that group members can plan early
02	Frequent requirement changes	0.50	9.0	4.5	• Sign off on the initial requirements • Employ prototyping
03	Working on new technology	0.40	8.0	3.2	• Training in new technology planned • Develop a proof-of-concept application
04	Change in customer coordinator	0.50	5.0	2.5	• Better status reporting
05	Failure to meet performance requirements	0.50	5.0	2.5	• Better design will be done to ensure that performance criteria are satisfied; the design will be reviewed by the technical group

mitigation steps. In addition, developing a proof-of-concept application is proposed as a mitigation step.

Note that once these options are accepted as the risk mitigation steps, they influence the detailed schedule of the project—the schedule must include time for appropriate training and proof-of-concept building activities. This need will arise with many risk mitigation steps. As they represent some actions to be taken in the project, and the detailed project schedule represents most of the actions to be done in a project, the risk mitigation steps will frequently change the detailed project schedule, adding to the overall effort requirement of the project.

Example 2. This project used the rating system for its risk management. The different ratings and the risk mitigation steps are shown in Table 8.5. This risk management plan is a part of the project management plan for the project and has been extracted from it.

Table 8.5 Risk Management Plan for Example 2

Sl #	Risk	Prob- ability	Conse- quences	Risk Exposure	Mitigation Plan
1	Failure to meet the high perfor- mance requirements	High	High	High	• Indicate expected performance to clients through prototypes
					• Use tips from Body of Knowledge data- base to improve per- formance
					• Make team aware of the requirements
					• Update the review checklist to look for performance pitfalls
					• Study and improve performance con- stantly
					• Follow guidelines from earlier perfor- mance studies
					• Test application for meeting perfor- mance expectations during integration and system testing

Table 8.5 Risk Management Plan for Example 2 (*continued*)

SI #	Risk	Prob-ability	Conse-quences	Risk Exposure	Mitigation Plan
2	Availability of persons with mixed process types	Medium	Medium	Medium	• Train resources • Prototype review with customer • Coding practices
3	Complexity of application requirements	Medium	Medium	Medium	• Ongoing knowledge transfer • Deploy persons with prior experience with the application
4	Manpower attrition	Medium	Medium	Medium	• Train a core group of four people • Rotate onsite assignments among people • Identify backups for key roles
5	Unclear requirements	Medium	Medium	Medium	• Prototype review • Midstage review
6	Reconciliation of changes done in onsite main-tenance during off-shore development	Medium	Low	Medium	• Configuration management plan and adherence to well-defined reconciliation approach • Reconcile once per month (first Tuesday or its next working day) • Changes done after a cut-off date will not be reconciled

For this project, all risks mentioned in the risk management plan do not appear on the list of common risks. Both this example and the WAR project example strongly suggest that the proposed method of risk management does help in focusing the project's attention on risks and risk management, so that risks not listed in the table of common risks also get uncovered.

During the risk analysis done at project milestones, a reprioritization of risks may occur. In this project, when an analysis was done at a milestone about three months after the initial risk management plan was made, the risk perception had changed somewhat. The method for performing the risk analysis at a milestone is essentially the same as described earlier, except that more attention is given to the risks listed in the project plan (that is, greater emphasis is placed on the output of earlier risk analyses for the project). Some of the risks for which the exposure had changed are given in Table 8.6.

Based on the experience in the project so far, the project leader has decided that the consequences of change reconciliation are considerably less dire. For example, this situation may arise because reconciliation problems encountered so far have been less difficult than expected. Similarly, the perception of "manpower attrition" risk has increased—again, perhaps due to experience with team members so far and perhaps the fact that people leaving in the middle of the project is now perceived as a greater problem than at the start of the project. Whenever risks are analyzed, the risk mitigation plans may also change, depending on the current realities of the project and the nature of risks. In this project, there was no change in the risk mitigation plans.

Table 8.6   Risk Evolution for Example 2

SI #	Risk	Current Probability	Current Consequences	Current Risk Exposure
2	Manpower attrition	High	High	High
3	Reconciliation of changes created in onsite maintenance during off-shore development	Low	Low/medium	Low

8.5 Summary

A risk for a project is a condition whose occurrence is not certain, but which can adversely affect the project. This chapter discussed the general concept of risk and risk management for software projects. It also described how risk management is done at Infosys. For risk assessment, risks are first identified and then prioritized. For risk identification, a list of commonly occurring risks in projects is compiled. This list forms the starting point for identifying risks in a project. The project leader has to look ahead and try to visualize all that can go wrong in a project so as to identify risks.

For risk prioritization, a simple mechanism is used. The probabilities of risks are classified into three categories: low, medium, and high. The effects of risks are also classified, as low, medium, high, or very high. Once the probability and potential consequences are categorized, risk prioritization can be done easily. A risk with high probability and high consequences is clearly a very high risk. A risk with a high probability (or consequences) and medium consequences (or probability) is also a high risk. Risks with low probability and consequences are low risks. This method does not allow for strict and full prioritization, but it does enable the identification of the top few risks that need to be managed in a project, which is what is needed in most projects. If prioritization is important, however, numbers can be assigned to each of the two factors to obtain a value for risk exposure, which can then be used for prioritization purposes.

Risk management requires that once the risks are identified and prioritized, something be done for the top few risks so that they have minimal consequences. The risk mitigation steps must be carefully planned. During the project, these steps have to be executed and their execution monitored. Risks themselves need to be monitored and reevaluated periodically to see whether the risk mitigation steps are having some effect and to rejudge the risk perception. This task involves reevaluating risks at milestones and reporting their status.

References

[1] B. Boehm. A spiral model of software development and enhancement. *IEEE Computer,* pp. 61–72, May 1988.

[2] B. Boehm. *Tutorial: Software Risk Management.* IEEE Computer Society, 1989.

[3] N. Brown. Industrial-strength management strategies. *IEEE Software,* pp. 94–103, July 1996.

[4] M. Carr, et al. *Taxonomy-based Risk Identification.* Technical Report, CMU/SEI-93-TR-006, 1993.

[5] R. Charette. *Software Engineering Risk Analysis and Management.* McGraw Hill, 1989.

[6] R. N. Charette. Large-scale project management is risk management. *IEEE Software,* pp. 110–117, July 1996.

[7] E. M. Hall. *Managing Risk—Methods for Software Systems Development.* Addison-Wesley, 1998.

9

Project Management Plan

In earlier chapters, we discussed how effort and schedule estimation, defect estimation, and risk management are done. The outputs from the planning activity are put together in a project management plan document, which is the main document guiding the project, along with the project schedule. Three types of personnel use the project management plan. First is the business manager of the project, to whom the project leader reports. For this manager, the plan provides an overall view of how the project is to be managed, what the commitments are, who the people are, and so on. Second is the project leader, who is also the owner of this document. Requiring that this document be in a certain format ensures that the project leader will take a comprehensive view of the project while planning. The plan also acts as the reference for the project leader when actually managing the project. Third is the developers in the project. To them, the plan provides a comprehensive view of the project, its goals, its commitments, and their roles in the project.

The project management plan plays a key role in properly managing a project. It is required by the Software Project Planning KPA of CMM level 2 as well as the Integrated Software Management KPA of CMM level 3. As the plan may also contain quantitative goals and outline quantitative approaches for monitoring, it also satisfies some requirements of the Quantitative Process Management and Software Quality Management KPAs of level 4. Because the plan specifies which documents and work products will be reviewed and the method of review, it satisfies some practices for the Peer Review KPA of level 3 as well. In addition, the plan indicates which mechanisms will be used for project tracking, thereby satisfying some aspects of the Project Tracking and Oversight KPA of level 2. Escalation of issues is also planned, which helps in implementing Intergroup Coordination KPA (level 3) requirements. In this chapter, we briefly discuss the contents of a project management plan at Infosys, and then give the project management plan for the WAR case study.

9.1 Project Management Plan

The project management plan (PMP) document must provide the necessary information to all three sets of people mentioned earlier. Infosys's PMP includes four major sections. The first section consists of the project summary, which gives overall information about the project. The second section, entitled project planning, describes the outputs of various planning activities, including things like process tailoring, estimates and basis for estimates, the risk management plan, and more. The third section, entitled project tracking, specifies all mechanisms to be used in the project for tracking. The final section describes the roles and responsibilities of the various people involved.

9.1.1 Project Summary

The project summary section gives a high-level overview of the project. It includes information on the start and end dates of the project, the project leader, contacts at the customer end, project objectives, major commitments made to the customer, and assumptions made. The assumptions made must be explicitly listed because they frequently serve as the source of risks in the project and can aid in risk management. When describing the commitments to the customer, all intermediate commitments are mentioned as milestones. They are "external milestones" for the project ("external" because the project does not have any control over them).

Details of billing may also be described (so that the business manager can track them). The objectives of the project from the customer's perspective as well as from Infosys's perspective are mentioned so that it is clear to all why the project is being executed.

9.1.2 Project Planning

The project planning section gives outputs of executing the various project-planning procedures. It also specifies the life cycle of the project. The tailoring guidelines permit the life-cycle process to be modified in a controlled manner. If, however, a project needs a process that cannot be obtained by applying tailoring guidelines to the standard process, then the necessary modifications to the process can be made. These "deviations" are highlighted in the PMP as "tailoring notes." Because the plan must be reviewed by the SEPG and approved by the business manager to whom the project leader reports, explicitly mentioning these deviations provides the necessary visibility for approval from SEPG and senior management.

Requirements, of course, may change. Unless they are tightly controlled, however, requirement changes can easily have adverse effects on the project. The issue of requirement changes was discussed earlier in Chapter 3. To keep a sharp focus on such changes, the change management process that a project will follow is specified in its PMP, along with the thresholds beyond which special actions will be taken.

An important part of the planning section is effort estimation. The estimation approach has been discussed earlier in this book. In the PMP, the estimates and their basis are captured. The development environment needed, tools employed, and any other requirements for the project are captured as well, along with the project-specific training plan. The quality plan and the risk management plan are also given in the PMP. The methods for developing these plans were discussed in Chapters 7 and 8.

The PMP also lists project milestones. These milestones are separate from the external milestones, as the former are used primarily for project management purposes whereas the latter are customer-driven. Milestone analysis (discussed in Chapter 13) occurs at project milestones. This analysis plays an important role in providing visibility to project management, which may potentially lead to management intervention. For a project, it is desirable that the detailed analysis performed at milestones be done reasonably frequently so that timely intervention in the form of corrective actions is possible. Hence project milestones are generally specified so that they are about three to five weeks apart. For each milestone, the schedule, effort and defect deviation limits are outlined. If the actual deviates from the estimated by more than the limit specified in the plan at that milestone, then this fact must be brought to the attention of the business manager and the project leader must take some corrective action.

9.1.3 Project Tracking

Project tracking involves monitoring the activities, issues, quality, and other aspects of the project. We will discuss this activity in more detail in Part III of the book. In the PMP, how activities, issues, and customer feedback will be tracked is specified. Policies regarding who will log the information, who will review it, who will close the activities, when they will be escalated, and so on are mentioned. The frequency of the various types of status reporting is also specified.

The focus of the project tracking mechanisms is capturing and resolving problems at the project level. If problems cannot be solved at the project level, however, then mechanisms must exist to take them to the "higher-ups" for resolution, so that the project is not delayed by unresolved problems. For this purpose, the escalation channel—at both the customer's and Infosys's ends—are specified in the PMP, along with policies regarding when they are to be deployed.

9.1.4 Team

The project team must be properly organized to achieve optimal performance. At Infosys, generally a hierarchical team structure is employed; this team is headed by a project leader (PL). The PL reports to the business manager (BM) and to the customer representative. (The frequency and nature of reporting are discussed in the tracking section.) The PL may have either module leaders or developers (DVs) as subordinates. In addition, the configuration controller (CC) and the database administrator (DBA) typically report to the PL.

As discussed in Chapter 1, an SEPG member known as the software quality advisor is associated with each project. The quality advisor interacts intensively with the PL (and with the CC), but does not report to the PL. Instead, the quality advisor has an independent reporting channel.

The team organization for the project is specified in the PMP. The logical responsibilities of each person are detailed, along with the start and end date for each person. A team member may have multiple responsibilities. Finally, the implications and responsibilities of each role in the project are specified.

9.2 Example: Project Plan of WAR 2.0

The project plan for our case study—the WAR project—is given in this section. The first section of the PMP gives the main players, milestones, and an overview of the project. Section 2 contains details about planning. For example, it states that the "development process" will be used and specifies the deviations that the project process has from the standard process. For requirements change management, the plan states that if more than five changes have occurred, if a major design change is necessary, or if a change takes more than two days, then reestimation and rescheduling will be done; this fact will also be highlighted in status reports. The size and effort estimates, as discussed earlier, appear in the plan. The quality plan is also included. The training plan clearly focuses on training in the new technology, as this training constitutes one of the risk mitigation steps.

The project tracking section (section 3) mentions that Microsoft Project (MSP) will be used for task scheduling, assignment, and status monitoring. The in-house developed tool, BugsBunny, will be used for tracking issues local to the project. The PL is responsible for reviewing and ensuring that these problems are resolved, except for the issues relating to the business manager. Bugs-Bunny will also be used for tracking customer complaints and feedback. Status reports will be sent every fortnight, and the customer will receive a report at each milestone. Detailed analysis is planned at milestones. Escalation channels at both ends are established.

Section 4 specifies the team structure as well as the roles and responsibilities of each person on the team.

Project Management Plan for WAR 2.0

1. PROJECT SUMMARY

1.1 Project Overview

Project Code	Module Code/ Name	Customer	Project Authorization Reference
MIS	WAR20—Weekly Activity Report Version 2.0	Infosys	

Project Leader (PL)	Configuration Controller (CC)	Business Manager (BM)	Backup PL	Backup CC
Dev	Vasu	Sastry	Ram	Rishi

Project Start Date	Project End Date	Total Estimated Effort
21-Oct-98	10-June-1998	

PROJECT CONTACT PERSONNEL			
Name and Designation	**Phone Number**	**Fax Number**	**E-Mail ID**
(Customer's Representative)			
Dev (PL)	—	—	—

BILLING SCHEDULE			
SI # **Date**	**Milestone**	**Amount**	**Percentage of Total Revenue**
NA	NA	NA	NA

(continued)

Customer's Objectives
• Should overcome some of the existing problems with some enhancements
• Should allow for platform independence
• Should facilitate entry of WAR from all development centers and customer's sites
• Should allow contractor to submit WARs

Infosys's Objectives
• Should be executed at CMM level 4
• Should arrive at and obtain Web-based migration architecture
• Should produce reusable model/code/design ideas and define development standards
• Should gain experience in application development on the Web

1.2   Commitments Made to the Customer

SI #	Milestones	Deliverables	Delivery Date	Responsible Person
1	Requirement	Requirements specification document + prototype	Dec 1	PL
2	Functional specifications	Functional specifications document + prototype	Jan 2	PL
3	Architecture and high-level design	Design document	Jan 15	PL
4	Database design	Database design document	Jan 27	PL

SI #	Milestones	Deliverables	Delivery Date	Responsible Person
5	Detailed design	Detailed design document	Feb 12	PL
6	Test case design	Test plan document	Feb 17	PL
7	Build	Code/modules	April 14	PL
8	System testing	Test results	April 25	PL
9	Acceptance testing	Test results	May 6	Customer's represen-tative
10	Implementation study	Implementation plan	May 13	PL
11	Pilot run	Pilot results	June 10	PL

1.3 Assumptions

SI #	Assumptions Made in Planning
1	All development centers are connected via 64kbps (WAN)
2	Hardware, Web server, and database servers are in place by release date
3	Quality department will identify pilot projects and prepare plan for pilot run

2. PROJECT PLANNING

2.1 Project Process

2.1.1 Standard Process Followed
Development process

(continued)

2.1.2 Tailoring Notes—Deviations

LC Stage	Added/Modified/Deleted	Reasons for Deviations
Detailed design	Added a new step—develop proof of concept	The project employs a new technology
Architecture design	Added—evaluation of available options for transaction management	Information about the different transaction processors available for DCOM is not available

2.1.3 Requirements Change Management

The following process will be followed for every requirement change request:

1. Requests will be logged into BugsBunny.
2. Impact analysis will be done and then reviewed.
3. Based on the review result, a decision will be taken. Possible decisions are to add to the current release, to postpone until the next release, or to not be included.

Minor change requests will be accommodated without changing the project plan. If the following criterion holds, then the project estimates must be redone:

The number of requirements changes is greater than five, or any major design change is necessary, or the effort for any change takes more than two days.

2.2   Effort Estimation

This estimation is preliminary. A better estimate can be developed only after the technology/architecture design is over (part of HLD). A bottom-up estimation method is followed. The process database and process capability baseline are the main sources of data.

BASIS FOR ESTIMATION		
Classification/ Type	Classification Criteria	Build Effort (Person-Days)
Simple	Programs with minimum business logic, not more than 2–3 table access, and very little data display	4

BASIS FOR ESTIMATION (*continued*)		
Classification/ Type	Classification Criteria	Build Effort (Person-Days)
Medium	Programs with moderate business logic, 2–4 table access, and moderate data display	6
Complex	Programs with complex busi- ness logic, more than 4 table access, and much data display	12

MODULE DETAILS	
Program/ Function	Complexity
Entry of WAR	Medium—Planned/unplanned section
Activity list filter	Complex—Filter criteria for tasks
Submission of WAR	Simple—Workflow function
Review of WAR	Medium—Has one more screen for submitter list as compared with the entry of WAR function
Project-level setup	Medium—Project-level activity codes/module codes
Activity code setup	Simple—Corporate-level activity codes maintenance
Mail interface	Medium—Formatting data and sending mail
WAR remainder	Simple
Onsite WAR entry	Complex—Needs to be handled for various modes, should support four platforms and two layers (UI and data storage)
WAR data entry program	Medium—For entry of WAR for workers who have filled in WAR in a sheet or any other format that must be entered manually (VB Program)
Other systems interface	Medium—Interface to other systems like leave, HRIS, and INMASS
Project plan upload	Medium
Reporting module	Complex—Includes automatic generation of reports (scheduler) on specific intervals other than standard reports (assuming 10 reports)

(continued)

MODULE DETAILS (*continued*)	
Program/ Function	**Complexity**
Middle layer	Complex—Consists of the processing logic/database layer/system layer (might vary based on the architecture)
Architecture	Complex—Three phases (design/build/ implement— includes distributed databases, Web servers, and more)
Help	Simple
User preferences	Medium—User's default settings
Batch process	Medium—Static HTML generation in Web server for activities code, module, and more (to enhance performance)
Other system modification	Modify existing tables to new

BUILD EFFORT			
Complexity	**Number of Units**	**Build Effort/Unit (Person-Days)**	**Total Build Effort (Person-Days)**
Simple	4	4	16
Medium	10	6	60
Complex	5	12	60
Total	**16**	**—**	**136**

Stage	**Percentage of Effort (%)**	**Effort**
Requirements analysis	4	14
Design	20	68
Build	40	136
Testing	10	34
Acceptance	4	14
Project management	8	27
Training	5	17
Others	9	30
Total	**100**	**340**

With Visual Basic 5, the expected productivity is between 20 and 40 FP per person-month. Because this project involves a new technology, the productivity expected in the project will be toward the lower side. We expect to achieve a productivity of 22 FP/person-month. The size in FP can therefore be estimated from the effort estimates. Taking 22 working days in a month, we obtain the size in FP as 340/22 × 22 = 340 FP.

2.3 Development Environment

Hardware	Software
Intel Pentium PC running Windows NT, Windows 95	Netscape Enterprise Server 3.0 SQL Server 6.5 Java-enabled browser Microsoft Visual C++ 4.5 Microsoft Visual Basic 5.0

2.4 Tools

Tools List	
Tools to be developed in the project	—
Tools to be procured from external sources	VSS, Netscape Enterprise Server, SQL Server 6.5
In-house tools to be used in the project	BugsBunny, WAR-MSP, MS Project

2.5 Training Plan

Training Area Technical	Duration	Waiver Criteria
HTML, CGI	1 week—On the job for 1 person	Two team members already have this skill and do not need this training
Netscape Enterprise Server	2 days—On the job for 1 person	

(continued)

Training Area Technical	Duration	Waiver Criteria
Java/C++/object-oriented design	1 week—Mentoring for 1 person	No need to undergo this training if the developer is not involved in the middle layer
CORBA/Messaging Arch/DCOM	1 week—On the job for 1 person	No need to undergo this training if the developer is not involved in middle-layer construction

Business Domain		
Nil	—	—

Process-Related		
CMM level 4 process	2 days—Mentoring	
VSS	1 day—On the job	
Standards discussion	1 day—On the job	

2.6   Quality Plan

PROJECT QUALITY GOALS			
Goals	Target	Organization-wide Norms	Estimated Value
Defect injection	1 defect/FP or about 0.012 defect per person-hour	0.9–1.8 defects/FP	340 defects
Acceptance testing	8%	5%–10%	27 defects
System integration testing	12%	20%–28%	41 defects
Code review and user testing	50%	50%–70%	170 defects
Requirements review (including prototyping) + design review	30%	15%–20%	102 defects

Strategy to Achieve These Quality Goals

- An extensive detailed design will be done to offset the effects of the new technology.
- Complex programs will be group-reviewed.

REVIEWS		
Review Point	**Review Item**	**Type of Review**
End of project plan document	Project plan	Group review
End of configuration management (CM) plan	CM plan	One-person review
End of requirements specification (RS)	RS document	Group review
End of architecture design	Architecture document	Group review
End of high-level design	HLD document	Group review
End of user interface and navigation design	User interface and navigation document	Group review
End of detailed design (HLD)	Detailed design document	Group review
End of test case design	Test plan	Group review
During build	Complex code	Group review
During build	Medium complex code	One-person review
End system test plan	System test plan	Group review

(continued)

2.7   Project Milestones

SI #	Project Milestones	Schedule Deviation Limit	Effort Deviation Limit	Defects Deviation Limit
1	End of functional specifications	10%	25%	33%
2	End of high-level design	10%	25%	33%
3	End of detailed design	10%	25%	33%
4	End of build	10%	25%	33%
5	End of system testing	10%	25%	33%

2.8   Risk Management Plan

SI #	Risks	Probability	Consequences	Risk Exposure	Mitigation Plan
1	Availability of functional/ technical group for reviews	0.80	9.0	7.2	Development of possible dates for review at least one month early, so that group members can plan early
2	Too many requirement changes	0.50	9.0	4.5	Sign-off for the initial requirements Prototyping
3	New technology	0.40	8.0	3.2	Training in new technology planned
4	Change in customer coordinator	0.50	5.0	2.5	Better status reporting
5	Failure to meet performance requirements	0.50	5.0	2.5	Better design to ensure that the performance criterion is satisfied; review of design by the technical group

3.   PROJECT TRACKING

3.1   Task Tracking

Activity	Procedure
Task scheduling	• Project leader plans the tasks using MSP. These activities show up in the WAR system as planned activities for the team members
Task assignment	• Same as above
Task status tracking	• MSP updated once per week
	• Status report updated once per fortnight
Project meeting	• Development team will meet weekly to discuss the issues, project status, and plans for the next two weeks

3.2   Issues Tracking

Issues Types	Where Logged	Who Can Log	Who Reviews and When	Whose Bottom Line	When Escalated
Project internal issues	BugsBunny	Team	PL	PL	5 days
Customer issues	BugsBunny	Customer interface	PL	PL	3 days
Business manager issues	BugsBunny	BM/PL	BM/SBU head	BM	5 days
Issues with support services	Requirements tracker	PL/Team	PL	PL	3 days

(continued)

3.3   Customer Feedback

Item	Logging and Tracking Process
Customer feedback	BugsBunny
Customer complaints	BugsBunny

3.4   Status Reporting

STATUS REPORTS AND ANALYSES	
Report to	**Frequency**
Business manager	Once per fortnight
Customer	At the end of each phase
Business manager and SEPG	At milestones (milestone analysis)

3.5   Escalation Procedures

Threshold Period	Name of Person	Title of the Person
At Customer's End		
3 days	—	Senior project manager
7 days	—	Director/head
At Infosys's End		
3 days	—	Business manager

4   TEAM—WHO, WHAT, AND HOW

4.1   Project Organization

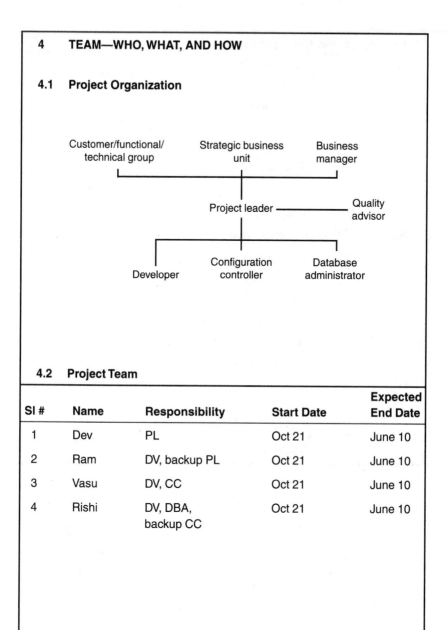

4.2   Project Team

SI #	Name	Responsibility	Start Date	Expected End Date
1	Dev	PL	Oct 21	June 10
2	Ram	DV, backup PL	Oct 21	June 10
3	Vasu	DV, CC	Oct 21	June 10
4	Rishi	DV, DBA, backup CC	Oct 21	June 10

(continued)

4.3   Roles and Responsibilities

Role	Responsibilities
BM	Coordination with SBU head
	Status tracking
	Resolving issues
Customer	Providing requirements
	Review coordination
	Acceptance test plan
	Acceptance
PL	Project management
	Specification documents
	Issue tracking
	Review
	Coordination with senior management
ML	Design, reviews, code reviews and coding
DV	Design and coding
CC	Configuration control activities
SQA	Compliance checks
	Review of project plan
	Data analysis

9.3 Summary

This chapter described the complete project management plan (PMP) document of a project at Infosys. This document outlines the various elements of the project plan, plans for tracking the project, and the team structure to be used. In earlier chapters, we discussed various aspects of planning; the PMP documents the outcome of these different aspects of planning. The PMP, along with the project schedule (which enumerates all tasks in the project), is the main document used for controlling the project.

The project management plan of the WAR project was also given in this chapter. Many of the elements that are included in the management plan—for example, effort estimation, quality planning, process tailoring, and risk management—were discussed earlier. The PMP specifies other aspects of project planning that are also important for the success of the project—requirements change management, escalation channels, thresholds for corrective actions, milestones, project tracking, and team structure.

10

Configuration Management

A software project produces a number of items during its execution, including various documents, programs, data, and manuals (also called work products). All of these items can be changed easily. This characteristic is a unique feature of software (as compared with products of various other engineering disciplines). It provides tremendous power and flexibility, but at the same time adds complexity in project management because anything can change at any time. In a software project, the requirements themselves may change at any time during the course of the project. To avoid losing control of the project in the face of changes, it is essential that changes be properly controlled and managed. Configuration management (CM)—also known as software configuration management (SCM)—is the aspect of project management that focuses exclusively on systematically controlling the changes that occur during the project [1, 2]. It consists of a set of activities performed to identify and organize software items and to control their modification.

CM is also needed to satisfy one of the basic objectives of a project—delivery of a high-quality software product to the client. What is this "software" that is delivered? At the least, it contains the various source or object files that make up the source or object code, scripts to build the working system from these files, and associated documentation. In a project, the sources and documentation are usually maintained as many separate files. This approach is taken for project management as well as product management reasons. As the project progresses, the files change, leading to different versions. In this situation, even constructing the system from its parts is a difficult task: How does one ensure that the appropriate versions of sources are combined and that no source is missed? Also, how does one make sure that the correct versions of the documents, which are consistent with the final source being delivered, are sent? For these types of situations, items and their versions must be properly tracked, along with the version of the software product. Without this information, delivering the "final" system itself will become an onerous task. This activity is not handled by regular project management or the development processes, but rather is considered a part of CM.

Software configuration management is best viewed as a separate process. It needs to remain separate because most process models for software development cannot accommodate changes at any time during the project and view software as a logical entity rather than a collection of items. Changes do occur, however, and a logical entity is usually kept as a collection of many smaller units. The software has to be produced and objectives of the project have to be met even when changes take place, and software is maintained as multiple items. This approach requires a proper process to handle and implement changes to the various items produced during the project, known as the CM process. CM is a very important activity in a project and a requirement at CMM level 2 (the Software Configuration Management KPA).

One of the most important activities in CM is proper planning for managing the configuration. CM planning is often considered to be a part of project planning. Although a CM plan can be made a part of the project management plan, this book views it as a separate document focusing on a specific aspect of management. This chapter first discusses some general concepts relating to CM and then describes the CM process followed at Infosys.

10.1 Configuration Management Concepts

A primary objective of CM is to manage the evolving configuration of the software system [1]. In a project, a program's evolution takes it through many states. At the beginning, when a programmer develops it, the program is under development (or "private"). Once the programmer is satisfied with the program, the program moves into the "ready for UT" state, implying that the program is now ready for unit testing (UT). Only when the program reaches this state can it be unit-tested. After it has been unit tested, the programmer must fix any defects found. The programmer has to make a copy in a private area to correct the defects.

If the UT succeeds, however, then its state changes to "ready for ST," implying that the program can now be used for system testing (ST). Only when all programs that are needed for ST reach this state can the ST activity commence. Just as with "ready for UT" state, if defects are found, the state of a program reverts back to "private"; otherwise it moves to "ready for AT," implying that the program is ready for acceptance testing (AT). When all programs needed for the system reach this state, the AT effort can proceed. If it succeeds, then the state of all programs changes to "ready for release," implying that they can now be released for "production use." Once a program is released, and is in production use, then all the programs (and associated documentation) move to "baselined" state, which represents the state of the production system.

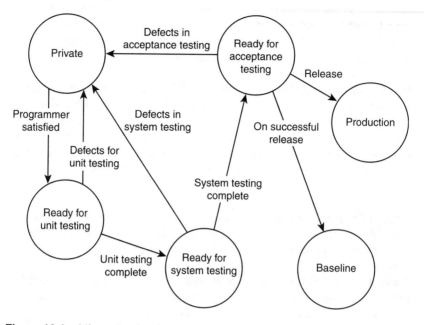

Figure 10.1   Life cycle of an item

Figure 10.1 provides the overall state diagram of a program, which represents its life cycle. This life cycle is more general and detailed than the one described in [4].

Clearly, the state information about programs must be maintained to properly manage the evolution of programs. It enables a tester to decide when to unit-test a program or when to perform system testing. The CM process has to ensure that this state transition diagram is implemented and that the state of a program remains visible.

In addition to the changes that take place during the "normal" software development course, requirement change requests may arise, whose implementation may alter programs. The existence of a large number of items in a project, plus the possiblity of changes to them, can create situations that require some actions; these actions, in turn, can be performed only if proper support is available from the CM process. To better understand CM, let us consider what functionality a project requires from it. Although this requirement can depend on the nature of the project and the exact situation, some general functions needed can be specified. Below, we discuss some of these functions and give some scenarios where they might be needed. These functions are more detailed than the CM functions defined in [3].

Give States of Programs.   This information is needed to decide when to start testing or when to release the software.

Give Latest Version of a Program.   Suppose that a program must be modified. Clearly, the modification has to be carried out in the latest copy of that program; otherwise, changes made earlier may be lost.

Handle Concurrent Update Requests.   Two programmers, in response to two different change requests, might change the same program concurrently. The change "written" later could potentially "overwrite" the change made earlier. Avoiding such a situation requires access control such that only one person can make changes to a program at any given time. If multiple parallel changes are allowed, then reconciliation procedures should ensure that both changes are reflected in the final version of the program.

Undo a Program Change.   A change is made to a program (to implement some change request), but later a need arises to "undo" this change request. Support for this function requires proper version control.

Prevent Unauthorized Changes or Deletions.   A programmer may decide to change some programs, only to discover that the change has adverse side effects. Access control mechanisms are needed to disallow unapproved changes.

Provide Traceability Between Requirement Change Requests and Program Changes.   Suppose a requirement change request dictates that three programs be modified, and these modifications have been assigned to three different team members. How does a project leader ensure that this change request has been properly implemented—that is, that all programs have been changed and that the changed programs have gone through their life cycle and are in a "ready for release" state? Answering this question requires some mechanism to track change requests that is capable of specifying all programs to be changed as well as the state of each program.

Undo a Requirement Change.   A requirement change request that was implemented (by changing many programs) may later need to be "undone" (perhaps because the users do not like the new features). This procedure requires a mechanism to identify all changes made for a change request.

Show Associated Changes.   Suppose that a bug is found in a program, and it is suspected that this bug came from the implementation of a change request. Hence it is desirable to review all changes made as a result of that change request. This effort requires mechanisms to trace a change in a program to a change request and to identify all changes made for a request.

Gather All Sources, Documents, and Other Information for the Current System.   As a result of file corruption or a system crash, it might be necessary to recover all files. Similarly, some change to an existing system (that is in operation) might be needed, making it is essential to obtain all source files and documents that represent the current system. A baseline can accomplish this goal.

The preceding items describe some of the more frequently occurring scenarios in a project that require support from the CM process. In a product scenario where multiple versions of a software product coexist, each utilizing a different version of the programs, other situations related to changes might come up that require the CM to have additional functionality (for example, handling variance [4]). We consider that the main purpose of CM is to provide various mechanisms that can support the functionality needed to handle the type of scenarios discussed above. The mechanisms commonly used to provide the necessary functionality include the following:

- Naming conventions and organization of files (and maintenance of state information)
- Version control
- Change request traceability
- Access control
- Reconciliation procedures
- Modification log in programs

Naming program files (and document files) according to some standard naming conventions and keeping the files in preplanned directories helps in finding a desired file quickly. Proper naming also helps to readily understand the nature of those contents without looking at those contents (for example, by having standards for extensions). In addition, segregating programs in different states into separate directories helps to identify the program state easily.

Version control is a key issue for CM [1, 2, 4], and many tools are available to help manage the various versions of programs. Without such a mechanism, many of the required CM functions cannot be supported. Version control helps preserve older versions of the programs whenever programs are changed.

A change request traceability mechanism provides mapping from a requirement change request to subsequent changes in the programs, which helps in managing requirement changes. For tracing a change back to the change request, the modification log mechanism is useful.

Access control mechanisms ensure that only authorized people can modify some files and that only one person can modify a file at any given time. Reconciliation procedures specify how two changes made independently to a program can be merged to create a new version that reflects both.

If these mechanisms are provided, then the scenarios given earlier can be handled satisfactorily. Some of these scenarios will necessitate the use of more than one mechanism. For example, undoing a requirement change will involve a mechanism to show the traceability of a requirement change to subsequent changes in programs as well as a version control mechanism to actually undo the changes. The dependence graph shown in Figure 10.2 indicates which mechanisms are used for implementing different functionalities.

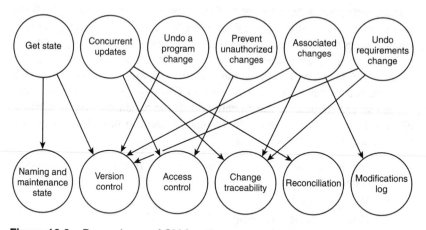

Figure 10.2   Dependence of CM functions on mechanisms

Some CM mechanisms may be supported by a tool, whereas others may require that the users perform them explicitly. For example, version control may be carried out by a tool, but capturing the state of a program may require the programmer to explicitly maintain this information. The CM process defines all steps needed to implement such mechanisms and explains how these mechanisms are to be used in a project.

The discussion so far has focused on programs. The documents that are produced in a project (for example, requirements document, design document, plans) also need configuration management. During the normal course of a project, a document passes through three states: "under development," "under review," and "baselined." The state transition is straightforward, and similar to the one proposed in [4]. The CM process must also implement the state diagram for documents. The rest of the chapter will focus primarily on the CM issues relating to programs, although it briefly discusses the document control procedures.

10.2 Configuration Management Process

The CM process defines the sequence of activities that need to be performed in support of the CM mechanisms. As with the project management process, the first stage in the CM process is planning—identifying those items that need to be under CM (known as configuration items), locations to store them, procedures for change control, and so on. Then the process has to be executed, perhaps by deploying some tool (the use of which also has to be planned). Any CM process, regardless of whether it uses a tool, requires self-discipline from the project personnel in terms of maintaining versions, storing items in proper locations, and making changes properly. Monitoring the status of the configuration items is therefore important.

At Infosys, the main stages in the CM process are as follows:

Plan and set up configuration management.

Perform configuration control.

Monitor the status of configuration items.

In addition to these steps, CM audits are performed to aid in the implementation of the CM process. The first phase is the most important, as all decisions regarding items, procedures to be used for different aspects of CM, and other issues are decided at that point.

10.2.1 Plan and Set Up Configuration Management

Planning for configuration management involves identifying the configuration items and specifying the procedures to be used for controlling and implementing changes to these configuration items. Identifying configuration items is a fundamental activity in any type of CM [2, 3, 4]. If team members do not have a clear idea about the items under the control of CM, it will be much more difficult to implement a desired change. Typical examples of configuration items include requirements specifications, design documents, source code, test plans, test scripts, test procedures, test data, standards used in the project (such as coding standards and design standards), the acceptance plan, documents such as the CM plan and the project plan, user documentation such as the user manual, documents such as the training material, contract documents (including support tools such as a compiler or in-house tools), quality records (review records, test records), and CM records (release records, status tracking records). Any customer-supplied products or purchased items that will be part of the delivery (called "included software product") are also configuration items.

During planning, the types of items that come under the aegis of CM are identified, but a detailed list of items is not prepared. This omission reflects the fact that all items may not be known during CM planning (which occurs at the beginning of the project). To facilitate proper naming of configuration items, the naming conventions for CM items are decided during the CM planning stages. In addition to naming standards, version numbering must be planned. When a configuration item is changed, the old item is not replaced with the new copy; instead, the old copy is maintained and a new one is created. This approach results in multiple versions of an item, so policies for version number assignment are needed. If a CM tool is being used, then sometimes the tool handles the version numbering. Otherwise, it has to be explicitly done in the project.

As discussed earlier, a program could be in different states. The CM process must control the various states of the programs, and the transition between those states. During planning, it must be decided how to maintain the state of a program. One way of collecting items in different states is to create separate directories for them. All items in a certain state reside in the directory for that state. When the state of a program changes, that program is moved from the directory for the old state to the directory for the new state. This approach is a general one and does not require the use of any tool for maintaining the state information. If some CM tool is available, however, then the directory structure needed for managing the states of programs depends on the tool. During the planning phase, the directory structure employed for managing the states has to be set, keeping the requirements of the CM tool, if any, in mind.

The planning is done by the project leader and the configuration controller (CC) (or the configuration control board [CCB]). It can be begun only when the project has been initiated and the operating environment and requirements specifications are clearly documented. The activities in this stage include the following:

Identify configuration items, including customer-supplied and purchased items.

Define a naming and numbering scheme for the configuration items.

Define the directory structure needed for CM.

Define access restrictions.

Define change control procedures.

Identify and define the responsibility and authority for the CC/CCB.

Define a method for tracking the status of configuration items.

Define a backup procedure.

Define a reconciliation procedure, if needed.

Define a release procedure.

Define an archival procedure.

Identify points at which the configuration items will be moved to the baseline.

The output of this phase is the CM plan. We have already discussed the first few planning activities. As we have seen, it is important that configuration items are managed properly. Frequently, a configuration controller or a configuration control board becomes involved in the project.

The CC is responsible for the implementation of the CM activities within the project. Depending on the size of the system under development, his or her role may be a part-time or full-time job. The CC could also be responsible for managing the release, archiving of the release, retrieving and releasing appropriate versions when required, and more.

In certain cases, where there are large teams or where two or more teams/ groups are involved in the development of the same or different portions of the software or interfacing systems, it may be necessary to have a CCB. This board includes representatives from each of the teams. A CCB (or a CC) is considered essential for CM [3], and the CM plan must clearly define the roles and responsibilities of the CC/CCB. These duties will also depend on the type of file system and the nature of tools being used.

As noted earlier, CM requires that access to some items in some states remain restricted. For example, the access and right to modify a program in the baseline must not be given to all programmers. Planning activities must therefore specify the access rights of the CC, the project leader, and the developers.

Policies and procedures for change control are also established during planning. The changes made to a program to fix bugs found during the various testing activities are generally managed by controlling the state transition of programs. A requirement change request, however, may necessitate that many programs be changed. For this reason, an impact analysis is carried out to decide which programs need to be changed and how the change request will affect the project (as discussed in Chapter 3). Once the impact analysis is complete, the changes to the different programs have to be properly implemented. Before the change can be "released," it must be ascertained that the different programs have been modified properly and that they have gone through their life cycle (that is, through unit testing, system testing, and so on). One method for implementing this mechanism is a spreadsheet developed for each change request. Such a spreadsheet lists all items that have to be changed as well as the directory for each item (thereby giving its state). It would typically have the following contents:

Date	Work Name	Product	Area			
			Development	Unit Test	System Test	Baseline

Note that a different spreadsheet is needed for each change request. A similar mechanism is used for keeping a global view of the state of the various programs. The directory structure mechanism, although it defines the state of each program, does not easily lend itself to determining the current state of a program. To give a global view of the state of all programs, a table can be maintained that lists each program in the project and its current state.

If concurrent updates to programs are to be allowed, then reconciliation procedures must be specified. Concurrent updates are sometimes necessary. For example, consider the situation where a change request is being implemented and another high-priority change request comes in. Clearly, that change request cannot be put on hold until the first one is finished. Similarly, while some change request is being implemented, if problems occur in the working system, then changes must be made immediately to ensure that the system can continue to function. For such situations, reconciliation procedures are needed. One possible procedure is to state that the differences between the original version and the new versions will be examined, and the changes in the version with fewer changes will be merged in the other version. If the changes affect different parts of the program, merging is straightforward; some CM tools readily support this capability. Otherwise, the programmer must review the overlap and then accommodate both changes.

All elements of the plan have to be documented in the CM plan. A template for documenting the CM plan has been provided that defines all the activities that need to be specified in the plan. Section 10.4 includes the CM plan for the WAR project, which utilizes this template.

10.2.2 Perform Configuration Control

Although configuration control activities are undertaken during the execution phase of the project, we discuss them here along with other aspects of CM. Two main configuration control activities are performed: one that deals with managing the state transitions of programs (and documents), and one that deals with managing the change requests that must be implemented.

State transition management involves moving the items from one directory to another when the state changes, creating versions when changes are made, and ensuring that each program (and document) goes through its life cycle and reaches the baseline. Once all items are in the baseline, the software is ready for production use.

Frequently, tools are used to manage the states and versions of items and access to them (sometimes collectively dubbed library management [4]). Many CM tools employ the check-in/check-out procedure for controlling the access and handling version control. The basic idea behind this approach is as follows. A program is considered to be in a "controlled environment" when it is in any state in which others can use it. Once a program is in the controlled environment, it cannot be modified without proper "authorization," even by the original author, as others may be using that program. To make an approved change, the program is checked out of the controlled environment. Checking out essentially implies making a copy of the item, without destroying the earlier version, and making a note that the item has been checked out so that multiple people do not check an item out for modification (if this step is allowed for some reason, then reconciliation must be done when changes are made).

An item is modified after it has been checked out. These modifications must then be reflected in the controlled environment, so others have the benefit of the new version and the change request (which may have forced the changes) can be truly implemented. Unfortunately, changes to items in a controlled environment cannot be made easily, because other team members may be using the items. As a result, some checks are done to ensure that the changed item is suitable before it is checked back in. Generally, when an item is checked back into the controlled environment, the older copy is not destroyed; instead a new version of the item is created. The checking-in ability may be restricted to the CC or the project leader. This limitation makes it possible to roll back the changes, if the need arises.

To provide the information regarding what changes have been made, a modification log may be kept in the program source itself. This log essentially identifies the start and end of a change and includes a reference to the change request that prompted it. The checking in, checking out, version maintenance, and creation of a modification log can be done effectively through the use of proper CM tools. Various tools are available that perform many aspects of this CM library function.

To implement requirement changes, which in turn trigger changes to configuration items, a change request is first analyzed by performing an impact analysis. This analysis determines the programs and documents that need to be changed to carry out the change request and the cost and schedule implications of making the change. Impact analysis was discussed in Chapter 3. Once the change is approved by the project leader and the CC, then all programs and documents identified in the impact analysis must be changed appropriately. The following activities are part of implementing a change request:

Accept the change request (with impact analysis).

Set up a tracking mechanism.

Check out configuration items that need to be changed and perform the changes.

Check in configuration items.

Take the item through its life cycle.

Earlier, we discussed the need for a tracking mechanism, and considered one spreadsheet-based mechanism, which lists all programs being changed and their status. To implement a change, the modifications to different items are assigned as tasks to members of the team, who check the items out so as to make these changes. After a team member makes a change, the changed program (or document) can be viewed as a new program, which has to go through different states (representing the life cycle of the program) before it can become part of the final in-operation system. When a check-in, check-out mechanism is being used, then the state transition of the program begins after it has been checked back in. Once all altered programs reach the baseline, and the documents associated with the programs also reach the baseline (after following their life cycle), the change request is considered to be fully implemented.

10.2.3 Status Monitoring and Audits

A configuration item could exist in one of several states. The set of possible states for an item varies according to whether it is a program or a document and what type of tools are being used for CM. It is important to accurately represent the state of each item. State-related mistakes can lead to problems. For example, if a program has not been unit-tested but is moved to the state "ready for release," it can cause problems. Similarly, if the fact that a program has been checked out from the baseline to implement some change is not reflected, then the software might be delivered without that change. When implementing a requirement change request, it is also important that the mechanisms used to capture the state accrately represent that state.

Whenever a mechanism based on a directory structure is used to represent the state of a program, mistakes are possible. This type of mechanism requires that the programs be moved properly from one directory to another when their state changes and that this change of state be reflected in the master table that maintains the states of the various items. To minimize mistakes and catch any errors early, regular status checking of the configuration items is done. A report may be produced about the discrepancies, and all such discrepancies must be resolved.

In addition to checking the status of the items, the status of change requests must be checked. To accomplish this goal, change requests that have been received since the last CM status monitoring operation are examined. For each change request, the state of the item as mentioned in the change request records is compared with the actual state. Checks may also be done to ensure that all modified items go through their full life cycle (that is, the state diagram) before they are incorporated in the baseline.

Finally, a configuration audit may be performed. As in other audits, the main focus here is to ensure that the CM process of the project is indeed being followed. The baseline for the system may also be audited to ensure that its integrity is not being violated and that movement of items to and from the baseline occurs in a manner consistent with the CM plans.

10.3 Document Control

In any organization, documents have to be created, distributed, and maintained so as to support easy, but controlled access. The two major types of documents that need to be controlled are those related to process definition (for example, quality system documentation) and project documents (such as plans, work products documents, and review records). Here we briefly discuss how documents are controlled, numbered, named, circulated, and otherwise managed, focusing primarily on documents that are not work products of a project.

Once created, documents have to be reviewed and authorized. The review is done by someone other than the author of the document. Once a document has been reviewed and approved, it may be baselined. Even after being baselined, the document may be altered. The procedure for such a change requires that a modification request be first raised. Once the request is accepted, the change is evaluated and affected documents are identified. The request for the change is logged.

The following general rules for controlling changes to documents apply:

- Any change that affects the form, fit, or function of the document is considered a major change; otherwise, it is a minor change. Minor changes may be accumulated before a document is actually taken up for modification.
- Approval of changes is done by the same function that performed the original approval, unless specifically designated otherwise.
- The version number of the next issue of the document is determined by the extent of changes. Each set of modifications is accompanied by a change in the version number.
- A revision list is maintained in the document itself, which gives a history of changes made to the document.

A document-numbering scheme is also recommended so that each document has a unique reference number. To ensure some consistency, documentation standards have been specified. These standards provide a framework for the layout and design of documents generated within the organization. A documentation standard is a set of detailed guidelines specifying not only the document structure, but also the format of pages, titles, and other components, the use of font sizes and styles, section numbering, and so on. For example, Infosys standards require that any document should include the following sections:

Title page

Revision list

Table of contents

Main body of the document

References (if necessary)

Appendices (if necessary)

Index (if necessary)

The title page should contain the title of the document, its version number, the name of the author, the name (and signature) of the authorizer, and the date of issue. The version number is a two-digit number, followed by a period, followed by another two-digit number. The first number indicates the version of the document, and the second number identifies the revision within this version.

The revision list gives the history of revisions to the document. It contains one item for each revision of the document. An item in the list specifies the version number of the document, the date of modification, the author who made the modification, and the changes incorporated in the revision. The revision list as a whole gives the history of how the document evolved to its current state.

The table of contents contains entries for all chapters and the main sections and subsections within each chapter. The main body of the document can be organized either like a book—with chapters and sections and subsections within each chapter—or like an article—with sections and subsections.

Document control also addresses the issue of circulation and access. Document circulation requirements fall in one of the following three categories:

- **Proprietary:** Circulation is restricted to a defined set of individuals. In this case, a master is maintained, with a set of copies remaining under restricted distribution. Examples include quality system documents and contracts.
- **Limited:** Circulation is limited to the group of individuals whose duties are directly related to the documents. Examples include the requirements specification document, design documents, project standards documents, plan documents, and user manuals.
- **Unlimited:** These documents are intended for general circulation. Examples include the marketing documents, yearly reports, and press releases.

Copies of any type of document could be either controlled or uncontrolled. *Controlled copies* are issued to a limited set of people. Each controlled copy bears a unique number and is assigned to an individual by name; that information is clearly marked as a controlled copy. A *master distribution list* of controlled copies is maintained by the issuing authority, which specifies the people to whom copies of the document should be sent. This system ensures the correct distribution of new copies and the withdrawal of superseded copies. The master distribution list also includes the version/revision number and copy number of the document issued to the different people on the list. *Uncontrolled copies* are created for a specific reason and are expected to be destroyed after their purpose is fulfilled. The copies are clearly marked as uncontrolled.

10.4 Example: Configuration Management Plan of the WAR Project

The CM plan of the WAR project, which uses the standard CM plan template, is given in this section. The CM plan document introduces the project (section 1), its environment (section 2), the responsibilities of the configuration controller (section 3), and the type of access restrictions (section 4). This information is followed by the configuration identification section (section 5), which specifies the types of program sources and the documents subject to CM. It states that all source code, HTML files, GIF files, scripts, and components are configuration items. For documents under the aegis of CM, the plan states that the requirements document, design documents, test plans, and so on are all configuration items. The plan also gives the naming convention for the various files.

Next, the plan specifies the directory structure to be used in the project for managing the evolution of configuration items and organizing those items (section 6). It indicates that each person on the project will have one directory in his or her personal area in which any source currently under development will be kept, and another directory in which any document currently under development will be kept (a different directory for static Web files and CGI scripts is used, because working on these items requires a different environment). These areas are uncontrolled. Document and source code control in this project is done through the Visual Source Safe (VSS) configuration management tool of Microsoft.

The directory structure within the controlled area (that is, under the control of VSS), along with access rights for each directory, is also given. One directory (*Docs*) holds all documents that any project person can check out and check in. With this structure, a person working on an existing document will check out the document from this area in his or her private area, update it, and then check the document back in. While the item remains checked out, VSS prevents any other person from checking out that item, thereby ensuring that only one modification is happening at a given time. When checking in the item, VSS ensures that the item is updated along with the version number and that sufficient information is kept for extracting an older version of the document, if needed. After a check-in, VSS makes sure that any subsequent check-out gives the latest version of the item.

A separate directory, *DvlpSource,* holds the sources. Once a developer has created some code and is satisfied with it, he or she checks it into *DvlpSource.* Later, if the programmer needs to modify the code, he or she checks it out, modifies it, and then checks it back in. A separate test area (COMTEST) holds sources for testing. For unit testing, for example, the source will be checked out from the *DvlpSource* area and kept in the COMTEST area. Once testing is complete and the defects are recorded, the source is deleted from the test area. If any defects are found in a source, the developer will check it out from the *Dvlp-Source* area, modify it, and check it back in (after which the source will go through the unit testing cycle again). Once a unit has been successfully tested, it is copied from the *DvlpSource* area to the *SecureSource* area. This controlled area has a more stringent access restriction—only the project leader or the CC can check in, check out, and add to this directory.

System testing involves sources in the *SecureSource* area. That is, sources are checked out from this area in the COMTEST area. When all sources are in *SecureSource,* system testing can be performed. If defects are found, their sources are identified, and the sources go through the change cycle again (copy from *DvlpSource* to private area, modify, check back into *DvlpSource,* perform unit testing, and, when successful, copy into *SecureSource*).

When the system testing is complete and the system is ready for release and acceptance testing, it is placed in the release area on the test server. Before being designated for operational use, the software is tested with *testdb,* which is created by copying the corporate database onto a local Web server. This step ensures that the system will work with real data. If this "trial release" is success-ful, the system is deemed ready for release and the CC is informed about the release. The person who is in charge of releasing the software to the users then copies the necessary files to release the system to the users.

After sources and documents are delivered and the system is deployed, all sources and documents are baselined by moving them into baseline directories. These sources and documents consist of the ones that make up the final system that is in production use. Later, for any enhancements or modifications, the con-tents of the baseline become the starting point—they will be copied from the baseline to the *DvlpSource* area.

The configuration control process section of Infosys's plan (section 7) describes the configuration control process. The section also defines the testing step that is undertaken by the person responsible for the release, before the release occurs. This step cannot be done by the project, as it involves copying data from the corporate database, to which the project does not have access. Section 7 also defines when different elements should be moved into the base-line. The version-numbering scheme for documents and sources is specified as well; it is the standard numbering scheme.

Configuration Management Plan—WAR 2.0

1. Introduction
Omitted

2. CM Environment
- Hardware: Digital, IBM, Acer servers; IBM-compatible PCs
- Operating system: Windows NT on servers, Windows 95 on PCs
- Other software/tools: MS SQL Server 6.5, Netscape Fastrack Server 2.0, MS Visual Basic 5.0, MS Office 97, MS Transaction Server 2.0, MS Project 4.0, Visual Source Safe

3. CC Responsibilities
The responsibilities of the CC are to create executables for release, to baseline code and documents, to release projects to file servers, and to properly control the sources and documents.

4. Access/Authority
The access privileges of members of the WAR project team for the various data storage locations are given here. The directory structure is specified later in the document.

4.1 Directories
- Development directory: Developers will have read/write permission on their own directory.
- Test directory (COMTEST): All developers/PL/DBA/CC will have read/write permission.
- Release directory: Only the CC and PL will have read/write permission.
- Project baseline directory: CC has read/write access; developers have read access only.

4.2 VSS (Development)
As given below

4.3 Database Servers
- Data on test server: Full access to all developers.
- *testdb* on test release server: Access only to DBA.
- *corpdata* on production server: Access only to DBA.

5. Configuration Identification

5.1 Configuration Item Types

5.1.1   Software Sources
The configuration of the following types of sources is controlled: source code, HTMLs, GIFs, HTML templates, Word document templates, scripts to create/ modify database objects, COM/DCOM/ActiveX components

5.1.2 Documents

- Requirements specifications
- Design documents
- Functional specifications
- Test plans
- Release notes
- Project plan
- Review records
- Quality documents
- CM plan

5.2 Naming Schemes/Conventions

5.2.1 Documents
The following naming convention will be used.

Directory	Document	File Name
PROP	Proposal document	PROP.DOC
PROJPLAN	Project plan	PROJPLAN.DOC
TGUID	Tailoring guidelines	TGUID.DOC
RS	Requirements specification	RS.DOC
DES	Architecture design	ARCHDES.DOC
	Functional design	FUNCDES.DOC
	Database design	DBDES.DOC
	High-level design	HLDES.DOC
	Detailed design	DETDES.DOC
	Program specifications	PRGSPEC.DOC
TESTPLAN	Unit test plan	*xxx*UT.DOC, where *xxx* is the short program name
	Integration test plan	ITEST.DOC
	System test plan	STEST.DOC

5.2.2 Software Sources
A descriptive name for the program, form, HTML, class, or image is given. The default extension of the item are used—for example, .bas for Visual Basic source files, .html for HTML files, and .htx for HTML templates.

6. Directory Structure

6.1 Development

The following directory structure will be maintained by developers for work area:

F:*DeveloperLanid**WAR20*\WORK: Working directory.

F:*DeveloperLanid**WAR20*\DOC: Project-related documents, reports, and so on.

C:\Netscape\Docs\Work*WAR20:* For HTMLs, GIFs, Java classes, and other static files.

C:\Netscape\cgi-bin\Work*WAR20:* For CGI-bin executables.

Version control of all new project development and enhancements would be done using Microsoft Visual Source Safe (VSS). In VSS, the following directory structure would be maintained:

- $/*WAR20/Docs:* Document directory. All developers will have check-in, check-out, and add rights to this directory
- $/*WAR20/DvlpSource:* Directory for source code during development. All developers of the project will have check-in, check-out, and add rights to this directory.
- $/*WAR20/SecureSource:* Secure directory for source code that has passed unit testing. Only the PL for the project and the CC have check-in, check-out, and add access to this directory.

6.2 Testing

Independent testing will be carried out in a separate area. The relevant directories are as follows:

F:\APPL\COMTEST*WAR20**SOURCE*

C:\Netscape\Docs\Comtest*WAR20*

C:\Netscape\Cgi-bin\Comtest*WAR20*

The CC is responsible for moving files from the development area to the testing area. After the testing is complete (according to the testing procedure as outlined in the project plan) and a defect report is submitted to the PL, the tester removes the programs from these directories.

6.3 Release

After development and testing, the project leader makes a release note as per release procedure and moves the programs and documents that are ready for release to the following directories:

F:\APPL\SECURITY*WAR20*\Docs: For documents.

F:\APPL\SECURITY*WAR20*\Source: For source code.

F:\APPL\SECURITY*WAR20*\Scripts: For DDL scripts.

C:\Netscape\Docs\Security*WAR20:* For Web-based applications.

6.4 Baseline

The baseline will be maintained on a file system. VSS is used only for version control during the development of a project. After the development is complete and the software is released, the final code and documents are transferred to the baseline and all other occurrences of them are removed. Documents, source code, and scripts will be maintained in the baseline in the following directories:

\\ITL_MIS_SERVER\Baseline*WAR20*\Docs\

\\ITL_MIS_SERVER\Baseline*WAR20*\Source\

\\ITL_MIS_SERVER\Baseline*WAR20*\Scripts\

\\ITL_MIS_SERVER\Baseline\Web*WAR20*\Docs\

\\ITL_MIS_SERVER\Baseline\Web*WAR20*\Source\

\\ITL_MIS_SERVER\Baseline\Web*WAR20*\Scripts\

\\ITL_MIS_SERVER\Baseline\Web*WAR20*\Static\

7. Configuration Control

7.1 Configuration Control Process

Each developer will create a directory called F:*DeveloperLoginId*\WAR20\ WORK and set it as the "working directory." At the beginning of each day, the developer will check out the files required from VSS. At the end of the day, the developer will check in all files. When the development is complete, the CC moves the code to the *Secure* directory under VSS.

When coding and unit testing of the entire project are completed successfully, the PL will write the draft release note. After approval, the CC will copy all documents, sources, and database object creation scripts to the COMTEST area. The DBA will be informed and will create/modify the database objects in *testdb*. The CC will create the executables to connect to *testdb*.

The project will then be handed over to the independent tester, who will test the project as per the test plan. After the testing is complete, the tester will submit the defect report to the PL. The CC will remove all configuration items from the COMTEST area. The PL will ensure that all defects are fixed. After the independent testing is complete and no more defects are reported or if the release is authorized, the CC will copy the documents, sources, and the database object creation scripts to the SECURITY area. The DBA will then release the application as defined in the release note

7.2 Baseline for Configuration Items

Configuration Item	Baseline
Requirements specification	Before HLD
Test plan	Before coding
High-level design	Before program specifications

Configuration Item	Baseline
Database design	Before coding
Functional specification	Before program specifications
Prototype (if any)	Before program specifications
Program specification	Before coding
Source code	After acceptance

7.3 Procedure for Version/Revision Numbering

Standard version numbering will be used (of the form *mm.nn*, where *mm* denotes the version number and *nn* denotes the revision number for that version).

10.5 Summary

This chapter discussed configuration management (CM) in software projects. Software configuration management is an important issue, because a software product typically consists of many programs and documents, and these items may change frequently. Changes occur due to two primary reasons: identification of defects and requirement change requests. A program generally exists in many states in its evolution before it becomes part of the final system to be delivered. A typical state sequence is "private" to "ready for unit testing" to "ready for system testing" to "ready for acceptance testing" to "ready for deployment" to "in baseline." It is important to maintain the state of the different items accurately—which is where the CM process comes into play.

One way to view the CM activity is by noting that the CM process must provide mechanisms that can support the functionality needed by projects to handle different scenarios. Examples of this functionality include the ability to undo a change, obtain the latest version of a program, and find the status of a program. Examples of the mechanisms provided by the CM process include version control, change request tracking, and capture of the state information of an item.

At Infosys, the first phase of the CM process occurs during the project planning stages. A complete plan is developed that lists the configuration items, where they will be stored, how changes to them will be managed, and so on. Next, the configuration control activities are performed. They involve managing the state changes of the items, managing changes, and so on. Finally, the last phase involves status checking, which is done periodically to verify that the states of the different items are consistent with what they should be.

Closely associated with CM is document control—documents are also configuration items. This chapter briefly discussed the document control procedures and conventions of Infosys.

Finally, the chapter provided the CM plan of the WAR project as an example. The plan describes the naming convention, directory structure to be used, tool that will be employed, access control, and configuration control procedures.

References

[1] E. H. Bersoff, V. D. Henderson, and S. G. Siegel. Software configuration management: A tutorial. *IEEE Computer,* pp 6–14, Jan. 1979.
[2] E. H. Bersoff. Elements of software configuration management. *IEEE Transactions on Software Engineering,* pp. 79–87, Jan. 1984.
[3] W. Humphrey. *Managing the Software Process.* Addison-Wesley, 1989.
[4] D. Whitgift. *Methods and Tools for Software Configuration Management.* John Wiley and Sons, 1991.

## PART III

Project Execution and Termination

11

Life Cycle Execution

Executing the life cycle (LC) for the project is, of course, an important activity. It is also the longest activity during which the project's process is executed. The LC execution comprises the main engineering activities for building software. Thus the LC for a development project consists of activities like design, coding, integration, and testing. Proper LC execution is the focus of the Software Product Engineering KPA of level 3 of the CMM.

For an organization that follows the process-oriented approach, at least two approaches can be followed for the life cycle. The first approach is to have a detailed process definition for each stage with support material describing how each step is to be executed. In other words, one can standardize some methodologies and then define detailed processes for these methodologies, along with support material for the processes. The intent behind this approach is that the process documentation be detailed enough and supported well enough that a new person can learn the methodology and execute the process effectively by using the documentation.

The second approach is to focus on the output and its quality rather than the detailed methodology for that stage. Thus the output of a stage is of primary importance, and the detailed steps are used for guidance. This approach requires a clear elucidation of the expected output and a strategy for judging its quality.

Infosys follows a mixed approach. The process steps are defined, but only limited guidance is given on how to use them. It is assumed that this knowledge is acquired through classroom and on-the-job training. During the LC execution in a project, the focus is on the outputs of the phases in the LC, whose form is generally specified through templates. For evaluating the outputs, checklists for review have been provided. Thus the main sources supporting LC execution are as follows:

- Activities checklists: The lowest-level activities for a process definition.
- Guidelines: Describe the methodology for executing some phases. Published methodologies may also be used.

- Templates: Define the structure and contents of the outputs of some stages.
- Review checklists: List the issues to look for while reviewing the output of a stage.

The total support material for LC stages is obviously quite large. Hence, what to cover is a much more difficult question for this chapter than for other chapters. The high-level process for the stages was described in Chapter 4. We can give all checklists, guidelines, and other documents necessary for the major phases, but that exercise is likely to become unwieldy and possibly uninteresting. We can illustrate the templates and the process execution by giving all work products generated by the case study, but that tactic is not feasible—the work products, even for a small project like WAR, will occupy more than 100 pages. We resolve this dilemma by giving only portions of the work products of the WAR project. These examples will illustrate the documents produced during a project as well as the project outputs. As the main purpose of the case study is to illustrate the use of various processes, this approach should be a satisfactory compromise.

11.1 High-Level Design

High-level design is the stage of the life cycle when a logical view of the computer implementation of the solution to the customer requirements is developed. It gives the solution at a high level of abstraction. The main outputs of this phase are the documents describing the functional design and the database design. Sometimes, a document describing the operating environment architecture may be produced as well. In this section, we show parts of the functional design architecture and parts of the database design document for the WAR project. The WAR project used a component architecture, so the template for architecture specification was modified for this purpose.

The functional architecture design document of WAR defines the project's overall layered architecture and specifies how parameters will be passed between the different layers. It then specifies the components that have been identified in the application layer. For each component, the classes in the component and the methods in the classes are defined. Brief specifications of only a few components are given here. Besides the component specification, the document includes information explaining how security is to be handled, what validations must be done, what exceptions the system must handle, and so on; this information has been omitted here.

The database design indicates the tables needed in the system, the attributes of each table, the primary key, the foreign keys, and more. Specifications of only a few of these items are given here. Besides the tables, the stored proce- dures are identified, along with the different views to be provided and the neces- sary triggers. More than 30 stored procedures are specified in the design—their specification has been omitted.

Functional Architecture Design of WAR

WAR 2.0 is a Web-based application that consists of four layers/tiers.

1. The user tier (a user workstation having a Java-enabled browser)
2. The Web server, called the client
3. The application server (the middle tier, which isolates the user from the database)
4. The database server (the back end)

The client is a 32-bit CGI executable to be developed using Microsoft Visual Basic 5.0 Enterprise Edition. The Web client will be installed on a Windows NT 4.0 server. The client communicates with the various compo- nents available in the middle tier using the *Distributed Component Object Model (DCOM)*. As prototyping was done for this layer, no separate high- level specifications have been written. The database server uses the MS SQL Server 6.5 relational database management system. The database design is given in a separate document.

Components

Most components have one class, although some have multiple classes. There are a total of eight components in the system. A few components, their classes, and methods for the classes are specified here.

Component UserPreferences

This component retrieves and saves the preferences set by the user.
Class ***clsUserPreferences:*** Creates a template to retrieve and save the user settings onto the database for a given user ID.
Methods: *fnGetUserPreferences, fnGetWarsToBeAuthorized.*

Component WAREntryReview

This component handles the functionality of WAR entry and review screens.

Class ***clsGetWAREntryData:*** Creates a template to retrieve and save the WAR entry details, and a mail interface for the various users.

Methods: *fnCheckMyWARStatus, fnGetMultipleWARStatus, fnGetPlanned Detail, fnGetUnPlannedDetails, fnGetAuthIdProject.*

Class *clsGetWARReviewData:* Creates a template to review a WAR, save review status and comments, reopen the authorized WAR, and have a mail interface.

Methods: *fnCheckWARSubmittedToMe, fnSaveWARReview, fnInsertRecordIntoMailRequest.*

Database Design Document of WAR

1. Tables

There are a total of 19 tables in this application, and the application accesses 11 external tables. The definition of a few tables is given here.

WARMstActGroupCode: All of the activity group codes are recorded in this table.

Attributes/Fields

#	Primary Key	Column Name	Data Type	Size	Nulls	Default	Check Constraint
1	Y	txtActGroupCode	char	8	N		
2		txtActGroup Description	char	50	N		
3		dtLastModified	Datetime		N	today	

Indexes

#	Column Names	Clustered/Nonclustered
Primary_key	txtActGroupCode	Clustered

WARMstActivityCode: All of the WAR activity codes are recorded in this table.

Attributes/Fields

#	Primary Key	Column Name	Data Type	Size	Nulls	Default	Check Constraint
1	Y	TxtActCode	char	8	N		
2		TxtActDescription	Varchar	40	N		
3		TxtActGroupCode	char	8	N		
4		DtLastModified	Datetime		N	today	

Indexes

#	Column Names	Clustered/Nonclustered
Primary_key	txtActCode	Clustered

Foreign Keys

#	Referenced Table	Key Columns	Foreign Key Column
1	WARMstActGroupCode	TxtActGroupCode	txtActGroupCode

2. Stored Procedures

More than 30 stored procedures exist for activities like adding, deleting, and storing. Examples of stored procedures include *spWARGetCorpCodes, spWARGetNotSubmittedList, spWARGetPlanForWeek, spWARGetProjAct Codes,* and *spWARGetUnPlanDetails.* Their specifications have been omitted here.

11.2 Detailed Design

Detailed design, as mentioned earlier while discussing the development process, has two main outputs: the logic design of the components identified in the high-level design, and the unit test plan for the units in the system. We focus on the logic design only; unit test planning is similar to system test planning, which is discussed later in the chapter.

During the logic design, an implementation must be specified for the modules identified during the high-level design. All details regarding the implementation of each module have to be worked out during the detailed design. All algorithm and data structure issues are resolved during this phase as well. With the output of the detailed design phase, the task during the coding stage is to write the specified logic in the chosen programming language.

Detailed designs can become quite large, because the logic for each component must be specified. If we assume that only the logic of the important modules is specified (say 50% of the modules) and that the logic description is 20% of the size of the programs (in LOC), the size of the detailed design document for a system with 40,000 LOC will be around 4,000 lines—about 100 pages! For the WAR project, the detailed design specifies the logic of most modules. Here we give the detailed design of a few methods of one class to illustrate the nature of the detailed design documents.

Class clsSetup of Component ComSetup

Private Function *fnGetUserPreferences* (*strUserId* **As String**) **As Variant**
    Instantiate the class *clsUserPreferences* belonging to the component
        comUserPreferences and reference it by an object variable
        l_obj UserPref.
    Invoke the method *fnGetUserPreferences(strUserId)* using *l_objUser*
        Pref.
    Assign the result to a safe array *l_varUserPreferences.*
        fnGetUserPreferences returns this safe array.

Private Function *fnGetUserPermissions* (*strUserId* **As String**, *strContext* **As String**, *strProject* **As String**) **As String**
    Obtain the RDO environment and connection.
    Create the SQL: *strSQL = "spWARGetUserPermission"* + *strProject.*
    Execute the SQL.
    Obtain the result in an RDOResultset.
    Obtain the result set in an safe array.
        fnGetUserPermission returns the permission using the safe array.
        Permissions could be "Auth" or "NotAuth."
    Close the RDO connection.

Private Function *fnGetProjectInfo* (**ByVal** *strProject* **As String**) **As Variant**
    Instantiate the class *clsCache* belonging to the component *comCache*
        and reference it by an object variable *l_objCache.*
    Invoke the method *fnGetProjectInfo(strProject)* using *l_objCache.*
    Assign the result to a safe array *l_varProjectInfo.*
        fnGetUserPreferences returns this safe array.

Private Function *fnGetActivityCodes* (***ByVal*** *strProject* ***As String***) **As Variant**
    Obtain the RDO environment and connection.
    Create the SQL: *strSQL = "spWARGetActivityCodes"* + *strProject.*
    Execute the SQL.
    Obtain the result in an RDOResultset.
    Obtain the result set in an safe array.
        fnGetActivityCodes returns this safe array.
    Close the RDO connection

11.3 Build

The main activity in the build phase consists of coding and unit testing of the coded modules. Coding entails converting the logic, as specified in the detailed design, into the chosen programming language. Coding standards for the selected programming language play an important role here. We do not show code of any modules here. Instead, we give the checklist for code review, which reflects the important coding issues. The output of the review is reported using the standard data collection forms for reviews, which will be discussed in the next chapter.

Code Review Checklist

Completeness

1. Does the program handle all conditions, functions, and updates given in the specifications?
2. Are inline comments used judiciously?
3. Are all design issues handled?
4. Have all user interface issues been handled?
5. Are all boundary testing/debugging conditions addressed?

Logic and Correctness

1. Are input parameters checked?
2. Are subscript out-of-range conditions checked?
3. Are results of error checks reported to the calling programs?
4. Are code layout and coding standards satisfied?
5. Is any hard-coding done?
6. Is any unwarranted coding done?
7. Are any uninitialized variables present?
8. Are any nonterminating loops present?
9. Does each program have one entry and one exit point?
10. Are all declared variables used?
11. Is the program logic correct?
12. Is the program modular?
13. Is the code reusable?

Reliability, Portability, and Consistency

1. Have performance/efficiency checks been done?
2. Is code independent of the character and word size of the platform?
3. Are records updated/deleted in the same order throughout the system?
4. Is a similar style of coding followed throughout the system?
5. Do comments correspond to the logic being described?
6. Are error conditions comprehensively and consistently handled?

Code Review Checklist (continued)

Maintainability

1. Does the program have proper indentation?
2. Is there a description at the beginning of the program that gives details such as a description of program functionality, the author, called programs, calling programs, and so on?
3. Are the comments current and do they clarify the functions of each program/module?
4. Are the data names descriptive?

Traceability

1. Can the program source be traced to the program specifications?
2. Are all copy books used cross-referenced?

11.4 System Testing

System testing involves two different phases with two different outputs. The first phase is system test planning, and the second phase is the system testing activity. The system test planning phase must be done before the system testing activity, and it can take place any time after the high-level design has been completed. The system testing activity, however, can be performed only after all modules have been coded and unit tested—that is, after the completion of the build phase.

The output of the test planning stage is a test plan. During the system testing activity, the system test plan is executed, and the main output is the system test report. This report specifies which test cases passed and which test cases led to errors. Sometimes, only the error report is given at the end of testing. The results of system testing are then reviewed and approved, and those situations that are not really defects are eliminated. The defects found are logged in the defect control system (discussed in more detail in Chapter 13). The logged defects are then tracked to closure.

The system test plan defines the test environment, test parameters, test procedures, and stopping criteria. For the environment, all hardware, software, communication, and security level requirements of the environment are specified. The test procedures identify the features to be tested and the features not to be tested (along with the reason for not testing them). Features to be tested include user interfaces, hardware and software interfaces, communication interfaces, and business processes. For each feature, different test cases are specified. A test case gives the condition that needs to be tested as well as the expected results. It is important to make sure that there are sufficient test cases for all test conditions specified in the SRS. The test procedure section of the plan specifies the tools to be used and the procedures to be followed (this information is not included here).

If defects are found in the system testing, then those problems are logged and later fixed. Another round of system testing is then done. If more defects are found, then the entire cycle is repeated. The test stopping criteria specify when system testing activity stops.

Some portions of the system test plan of the WAR project are shown here. The intent, as with other phases, is to give parts of the work product to illustrate the nature and structure of the document.

System Test Plan for WAR 2.0

1.　Test Environment

1.1　Hardware
Server: Pentium-based server with 64MB RAM and 1GB of disk space
Middleware servers: Pentium-based servers with 32MB/64MB RAM
Client: IBM-compatible PCs with 16MB RAM

1.2　Software
Database server: SQL Server 6.5
Web server: Netscape Web server running on Windows NT 4.0
Middleware: Microsoft Transaction Server 2.0
Client layer: Netscape 3.0 or above, IE 3.0 or above

1.3　Communication
TCP/IP

1.4　Security Level
There will be three classes of users: Corporate Admin, Project Admin, and User.

- Corporate Admin will have rights to maintain the entire list of activity codes used across the company.

- Project Admin will have rights to define the group of activity codes/module codes for his or her project.

- User can enter, submit, and approve WARs.

---

2. Features to Be Tested

2.1 User Interfaces (total 10 cases)

	Condition to Be Tested	Expected Results
1	Navigational interfaces	Should be as consistent in all screens
2	Alignment of interface elements	-do-
3	Scrolling	-do-

2.2 Browsers/Operating System in Which All the Test Conditions Are to Be Tested

Browser: Netscape Navigator 3.0, Netscape Navigator Gold, Netscape Navigator 4.0, Internet Explorer 3.0, Internet Explorer 4.0
Operating System: Windows NT/95, Windows 3.1, Mac, some UNIX

2.3 Generic Test Conditions (total 10 cases)

	Condition to Be Tested	Expected Results
1	Click on all links	System should display appropriate screen; it should not display "Not found"
2	Use of empty values in mandatory fields	Appropriate error message should be displayed

2.4 Software Interfaces

	Condition to Be Tested	Expected Results
1	The application server running on the middle tier goes down	The application should be able to sense the condition and should give an appropriate message
2	The database server goes down	An appropriate message should be flashed to the user that the database server is down and should give proper instructions about when to try later

2.5 Security Check

	Condition to Be Tested	Expected Results
1	Log in with wrong user ID	The system should give an appropriate message and should not allow the user to enter the application
2	Provide wrong password	-do-

2.6   Communication Interfaces

	Condition to Be Tested	Expected Results
1	The machine on which the application server resides goes down	The application should not be abnormally terminated, but should give an appropriate message as to what has happened and what action needs to occur
2	The database server machine goes down	-do-

2.7   Offline and Other Processes (total 11 cases)

	Condition to Be Tested	Expected Results
1	WAR reminder	The system should automatically send reminders to all people who haven't sent WARs for a particular week
2	WAR upload program	This program should be very robust and reliable and fast enough

2.8   Business Processes

2.8.1   Inbox (total 8 cases)

	Condition to Be Tested	Expected Results
1	Log in as "1572" and click on "Inbox" main menu	System should display all WARs to be submitted and WARs to be authorized by user 1572
2	WARs to be submitted appear on-screen	System should display all pending WARs sorted by descending order, and only a maximum of eight week-ending dates should be displayed. If the number of WARs is greater than this value, then the program should display '..All..' link for all pending WARs
3	Select one week-ending date from the "WAR to be submitted" displayed list	System should show WAR entry screen for entry. Enter activity details, enter authorizer's ID as "Sastryms," and click on submit button. The program should save all the entries and show the details in read-only mode with a Cancel submission button

2.8.2   WAR Entry (total 35 test cases)

	Condition to Be Tested	Expected Results
1	Display of WAR entry screen	Project code and authorizer ID should be displayed as per the user preferences. Dates should be displayed in dd-mmm-yyyy format
2	Creation of new WAR	There should be a provision for the user to fill up another WAR for the same week-ending date. A textbox should be provided with a maximum length of eight characters and a Create/Update button
3	Display of planned activities	Should match the filter chosen in the user preferences. If an activity falls outside the filter chosen but has information logged against it, then that activity needs to be shown even though it doesn't satisfy the filter
4	Negative hours logged in	The hours should automatically be taken as positive and saved
5	WAR saved with a planned activity that has not been already saved and the number of hours logged in for that activity is nonzero	The system should save the activity and the number of hours logged in; it should bring up the screen showing the same

2.8.3   WAR Review (11 test cases)—Omitted

2.8.4   Setup (29 test cases)—Omitted

2.8.5   User Preferences (13 test cases)—Omitted

2.8.6   Upload Project Plan (11 test cases)—Omitted

2.8.7   Year Change and Y2K Test (4 test cases)—Omitted

2.8.8   Reports (20 test cases)—Omitted

The system test report gives the outcome of executing the system test plan. For each test case, it specifies whether the system behaved as expected. Frequently, the test plan is written in a manner such that there is space for specifying the test-cycle number and comments. In such cases, the system test plan document itself may be used to report the results of system testing. Alternatively, a separate test report may be written, which gives the defect found (and the test case that found it). While discussing the test plan for WAR, we have omitted some columns that allow the plan to be used simultaneously for reporting purposes. If this method is used, then the system test report has the following structure:

	Condition to be tested	Expected results	Condition satisfied? (Y/N)			Remarks
			1	2	3	

As discussed earlier, many cycles of system testing may be carried out; space is provided for reporting the results for each cycle. After each cycle is complete, the author tries to remove the defects before releasing the software for system testing again. The Remarks column of the report is used to describe the erroneous behavior and the conditions under which it occurs.

The other method of reporting system testing defects is to create another document listing the defects that are found during system testing. For each defect, the behavior observed is specified along with the conditions under which it was found (this information is needed by the author to identify the defect).

11.5 Acceptance and Installation

Whatever software is developed, it must be formally accepted by the customer to be considered successful. Usually, the customer does some acceptance testing in the environment in which the software will eventually operate. Acceptance testing works in the same way as system testing—an acceptance test plan is written and then executed. When the test results satisfy the acceptance criteria, the software is accepted. Unlike in system testing, however, the acceptance test plan is prepared by the customer and the testing is carried out by the customer, although the vendor that developed the software often helps in this testing. Consequently, the development process does not include any "prepare acceptance test plan" phase. Nevertheless, all defects found during acceptance testing have to be fixed by the development team, so acceptance testing is explicitly planned for in a project. After acceptance, the software has to be installed in the customer environment and put to production use.

Both acceptance testing and installation require instructions on how to "load" the software in the production environment. Without these directions, it will be difficult for the customer to operate the software, even for acceptance testing purposes. A "release note" is therefore prepared for the project. This document describes what directories to create, where to place which files, and what else to do to make the software system operational. For example, the WAR release note defines the tables in the system, the stored procedures, the strategy for populating the database, the software needed on the client and servers, and the locations (directories) where source files of the software are kept.

An acceptance test plan resembles the system test plan, except that it is completely derived from the requirements and its objective is to test whether the system implements those requirements. Hence, for each test case, the requirement number that the test case is trying to test is given. Armed with this information, the customer can perform simple completeness checks to ensure that there is some test case for each requirement. For the WAR project, the complete acceptance test plan includes approximately 50 test cases, each having many test conditions. As it is similar to the system test plan, the acceptance test plan is not shown here.

The acceptance test results are similar to the system test results. Many times when the system is distributed (as WAR is), acceptance testing may be done at different sites and then results from the various sites compiled into a single test report; this report is then given to the developers so they can fix the reported problems. Once the errors are identified, they may be entered in the defect control system and then tracked to closure. Results of performance testing may be documented and reported separately.

11.6 Summary

This chapter briefly discussed the execution of the technical life cycle of a project—that is, execution of the development process. These activities are performed in the project to engineer the software. At Infosys, support is provided in different ways for various stages in the process. Checklists for the activities in the process form the guidelines about how to perform those activities. Guidelines in the form of methodologies are also given for some activities and phases. Templates are provided for most work products—that is, for the outputs of the major phases in the project. Finally, checklists are provided for review, which highlight the areas of concern for that output and provide some guidelines for evaluating the output.

The chapter included some portions of the various outputs for the WAR project. The idea is not to have a complete discussion of the WAR software, but rather to illustrate what the various work products contain. In some cases, checklists were also given to illustrate the issues for a particular stage.

12

Peer Review

While software is being developed, defects are inevitably injected. That is, while the different stages of the process are being executed to produce the software, mistakes are made that result in defects. In fact, defects can be injected at any stage of the development process, not just in coding. Nevertheless, the basic goal of any development project remains to develop software that either has no defects or has as few defects as possible. To achieve this goal in the face of the fact that defects are introduced, the basic approach is to identify and remove the injected defects before delivering the software. In other words, defect removal is a necessary and very important activity while developing software. The defect injection and removal cycle was discussed in Chapter 7.

Two approaches are commonly used for identifying defects: reviews and testing. Whereas testing can be used for identifying defects only in executable systems, reviews are more general and can be applied even to documents or artifacts that cannot be executed. Reviews can be done in many different ways—a formal group review, also called inspection, is perhaps the best of these options for identifying defects.

Software inspections were first proposed by Fagan [2, 3]. Earlier inspections focused on code, but over the years this technique has spread to other work products. Today, software inspections are a recognized industry best practice with considerable data to prove that they improve quality and productivity (for example, see the reports in [5, 6, 11]). This fact may explain why inspections have been made a separate KPA in the CMM (testing, for example, is not a separate KPA but a part of the Software Product Engineering KPA). Several books on the topic describe in great detail how inspections should be conducted [1, 4, 5].

The group review is a review of a software work product by a group of peers following a clearly defined process. The basic goals of such reviews are to improve quality by finding defects and to improve productivity by finding defects in a cost-effective manner. Characteristics of group review include the following:

- A group review is conducted by technical people for technical people (that is, the review is done by peers).
- It is a structured process with defined roles for the participants.
- The reviewers are prepared in advance and have identified their concerns and questions before the group meeting starts.
- The focus is on identifying problems, not resolving them.
- The review data are recorded and used for monitoring the effectiveness of the group review process.

Because group reviews are performed by a group of people, they can be applied to any work product, something that cannot be done with testing. The main advantage of this flexibility is that defects introduced into work products created during the early parts of the life cycle can be detected in that work product itself, thereby not incurring the much higher cost of detecting defects in later stages. Defects may also arise in plans for the system—for example, the project management plan or testing plan. For example, in the project management plan, the process selected for the project might not be the best option; in a test plan, some important condition may be missed. These defects, which can affect the success of the project, can also be removed through group reviews.

Besides detecting defects in a cost-effective manner and helping to ensure that an output of a stage is correct, group reviews offer other advantages:

- Through reviews, the best talent in the organization can be utilized in a project, even without assigning those personnel to the project.
- Reviews provide people with a sense of achievement, participation, and recognition.
- Reviews help the participants develop their skills by reviewing the output of other people.
- The review process helps build team spirit.
- It helps in defect prevention by creating more awareness about defects and their types.

Most methods for inspections are similar, albeit with minor variations. Nevertheless, any organization starting inspections will have to adapt the process somewhat to suit that particular organization. This adaptation will require developing suitable guidelines for usage, creating acceptable forms for data collection, setting appropriate coverage and defect rates, and so on. In the rest of the chapter, we discuss the review process employed by Infosys, the company's policies for reviews, and the manner in which data are collected and employed. We also briefly consider how experimentation was used to help convince people about group reviews when they were initially introduced. Reviews are required at level 3 of the CMM (for the Peer Review KPA). Quantitative control of reviews based on past performance is also needed at level 4 in both the Quantitative Process Management and Software Quality Management KPAs.

12.1 Review Process

The group review process includes several stages: planning, preparation and overview, group review meeting, and rework and followup. These stages are generally executed in a linear order, as shown in Figure 12.1.

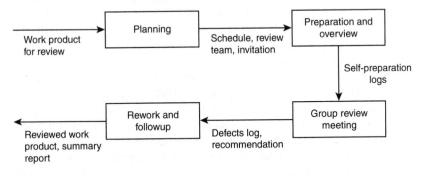

Figure 12.1   Review process

In some situations, a group review may be overkill, and a more limited form of group review may be more cost-effective. At Infosys, a one-person review is also done. The process for one-person review is defined later in this section. Policies explaining when to use a particular process are discussed later in the chapter.

12.1.1 Planning

The objective of the planning phase is to prepare for the group review by selecting the group review team and scheduling the review. Different persons have different responsibilities in this process. The author of the work product, for example, has to ensure that the work product is ready for group review and that all pertinent standards have been met or appropriate waivers obtained. The project leader, with the author's agreement, first selects the moderator; then, with moderator's agreement, the project leader selects the other reviewers. The moderator has the overall responsibility of ensuring that the review is done in a proper manner and that all steps in the review process are followed. The reviewers (also called inspectors) have the responsibility of identifying defects in the work product. Generally, the author is also one of the reviewers; the moderator may be a reviewer as well.

The major activities in the planning phase are as follows:

Verify entry criteria.

Select the group review team.

Prepare the group review package for distribution.

The first activity in this phase is to check that the entry criteria are satisfied by the work product. These criteria for different work products are given later. A project may specify its own criteria.

Once the work product is ready, the review team is formed. A special consideration while selecting a team is that, as far as possible, no superiors should be included because their presence might discourage the reviewers from raising issues or errors. If the author wants, however, the project leader can also take part. The moderator cannot be the reader, and the author cannot be the reader/moderator. Thus a group review involves the participation of at least two reviewers apart from the author.

Once the review team is selected, then the package that needs to be distributed for group review has to be prepared. This package includes the work product to be reviewed, the specifications for that work product, and relevant checklists and standards. The specifications for the work product are frequently the output of the previous phase and are needed to check the correctness of the current work product. For example, when a high-level design is to be reviewed, the package must include the requirements specification, without which checking the correctness of design may not be possible.

12.1.2   Overview and Preparation

The purpose of the overview and preparation phase is to deliver the package for review to the reviewers and to explain the work product, if necessary, so that the reviewers can prepare for the group review meeting by reviewing the material individually for defects. The entry criteria are that the group review package is ready for distribution and the group review team is identified; the exit criterion is that all reviewers submit the log of errors detected during their individual reviews to the moderator. The measurements needed include the effort for preparation, number of defects, number of issues, and severity of defects.

The major activities of this phase are as follows:

Call an opening meeting to describe the group review objectives.

Provide an overview of the work product and review process, if required.

Review the group review work product individually.

Record defects and issues and submit them to the moderator.

Record the time spent on preparation and submit it to the moderator.

The material may be distributed and explained in an opening meeting. The moderator opens this meeting with a brief statement on the work product to be inspected, the group review objectives, and, if needed, an overview of the group review process. The author may provide a brief tutorial on the work product, including a summary of any special considerations or areas that might be particularly difficult to understand. During this overview, anything unique about the project or the work product should be highlighted. This step is optional and can be omitted. In that case, the moderator simply provides a copy of the group review package to the reviewers.

Following the introductory meeting, the reviewers individually prepare for the group review. Where the work product is confusing or appears to have some defect, reviewers make notes with explanations in the self-preparation log. They also record the time spent in individual review in the log. A standard form may be used for this self-preparation log. The log may also be given to the author to permit study and consolidation of the various reviewers' findings. Relevant checklists, guidelines, and standards may be used during the individual reviews. Ideally, the preparation for reviews should be done in one continuous time span. The recommended time for preparation is one hour for every one hour of group review meeting scheduled.

12.1.3   Group Review Meeting

The basic purpose of the group review meeting is to come up with the final defect list, based on the initial list of defects and issues reported by the reviewers and the new ones found during the discussion in the meeting. The entry criterion is that the moderator is satisfied that all reviewers are ready for the meeting; the inputs include the group review package and self-preparation logs. The main outputs of this phase are the defects log and the issues log. The measurements made include the total effort spent on group review meeting, number of defects detected, type of defects detected, and origins of any defects.

In addition to the author and the moderator, the participants in the review include the scribe, the reader, and perhaps observers. These logical roles are generally played by the reviewers. The job of the scribe is to note all defects identified in the meeting and all issues raised. The main task of the reader is to present the work product to the review team, slowly going over each line and paraphrasing it. This approach keeps the attention of the review team focused on the line being discussed.

The major activities of the group review meeting are as follows:

Check the preparedness of the reviewers.

Conduct the group review meeting.

Record the defects.

Decide whether re-review is required.

Summarize the issues and action items.

Make review recommendations for the next stage.

Close the meeting.

The moderator first checks whether all reviewers are prepared. This verification involves a brief examination of the effort and defect data in the self-preparation logs to confirm that sufficient time and attention have gone into the preparation. When preparation is not adequate, the group review is deferred until all participants are fully prepared.

If everything is ready, the group review meeting is held. The moderator is in charge of the meeting and must make sure that the meeting stays focused on its basic purpose—defect identification—and does not degenerate into a general brainstorming session or personal attacks on the author. The meeting is conducted as follows. The reader goes over the work product line by line (or any other convenient small unit), paraphrasing each line to the team. At any line, if any reviewer has previously identified any issues or finds new issues in the meeting while listening to others, he or she raises the point. There could be a discussion on the issue raised, and other reviewers may agree or disagree with it. In any event, the author reviews the issue under discussion and either clarifies why it is not an issue or accepts it as a defect or open issue. The scribe records the issues and defects raised. At the end of the meeting, the scribe indicates the open issues and defects identified during the meeting that will be subject to a final review by the team members. Note that defects and issues are merely identified during the review process. It is not the purpose of the group to identify solutions—that action is done later by the author.

If few modifications are required for fixing the defects and addressing the issues, then the group review status is "accepted." If many modifications are required, a followup meeting by the moderator or a re-review might be necessary to verify whether the changes have been incorporated correctly. The moderator recommends what is to be done. Based on past data, guidelines have been provided for making recommendations, they are discussed in more detail in Section 12.1.7; later in this chapter. A summary of all issues raised is also made. Unlike defects, which are the responsibility of the author, issues may be assigned to different persons for resolution. That assignment may be made before closing the meeting. In addition, recommendations regarding reviews in the next stages may be made (for example, in a detailed design review, it may be recommended as to which code modules should undergo group reviews in the build phase).

12.1.4   Rework and Followup

The author has to perform rework to correct all defects raised during the group review meeting. The author may also have to redo the work product, if the moderator recommends that course of action. In addition, if the reviewers have been assigned some open issues, they must investigate those problems and give the investigation results to the author and the moderator.

In this phase, the author reviews the corrections with the moderator or in a re-review, if the moderator had earlier decided one was necessary. The scribe has to ensure that the group review report and minutes of the meetings are communicated to the group review team. The moderator ensures that the group review results and data are recorded and that the group review summary form is submitted to the SEPG and the project leader after all the issues and defects are closed.

Thus the major activities of this phase are as follows:

Perform rework to fix the defects detected.

Perform investigation and provide results to the author.

Prepare a summary report and send it to the SEPG.

12.1.5 Roles and Responsibilities

The group review process is a structured process with different people having different responsibilities. The key roles in a group review are those of the moderator, scribe, reviewer, reader, and author. A person can be assigned several of these logical roles, with the restrictions that the author cannot be the moderator or the reader, and the moderator cannot be the reader. This limitation implies that the minimum size of the group review team is three—the author, the moderator, and the reader. These three people are also reviewers and can assign the role of scribe to one of them. Here we briefly describe the main activities of the key roles in a group review.

The moderator has perhaps the most important role during a group review. He or she has the overall responsibility of ensuring that the review goes well. The moderator should undergo formal training on how to conduct reviews or should have experience in participating in a few reviews. The responsibilities of the moderator include the following duties:

- Assist the author in selecting the reviewers and arranging for their participation.
- Schedule the group review meeting.
- Conduct a pre-review session and ensure that the reviewers understand both their responsibilities and the group review process.
- Ensure that the entry criteria for the meeting are met.
- At the opening of group review meeting, ensure that all participants are prepared and have submitted self-preparation logs; otherwise, reschedule the group review.
- Conduct the group review in an orderly and efficient manner.
- Ensure that the group review starts and ends on time.
- Ensure that the meeting stays focused on the main task of defect identification.
- Ensure that all identified problems are recorded and resolution responsibilities are assigned.
- Track each problem to resolution or ensure that it is tracked by someone else.

- Ensure that the group review summary form is completed.
- Communicate the group review results to the SEPG and others.

During the meeting, the moderator must make sure that all participants contribute effectively, everyone is heard, agreement is reached on the findings of the review, and the interest level does not drop. A key responsibility is to ensure that the focus remains on problem identification and does not drift into problem resolution and that all reviewers concentrate on finding defects in the work product and do not indulge in finding faults with the author. Overall, orderly and amicable conduct of the meeting is largely the responsibility of the moderator. After the meeting, the moderator must make sure that all participants are satisfied, the review report is filled and communicated, and followup actions are taken.

The scribe is responsible for preparing the final report of the group review meeting, which records all defects and issues found during the meeting. The scribe must therefore know the work product well and clearly understand all issues raised during the meeting. It is the scribe's task to record all issues and defects precisely.

A reviewer is primarily responsible for finding defects. Generally, all members of the group review team are reviewers. All defects found in a group review are found either through individual review or through the group review meeting. The main duties of a reviewer are as follows:

- Be prepared for group review.
- Be objective; focus on issues rather than on people.
- Concentrate on problems and offer suggestions on style or problem solutions before or after the group review.
- Address major issues and submit minor items separately during preparation.
- If something is not clear, do not hesitate to stop progress until it is understood.
- When proved wrong, move on.

The reader paraphrases the work product, line by line, during the review meeting. Some meetings do not include paraphrasing, in which case the reader role may not be present. The main activity of the reader is to understand the matter reasonably well so that he or she can read it properly during the meeting. The reader also controls the speed of the review and must make sure that the pace of review is not so fast that defects are overlooked and not so slow that reviewers start losing interest and time is wasted.

The author is the person who produces the work product under review. Responsibilities of the author include the following:

- Ensure that the work is ready to be reviewed.
- Identify the review team in consultation with the project leader and the moderator.

- Provide copies of the group review package that is distributed to reviewers.
- Promptly resolve all identified issues.
- Remain objective and avoid being defensive.

12.1.6   One-Person Review

Group review is a highly effective way of identifying defects. Unfortunately, its cost is also high—many people spend time in preparation as well as in the review meeting. In addition, arranging group review meetings can be a complex logistical problem, with associated overheads. If the work product has many defects or is a critical one, then this cost is justified. Indeed, group reviews may turn out to be a cost-effective way of uncovering those defects. But what if the work product is relatively straightforward, is not likely to have many defects, and is not very critical? In this case, the group review effort may not be justified. Nevertheless, some review of such work products may be useful—not only to detect defects, but also to gain the psychological benefits that accrue when the author knows that someone else will be reviewing the product later.

For such situations, a one-person review may be more appropriate. That is, for work products of medium criticality or complexity, a one-person review may be substituted for a group review. One-person reviews are formal reviews but less costly than group reviews, as they do not involve a team for review.

The process for one-person review is somewhat similar to the group review process. The author, in consultation with the project leader, identifies the reviewer. The review is scheduled, and the reviewer receives the review package in advance. The reviewer reviews the work product individually and comes prepared to the meeting with the author. The review meeting has only two participants—the author and the reviewer. During the meeting, the issues log and the defects log are generated. The reviewer informs the project leader when the review is finished. The project leader is responsible for tracking defects to closure.

12.1.7   Guidelines for Work Products

All work products in a project may not undergo group review, as that approach may be prohibitively expensive and may not give commensurate returns. Some general guidelines for selection of work products for reviews are provided here. For a specific project, the actual criteria and the decision regarding the work products to be reviewed are left to the project leader and the team reviewing the work products of the early phases of the process. The reason is that, armed with the outcome of the reviews, better decisions can be made regarding what to review in the rest of the project and the method of review. As the work products of the early part of the life cycle are very critical and defects in them have a multiplier effect in the later stages, it is recommended that the following work products be group-reviewed:

- Project management plan
- Requirement specification
- System test plan
- High-level design
- Integration test plan

At the end of high-level design review, the group review team will make a recommendation for review of the detailed design. Similar recommendations are made for the code at the end of the review of the detailed design.

Table 12.1   Guidelines for Review of Work Products

Work Product	Focus	Entry Criteria	Participants
Requirements specification	Requirements meet the customer's needs. Requirements are implementable. Omissions, inconsistencies, and ambiguities in the requirements are targeted.	The documents conform to the standards.	Customer Designers Tester (system testing) Installation team member User documentation author
High-level design	The high-level design implements the requirements. The design is implementable. Omissions and other defects in the design are targeted.	The document conforms to the standards. The requirements have been reviewed and finalized.	Requirements author Detailed designer Developer
Code	The code implements the design. The code is complete and correct. Defects in the code.	The code compiles and passes style and other norms.	Designer Tester Developer
System test cases	The set of test cases checks all conditions in the requirements. System test cases are correct. Test cases are executable.	Requirements have been baselined. The system test plan is consistent with the standards.	Requirements author Tester Project leader
Project management plan	The project management plan meets project management and control needs. Completeness is provided. The project management plan is implementable. Omissions and ambiguities are targeted.	The project management plan follows the standard template.	Project leader SEPG member Another project leader

Although the review process is the same for any work product, some differences arise in terms of the focus of the review, entry criteria, and the constitution of the review team based on the nature of the work product. The checklists used also depend on the nature of the work product. The guidelines for a few of the work products are summarized in Table 12.1. Guidelines for other work products are similar.

12.2 Data Collection

Data collection is extremely important for reviews. Because reviews are largely human processes, if data are not properly recorded, the information can easily be lost. Besides logging the defects that are identified by the review process, effort data must also be captured. Detailed defect data are needed for tracking defects in the project. The overall defect and effort data are needed for analyzing the effectiveness of the review and for constructing the review capability baseline. Hence the summary data for each review are maintained in a review database, which is kept separate from the process database discussed in Chapter 5. In this section, we describe the key forms used for data collection during reviews.

12.2.1   Self-Preparation Log

The self-preparation log records all defects or issues found by a reviewer while doing his or her independent review. The effort spent during the review is recorded as well. Each reviewer prepares this log. Besides identifying the project, the work product, reviewer, and other facts, entries in the log specify the location of the issue or defect found by the reviewer and the assessment of the reviewer regarding the seriousness or criticality of the defect or issue. The form shown in Figure 12.2 may be used as is or implemented via a spreadsheet.

Project code:			
Work product ID:			
Reviewer name:			
Effort spent for preparation (hours):			
Issue list:			
SI #	Location	Description	Criticality/Seriousness

Figure 12.2   Self-preparation log

12.2.2 Group Review Meeting Log

The log of the group review meeting is prepared by the scribe. It lists the defects and issues that were identified during the meeting. Hence, it includes all defects found by individual reviewers in their self-reviews that were validated as defects or issues during the meeting as well as the additional defects found during the meeting. Unlike the self-preparation log, which lists defects as perceived by a reviewer, the group review meeting log lists only those defects that have been agreed to by the author. In other words, it lists actual defects found.

Besides the defect location and description, the severity of the defects is given in this log. The severity reflects the consensus of the group review team. The severity of a defect can be either critical, major, minor, or cosmetic. If it can be determined at which stage the defect was injected, then this information can also be recorded. The type of defect can be recorded, too. A defect can be of one of the following types: logic, standards, redundant code, user interface, documentation, traceability, consistency, portability, memory management, design issue, or performance.

Besides the defects, the issues raised are listed in a separate log. For each issue, a person is assigned to resolve it. The total effort spent (in person-hours) in the meeting is also recorded in this log.

The format of the log group review meeting is given in Figure 12.3. It may be implemented via a spreadsheet or some other mechanism.

Project code: Meeting type:
Moderator: Scribe:
Author: Reviewer(s):
SEPG member: Observer(s):
Date: Work product ID:
Effort spent on review meeting (person-hours):
Defects to be closed by (date):
Defect List:

Sl #	Defect Location	Type	Severity	Stage injected	Description

Open Issues Log:

Sl #	Issue Description	Assigned to	Targeted date	Closed date

Figure 12.3 Group review meeting log

This type of log forms the final, official output of the review. Defects listed in it must be removed and their proper removal verified. Defect removal is carried out by the author, and verification is done by the moderator (unless a re-review was recommended).

In addition, the issues listed in the issues log must be closed. Issues may be assigned to different reviewers for resolution. The resolution is then communicated to the author and the project leader.

12.2.3 Group Review Summary Report

The defects log is needed to track all defects to closure. For analyzing the effectiveness of a review, however, only summary-level information is needed. This information is also needed for updating the review baseline. For process improvement and understanding the point of view, the group review summary report is the most important element. Hence, this information is maintained in a separate review database, which is available for analysis.

The summary report describes the work product, the total effort spent and its breakup in the different review process activities, the total number of defects found for each category, and size of the work product being reviewed. If the types of defects were recorded, then the number of defects in each category can be recorded in the summary. Besides the data on effort and defects, the summary contains suggestions for the next phase. As mentioned earlier, though some general guidelines have been developed regarding when group review should be applied for a project, actual recommendations regarding the application of reviews are made during the reviews of earlier stages. These recommendations appear in the summary report. Finally, the summary indicates whether a re-review is needed. A completed summary report is shown later in this chapter.

12.3 Monitoring and Control

The review process provides a mechanism for detecting defects in an extremely cost-effective manner. On the other hand, if they are performed poorly, reviews may not detect many defects. In other words, the effectiveness of the review process depends on how well the process has been deployed. For example, if only 2 defects were found during the review of a 500-line program or a 20-page design document, the review clearly was not effective. The most common reason underlying a poor review is that the review is not done with proper focus and seriousness. Unless reviews are taken seriously, they will likely be a huge waste of time that do not give any due return, or they may become a step that is "ticked off" by performing it perfunctorily.

Statistical process control (SPC) through control charts can be an effective way of controlling reviews. Because the number of data points for reviews—

particularly for code reviews—can be large, statistical techniques can be applied with more confidence and rigor. In this section, we discuss how Infosys monitors and controls reviews using statistical techniques. The guidelines discussed here aid the moderator in evaluating the quality of a review and taking appropriate actions, when needed.

12.3.1 Review Capability Baseline

To apply SPC, as discussed in Chapter 5, critical performance parameters must be identified and then monitored. As the intent of reviews is to detect defects, the most significant parameter of interest is the number of defects found during reviews (per unit size of the work product). The review rate is perhaps the most important metric in terms of the effectiveness of reviews [3, 7]. For the review rate, the preparation rate and the meeting rate may be monitored separately. For the defect density, the density of different types of defects may be monitored separately. For these performance parameters, the control limits or natural variability limits must be determined, if SPC is to be applied.

At Infosys, the performance parameters for which control limits have been determined are the coverage rate during preparation, the coverage rate during the group review meeting, the defect density for minor or cosmetic defects, and the defect density for serious or major defects (the overall defect density is simply the sum of the two preceding defect densities). These limits are determined from past data in the same manner as the process capability baseline for the overall process (discussed in Chapter 5). Creating and maintaining this baseline is an important reason for collecting summary data on reviews. The group review capability baseline is given in Table 12.2.

The group review baseline in Table 12.2 gives, for the various types of work products, the coverage rate during preparation, the coverage rate during review, and the defect density for minor and critical defects (the overall defect density is the sum of the two). The defect density is normalized with respect to size, where size is measured in number of pages for all noncode work products and in lines of code for code work products. (For a design, size can be measured in terms of number of specification statements; for test cases, size can be measured in terms of number of test cases.) The coverage rate is stated in terms of size per unit effort, where effort is measured in person-hours. As we can see, the coverage rates and defect densities for documents are quite similar, but are different for code (where the unit of size is also different). The control charts (with the outliers) for specifications review and code review are shown in Figures 12.4 and 12.5 along with the control ranges.

The rates for one-person reviews can be expected to be different. Detailed design documents, test plans, and code are the work products that undergo this form of review regularly. Hence a one-person review baseline was developed for these work products. In the baseline for one-person review of documents,

Table 12.2   Review Capability Baseline

Review Item	Preparation Coverage Rate (if Different from Cover-age Rate)	Group Review Coverage Rate	Cosmetic/Minor Defect Density	Serious/Major Defect Density
Requirements		5–7 pages/hour	0.5–1.5 defects/page	0.1–0.3 defects/page
High-level design		4–5 pages/hour (or 200–250 specification statements/hour)	0.5–1.5 defects/page	0.1–0.3 defects/page
Detailed design		3–4 pages/hour (or 70–100 specification statements/hour)	0.5–1.5 defects/page	0.2–0.6 defects/page
Code	160–200 LOC/hour	110–150 LOC/hour	0.01–0.06 defects/LOC	0.01–0.06 defects/LOC
Integration test plan		5–7 pages/ hour	0.5–1.5 defects/page	0.1–0.3 defects/page
Integration test cases		3–4 pages/hour		
System test plan		5–7 pages/hour	0.5–1.5 defects/page	0.1–0.3 defects/page
System test cases		3–4 pages/hour		
Project management and configur-ation manage-ment plan	4–6 pages/hour	2–4 pages/hour	0.6–1.8 defects/page	0.1–0.3 defects/page

the coverage rate per hour is about twice the corresponding coverage rate of group reviews; the defect detection rate per page is about half of that found with group reviews. For code, the coverage rate per hour is about the same, but the defect detection rate per LOC is about 30% less.

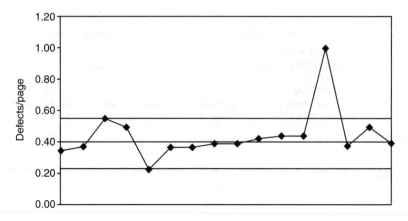

Figure 12.4   Review data for specifications

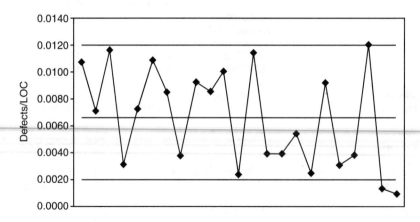

Figure 12.5   Review data for code

12.3.2   Analysis and Control Guidelines

The ranges given in the baseline can be used to determine whether the performance of the review falls within acceptable limits. To ensure that the performance of a review is checked with respect to the control limits after each review takes place, this check is specified as an exit criterion for the review process. Although the exit criteria can be defined as in-range checking of all of the various parameters, because detecting defects is the central purpose of reviews, the exit criterion is that the overall defect density should lie within the specified limits. (Checking that the defect densities for the two types of defects are within the appropriate ranges can also be used.) If the number of defects found during the review is within the range given in the baseline, the review is considered effective, the exit criteria are satisfied, and no further action is needed for this review.

If the density of defects found in a review is not within the range given in the capability baseline, then the exit criteria are not satisfied. In software, however, the fact that the performance has gone out of the specified range does not automatically mean process failure. Instead, the moderator has to critically evaluate the situation and decide on the next steps. The preparation rate and review rate become very useful here—if the review rate is "too fast" as compared with that given in the baseline, then the reason for review not being effective is relatively clear. The defect densities for minor and critical defects can also be useful in this analysis. Although the moderator can use any technique to determine the cause of performance deviation and the corrective and preventive actions that should be taken, a set of guidelines have been provided to help in this endeavor. These guidelines are given in Table 12.3.

Table 12.3   Analysis Guidelines for Review

Possible Reason	Actions to Consider
If Defects Found Are Less Than Norms	
Work product was very simple	Convert group reviews of similar work products to one-person reviews (refer to tailoring guidelines).
	Combine reviews (refer to tailoring guidelines).
Reviews may not be thorough	Check coverage rate; if too low, reschedule a review, perhaps with a different team.
Reviewers do not have sufficient training on group reviews or experience with the reviewed material	Schedule or conduct group review training.
	Re-review with a different team.
Work product is of very good quality	Confirm this fact by coverage rate, experience of the author, reviewers, and so on; see if this quality can be duplicated in other parts of the project.
	Revise defect prediction in downstream activities; see if there are general process improvement lessons.
If Defects Found Are More Than Norms	
Work product is of low quality	Examine training needs for author.
	Have the work product redone.
	Consider reassigning future tasks (that is, assign easier tasks only to the author).
Work product is very complex	Ensure good review or testing downstream (refer to tailoring guidelines).
	Increase estimates for system testing.
	Break the work product into smaller components.

(continued)

Table 12.3   Analysis Guidelines for Review *(continued)*

Possible Reason	Actions to Consider
If Defects Found Are More Than Norms	
Too many minor defects (and too few major defects)	Identify causes of minor defects; correct in the future by suitably enhancing checklists and making authors aware of the common causes.
	Reviewer may have insufficient understanding of the work product. If so, hold an overview meeting or have another review with different reviewers.
Reference document against which review was done is not precise and clear	Get the reference document reviewed and approved.
Reviewed modules are the first ones in the project	Analyze the defects, update the review checklist, and inform developers.
	Schedule training.

Table 12.3 includes two groups of guidelines: one set applicable when the defect density is below the range, and another set applicable when the defect density found is above the range. Both the situations suggest that something abnormal has taken place, and the situation has to be examined carefully. Some of the possible causes for why the situation might have occurred are given in Table 12.3; this information may be used by the project leader or the moderator to decide on the cause of the situation. Once the cause is identified, then the corrective actions for this review and any preventive actions for future reviews must be decided. Again, Table 12.3 gives some guidelines for different causes.

12.3.3   An Example

Consider the summary report for the group review of a project management plan given in Table 12.4.

As is clear from the report in Table 12.4, this summary covers a group review of a 14-page project management plan of a project. The total number of minor defects found was 16, and the total number of major defects found was 3. Thus the defect density found is $16/14 = 1.2$ minor defects per page and $3/14 = 0.2$ major defects per page. Both of these rates are within the range given in the capability baseline, so the exit criteria are satisfied and it can be assumed that the review was conducted properly. Although not needed for this review because the exit criteria are satisfied, other rates can also be checked. The review team had 4 members, each of whom spent 2.5 hours in individual review; the review meeting lasted 2.5 hours. Thus the coverage rate during preparation and review was $14/2.5 = 5.6$ pages per hour, which is within the range for preparation but somewhat higher for review.

Table 12.4   Summary Report of a Review

Group Review Summary Report	
Project	—
Work product type	Project plan, v. 1.0
Size of product	14 pages
Moderator	Meera
Reviewer(s)	Biju, Meera
Author	JC
Effort (Person-Hours)	
a. Overview meeting	0
b. Preparation	10 person-hours
c. Group review meeting	10 person-hours
Total Effort	20 person-hours
Defects	
Number of critical defects	0
Number of major defects	3
Number of minor defects	12
Number of cosmetic defects	4
Number of defects detected during preparation	—
Number of defects detected during group review meeting	—
Number of open issues raised	1
Total number of defects	19
Result	Moderator reexamination
Recommendations for Next Phase	
Units to undergo group review	N/A
Units to undergo one-person review	N/A
Comments (Moderator)	The plan has been well documented and presented.

Prepared by: Meera; **Date:** xx-xx-xxxx

12.4 Introduction of Reviews and the NAH Syndrome

Introducing group reviews in an organization that does not use them is one of the most challenging tasks before an SEPG. Reviews are, in many ways, counter-intuitive. A programmer may not understand how a review by a group of people can be more effective than testing. Even if one does believe that reviews can catch more defects, it is extremely difficult to believe that reviews can also be more cost-effective than testing. When human effort is the most critical resource in a project, it is not easy to accept the position that replacing testing (or complementing it) by a highly manpower intensive process will make the overall process more productive and improve quality. As a result, convincing people to use reviews is one of the most difficult process deployment tasks. One SEI report indicates that only 22% of software organizations employ some form of inspections [9].

Clearly, hard data are invaluable for proving the case. A fair amount of published data supports the claim that reviews can be cost-effective and can improve quality quite substantially. Most consultants and SEPGs use these data in an attempt to convince doubters that reviews can be good and should be used. Nevertheless, such published data from organizations around the world often fail to convince engineers that reviews can be good for their organization. One reason for this skepticism is the Not Applicable Here (NAH) syndrome—people believe that reviews are good for other organizations, but that the situation in their company is different and thus the reviews are not applicable [8].

If inspections are to be deployed in an organization, then the NAH syndrome must be overcome—both managers and developers need to be shown that inspections can really provide benefits. By definition, data from other organizations cannot be used to overcome the NAH syndrome. Instead, data from within the organization itself must be used to build a case for inspections. As the organization is not deploying inspections, and people are not fully in favor of inspection deployment, this information will have to be obtained by conducting some limited experiments. An experimental setup is therefore needed that can be quickly deployed in real-life scenarios to evaluate the suitability of inspections in the organization. In fairness, such an experiment cannot be conducted to "prove that inspections are useful" but only to evaluate the suitability of inspections as a technique to improve quality and/or productivity.

Infosys used a simple experiment in an attempt to overcome the NAH syndrome. This experiment is described in this section, along with the experiment results and the aftermath of the experiment. The experiment is quite general and simple and can be conducted easily by any organization. Further details of this endeavor appear in [8].

12.4.1 Experiment Design

Infosys's experiment focused on code inspections because coding is something to which developers can relate, and because coding is usually the source of the greatest number of errors. Historically, inspections started with code and only later were extended to design, requirements, test plans, and other items. Once a strong case can be built for code inspections, and they can be deployed, then the advantages of inspections will become obvious and build a case for inspections of other work products.

The purpose of the experiment was to demonstrate how inspection compares with unit testing. It had two objectives. First, it was intended to reveal how the defect detection capabilities of unit testing and inspection compare with each other in the context of Infosys. Second, it was planned to study the effects of inspections on the overall cost of development. One way to compare the defect detection capabilities of inspections and unit testing is to independently apply the two techniques on the same code and then compare the defects found by them. Infosys's experiment used this tactic. With some data about downstream testing effort, this type of experiment can also be used to study the effect on overall effort. The basic experiment steps are shown in the flow diagram in Figure 12.6.

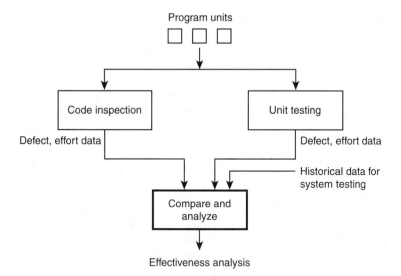

Figure 12.6 Steps in Infosys's experiment

For the experiment, some units were selected at random in a project. For each unit, two independent paths were followed during the experiment. In one, the unit was inspected; in the other, it was unit-tested. Clearly, the people inspecting the code and the people doing the unit testing in such an approach should be different and should not communicate with each other. For both paths, the effort spent and the defects detected were recorded and classified to understand how the nature of defects affected the detectability of the two techniques. As inspections were not being regularly conducted in Infosys, it was important to make sure that people had been properly trained in inspection and had done some exercises in inspection before beginning the actual experiment.

If the sets of defects found by those two approaches were not the same and one set was not a subset of the other, then one could claim that inspections do find a different set of defects than unit testing and that adding inspections will be beneficial. Understanding the cost implications is more difficult (and where most doubts arise). We must evaluate the effect on overall cost of the project if inspections are introduced as an extra step. This cost can be estimated based on past data for system testing (as illustrated later in this chapter).

12.4.2   Data from Experiment Deployment

For Infosys's experiment, six system enhancement requests (SERs) on a banking product were selected. Six developers were assigned one SER each. These developers were first trained in the inspection process; for practice, they were asked to inspect the implementation of an earlier SER that had some defects seeded in it.

The personnel divided into two groups of three developers. Each group formed an inspection team. Each developer was asked to implement the SER, compile his or her code, and do some self-testing, before submitting it. Once submitted, the SER went through two independent paths: inspections and unit testing. During the experiment, an inspection team inspected the code for the three SERs developed by the members of the group. In each inspection, the author acted as an inspector rather than the moderator or the reader. In parallel, the SERs were unit-tested independently by the module leader for the domain to which the SER belonged. The sizes of the different SERs, the total effort, and the number of defects found in the two paths are given in Table 12.5.

It is clear from Table 12.5 that the inspection route identified more defects than the unit-testing route did. This finding was consistently observed for all of the SERs. Overall, inspections caught about 2.5 times as many defects as unit testing did, although inspections consumed more effort than testing did. The number of defects detected per person-hour, however, are similar for inspection and unit testing—both detected about 1.9 defects per person-hour.

Now let us look at the nature of the defects found by the two approaches, shown in Table 12.6. This table shows that almost in all categories, inspections caught more defects than unit testing, particularly for categories related to quality attributes like "maintainability," "portability," and so on (as might be expected given that testing generally focuses on errors in functionality). The

Table 12.5 Effort and Defect Data

SER	Size (LOC)	Inspections		Unit Testing	
		Total Effort (Hours)	Total Number of Defects	Total Effort (Hours)	Total Number of Defects
1	968	8.0	8	2.0	4
2	432	5.0	8	1.5	3
3	85	4.0	4	1.5	1
4	667	6.5	26	1.5	7
5	50	12.5	3	1.5	0
6	408	2.5	5	2.5	5
Total	**2,610**	**27.5**	**54**	**10.5**	**20**

data also show that even in logic and interface defects (the focus of testing), inspections do better than unit testing. From these data, the case for adding inspections to improve the error detection capability is clear and convincing.

Table 12.6 Defect Distribution

Defect Type	Inspections	Unit Testing	Common Defects
Data	3	1	0
Function	4	2	0
Interface	14	11	7
Logic	12	5	4
Maintainability	11	0	0
Portability	5	0	0
Other	5	1	1
Total	**54**	**20**	**12**

This type of data, along with the data about average cost of identifying and fixing a defect in system testing, can be used to do the cost analysis. From past experience and data, it is known that it takes about 4 person-hours to identify and remove a defect during system testing. If a defect goes past system testing, it takes about 2 person-days (17 person-hours) to identify and remove it.

Testing will rarely catch maintainability and portability type defects. We assume that all logic, interface, function, and data defects that are not caught by unit testing are found later. The number of such defects (after eliminating common defects, which are also caught by unit testing) is $3 + 4 + (14 - 7) + (12 - 4) = 22$. If all of these defects are caught in system testing, then the system testing cost will increase by $22 \times 4 = 88$ hours, or about 11 person-days. If 75% of these errors are caught in system testing and 25% are caught later, the additional cost in system testing is $0.75 \times 22 \times 4 = 66$ hours (9.5 person-days); the additional cost of fixing defects found later is $0.25 \times 22 \times 2 = 11$ person-days. That is, an additional 20.5 person-days will be spent in fixing the extra defects, if no inspections are done.

Thus the cost saving due to inspections is 11 person-days if all defects are caught in system testing and 20.5 person-days if 25% of the defects are not caught in system testing. The cost of the inspections, which yielded these savings, is about 3.5 person-days. The case is very clear—if we spend one additional day in code inspection, in this product we can expect to save three to six days in defect fixing later in the development cycle!

12.4.3   Aftermath of the Experiment

Infosys's experiment lasted about two weeks, but had a very substantial effect on the organization. For some time, the SEPG had been trying to deploy formal inspections in the organization. The resistance had been quite stiff, however, and developers were not willing to believe that examining code written by others in a structured manner could help identify more defects and save costs.

The results of the experiment convinced developers and managers alike that inspections should be tried. The data from the experiment also indicated that the inspections would offer fewer benefits if the code was simple or small (in smaller SERs, the benefit was unimpressive). A policy decision was therefore taken by the banking product team to classify the SERs in three categories (simple, medium, and complex) and to consider formal inspections for all complex modules.

The climate for inspections changed considerably when the data from the inspections were presented to the developers and managers. The NAH syndrome was successfully overcome! The task of SEPG then changed to tackling the problem of how to train people and how to institute inspections on a company-wide scale, rather than fighting a psychological battle against closed minds.

12.5 Summary

The purpose of a group review is to detect defects in a work product, through a process of formal and structured review by a group of peers. Group reviews have been found to be very cost-effective and offer an advantage in that they can be applied to a work product that cannot be executed. They represent an important technique for improving both the quality of software and the productivity of the development process. The importance that CMM attaches to reviews can be seen by the fact that reviews form a separate KPA at level 3 of the CMM.

The group review process followed at Infosys is the standard group review (or inspection) process: planning, preparation or individual review, group review meeting, and followup. In planning, the team for group review is formed, the work product to be reviewed is identified, and the objectives of the review are set. In the preparation phase, each reviewer analyzes the work product individually and logs all defects and issues found. During the ensuing group meeting, one of the participants acts as a reader and goes over the work product line by line. The participants raise the issues or defects they have found. If an agreement is reached that the issue raised is indeed a defect or an issue to be resolved, it is noted by the scribe. The final list of issues and defects is prepared and given to the author, who removes the defects during the rework phase. During the review meeting and the individual reviews, the focus is exclusively on finding defects, rather than solving them. Defects are removed later by the author of the work product.

A one-person version of review also exists. Group review tends to be quite expensive in terms of effort, as a group of people must spend time reviewing a work product. For simple work products that may not have many defects, a one-person review may be more cost-effective. One such process has been proposed that is quite similar to group review except that only one other reviewer participates and the meeting involves only the reviewer and the author. The final list of defects is agreed upon during this meeting and resolved later by the author.

To help the moderator evaluate the effectiveness of a group review and take appropriate actions, a group review capability baseline has been developed based on data from past reviews. This baseline gives the acceptable range for parameters such as coverage rate and defect density for different types of reviews. If the defect density falls within the expected range, then the reviews were most likely done properly. If they do not, then there could be many reasons for this failure. A set of possible reasons and possible courses of action, based on past experience, was provided in this chapter.

Introducing group reviews into an organization that does not use them is a difficult challenge for the SEPG. One reason for this problem is the Not Applicable Here (NAH) syndrome. Even when people believe that reviews have provided good benefits to other organizations, they may insist that reviews will not be applicable for their organization. This skepticism makes it very difficult to change the method of executing projects and introduce reviews. One method for overcoming the NAH syndrome through experimentation within the organization was described, along with its result at Infosys.

References

[1] R. G. Ebenau and S. H. Strauss. *Software Inspection Process.* McGraw Hill, 1993.

[2] M. E. Fagan. Design and code inspections to reduce errors in program development. *IBM System Journal,* (3):182–211, 1976.

[3] M. E. Fagan. Advances in software inspections. *IEEE Transactions on Software Engineering,* SE-12(7):744–751, 1986.

[4] D. P. Freedman and G. M. Weinberg. *Handbook of Walkthroughs, Inspections, and Technical Reviews—Evaluating Programs, Projects, and Products.* Dorset House, 1990.

[5] T. Gilb and D. Graham. *Software Inspections.* Addison-Wesley, 1993.

[6] R. B. Grady and T. V. Slack. Key lessons learned in achieving widespread inspection use. *IEEE Software,* pp. 48–57, July 1994.

[7] W. E. Humphrey. *Managing the Software Process.* Addison-Wesley, 1989.

[8] P. Jalote and M. Haragopal. Overcoming the NAH syndrome for inspection deployment. *Proceedings of the 20th International Conference on Software Engineering,* pp. 371–378, 1998.

[9] D. H. Kitson and S. M. Masters. An analysis of SEI software process assessment results: 1987–1991. *Proceedings of the 15th International Conference on Software Engineering,* pp. 68–77, 1993.

[10] G. W. Russell. Experience with inspection in ultra-large-scale developments. *IEEE Software,* Jan. 1991.

[11] E. F. Weller. Lessons learned from three years of inspection data. *IEEE Software,* pp. 38–53, Sept. 1993.

13

Project Monitoring and Control

When a project is executing, it is important that it be properly monitored. Monitoring is intended to ensure that the project continues to move along a path that will lead to its successful completion. During project execution, how does a project manager know that the project is following the desired path? To determine this information, one must have visibility about the true status of the project [14]. As software itself is invisible, visibility in a software project is obtained by observing its effects [7]. Providing proper visibility is the main purpose of project monitoring.

Project monitoring has two key aspects. First, it is necessary to collect information or data about the current state of the project and interpret it to make some judgments about that state. If the current state is a "desired state," implying that the project is moving along the planned path, then monitoring provides assurance that things are indeed working well. But what if the monitoring data reveal that the state of the project is not "healthy"—that is, the project is not progressing as planned? Clearly, it must be followed by some actions to ensure that the course of the project is "corrected." That is, some control actions are applied to the project. The second aspect of project monitoring is therefore the application of proper controls to bring the project "back on track." This collection of data or information to provide the feedback about the current state and subsequent corrective actions, if needed, form a basic paradigm of project management and the foundation of any stable control system (the feedback loop is an essential component in control system theory). Figure 13.1 illustrates his control cycle [13].

Monitoring requires information about the actual state of the project. Perhaps the best approach is to quantitatively measure the parameters that reflect the "health" of the project and then use these measures to judge the actual health or progress of the project. For project management, this approach constitutes the main use of software metrics [3]. Once data are in hand, control in the

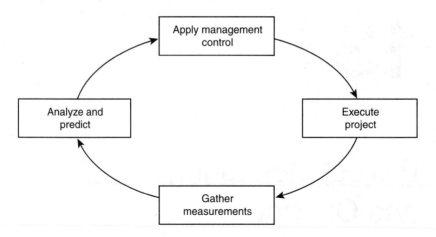

Figure 13.1   Project monitoring and control cycle

form of corrective actions can be applied to the project based on the interpretation, if needed.

Quantitatively monitoring and controlling a project are required at level 4 of the CMM, particularly within the Quantitative Process Management KPA. Quantitative control of quality is also a requirement of the Software Quality Management KPA of CMM level 4. Basic project tracking and control are required by the Software Project Tracking and Oversight KPA at level 2. Some aspects of monitoring discussed in this chapter, such as risk monitoring and establishment of thresholds for performance variation, are required by the Integrated Software Management KPA at level 3. This chapter first discusses how Infosys collects basic data, then considers how this information is used for monitoring and control.

13.1 Data Collection

The foundation of monitoring and control is information about the project obtained at different times during its execution. Although models or rules will be needed to analyze or interpret the data, the first question is which data to collect. In other words, the first issue for quantitative project monitoring and control is the selection of metrics whose values are needed for monitoring and the strategy for measuring those parameters. As discussed earlier in Chapter 5, the basic data for software engineering consist of effort, schedule, defects, and size [5, 12]. These data are the most commonly used in models and together can provide sufficient visibility into the project.

Collecting raw data for these key parameters is one of the most challenging activities in quantitative project management. This difficulty often arises because people resist providing data about their work, fearing that the data might be used against them. This and other people-related issues must be resolved if the measurement program is to succeed. Some of these issues are discussed in [5]. To ensure that data collection does not impose undue overhead, tools are very important; without them, a measurement program may not succeed [5, 8]. As the schedule is phrased in terms of calendar dates, information on it is relatively easy to collect. Hence data collection tends to focus on effort, defects, and size. In this section, we discuss how these metrics are collected in Infosys and what tools are used to aid in this collection. Later in the chapter, we discuss how these data are used for monitoring and control purposes.

13.1.1 Effort Data

Effort is a fundamental parameter of a software project because it determines the cost of the project. Earlier, we saw that estimating effort for a project is a key activity in project planning and an important issue in the contract between a vendor and a customer. Clearly, tracking of effort should be a key activity during monitoring.

Monitoring effort is essential for evaluating whether the project is executing within budget. That is, this information is needed to make statements like "The cost of the project is likely to be about 30% more than projected earlier" or "The project is likely to finish within budget." In addition, data from completed projects about total effort and effort distribution among different phases are needed to compute the values of various components of the process capability baseline (PCB). Carrying out these calculations requires effort collection methods such that total effort expended can be determined at any time in the project or, at least, at defined milestones. Furthermore, the effort expended in a project must be classified into different categories to facilitate the computation of the PCB.

To satisfy these requirements, the effort spent on various tasks by an employee are entered through the weekly activity report (WAR) system. This online system, developed locally, stores all WARs submitted by the employees in a centralized database. Each person submits his or her WAR for each week. On submission, the report goes to the individual's supervisor for approval. Once approved, the WAR submission is final and cannot be changed. As the data are entered weekly by all employees, online analysis is possible. Some analysis is provided by the WAR system itself; for more elaborate analysis, the data from the central database must be obtained and analyzed. Logging effort through WAR is backed by suitable management actions—everyone submits a WAR, including the CEO, and if a WAR is not submitted within some time period, leave is deducted.

A WAR entry by a person for a project consists of a sequence of records, one for each week. Each record is a list of items, with each item containing the following fields:

- Program code
- Module code
- Activity code
- Activity description
- Hours for Monday through Sunday

The activity code characterizes the type of activity. The program code and module code permit separation of effort data with respect to modules or programs—this consideration is important for component-level project monitoring. For creating the PCB and doing analysis regarding where the effort is going in projects (information that is also needed to identify potential areas for productivity improvement), activity codes are the key piece of data. For doing analysis and for comparing projects with one another, it is important that the activities against which effort is reported be standardized. Having a standardized set of activity codes also helps to achieve this goal. The activity codes used in Infosys's projects are given in Table 13.1.

Table 13.1   Activity Codes for Effort

Code	Description	Code	Description
C101	Contract preparation/review	C501	Coding and self-test
C102	Liaison with administration	C502	Code walkthrough
C103	Customer interface	C503	Independent unit test
C104	Obtain customer acceptance	C504	Prepare manuals
C199	Project initiation—catch-all	C505	Development of reusable code
C201	Customer interviews	C506	Rework after code walkthrough
C202	Prepare SRS	C507	Rework after independent test
C203	Obtain customer acceptance	C599	Build—catch-all
C204	SRS review	C601	Integration testing
C205	SRS rework	C602	System testing
C299	Requirements specifications—catch-all	C603	Test results analysis
C301	Planning/reviewing plans	C604	Integration test planning
C302	Project management and meetings	C605	Rework after integration testing
C303	Customer liaison	C605	Rework after system testing

Table 13.1   Activity Codes for Effort (*continued*)

Code	Description	Code	Description
C399	Project management—catch-all	C699	Testing and amplification; validation—catch-all
C401	Develop design and standards	C701	Develop acceptance and installation documents
C402	Develop/review high-level design	C702	Arrange for logistics
C403	Develop/review detailed design	C703	Acceptance testing
C404	Setup/maintenance of development environment	C704	Installation
C405	Test case design	C705	Customer training
C406	High-level design rework	C706	Rework after acceptance testing
C407	Detailed design review	C799	Acceptance—catch-all
C408	Detailed design rework	C801	Develop/review maintenance plan
C499	Design—catch-all	C802	Customer interaction activities
		C803	Warranty maintenance activities
		C899	Maintenance—catch-all

In the activity codes, the first digit specifies a particular phase. The other two digits identify activities of interest within the phase. For each phase, there is a code for "catch-all," which essentially captures the effort spent in that phase that does not have a further classification and falls under the "other" category. In many phases, a separate code for rework effort is provided. This classification helps in computing cost of quality (see Chapter 15). With this level of refinement, a phase-wise analysis or a subphase-wise analysis can be carried out on the effort data on a project. Special analyses for studying the effects of policies, tools, methodologies, and other factors on different activities of a project also become possible. The program code and module code, which are specified by the project, can be used to record effort data for different units in the project, thereby facilitating unit-wise analysis.

Through the use of activity codes, the effort spent is categorized in terms of activities. Unfortunately, this classification does not indicate whether the activities are planned. Ideally, all activities on a project should have been planned previously. In practice, this planning process is not possible; situations always come up in a project for which adequate planning was not done at a detailed level. Indeed, it may not even be possible to have a detailed plan for everything. Consider change requests—one cannot "schedule" change requests a priori in a plan. Hence some activities performed in a project will inevitably be "unplanned" and some part of the effort of a project will therefore be spent on unplanned tasks. If a project is spending a major portion of its effort in unplanned activities, however, then this effort is a source of concern as it may reflect poor project planning. In other words, besides monitoring total effort and effort expended in different phases and on different modules, it is also useful to study what portion of the effort is being spent in planned activities versus unplanned activities.

The WAR system provides this kind of analysis by connecting the Microsoft Project (MSP) depiction of the project with the WARs being submitted by project personnel. Project staff can begin submitting WARs for a project only after the MSP for the project has been submitted (once the MSP is submitted, the system knows which people are supposed to be working on the project). Planned activities are defined as those listed in the MSP and assigned to some authorized person in the project. Unplanned activities are all other project activities.

When entering the WAR for a week, the user works with a screen that is divided into two sections—planned activities and unplanned activities. All activities that are assigned in the MSP to a particular person for this week show up in his or her planned activities section for that project. The user cannot add activities or modify activities that show up in this section. He or she can enter only the hours spent each day for the different activities provided. To log the time spent on activities not listed in the planned section, the user can enter a code, its description, and the hours spent each day on these activities in the unplanned section for the project.

The WAR system provides some online analyses. Some of these analyses were discussed in the requirements specification of the WAR system, given in Chapter 3. For more elaborate analysis, such as that needed for computing the PCB or performing the closure, the WAR data must be assessed separately. Generally, the WAR data for a project are imported from the database into a spreadsheet, and then analysis is performed.

13.1.2   Defect Data

Defect information is another type of raw data that is of considerable importance in software projects. Because defects have a direct relationship with software quality, in many senses defect data are even more important than effort data. In the ISO 9001 standard, tracking of defects is mandatory and explicitly mentioned, whereas tracking of effort is not explicitly required. We consider a defect to be something that is found in some work product of the project, the presence of which can have adverse effects in achieving the goal of the project. Let us first understand the purpose of this information and what can be done with it.

Defect data are needed, first and foremost, for managing the project. A large software project may include thousands of defects that are found by different people at different stages of the project. Often the processes are such that the person who fixes a defect is different from the person who finds or reports the defect. Generally, a project will want to remove most or all of the defects found before the final delivery of the software. In such a scenario, defect reporting and "closing" cannot be done informally. The use of informal mechanisms may lead to defects being found but later forgotten, so defects may not be removed or extra effort may have to be spent in finding the defect again. Hence, at the very least, defects must be logged in and their closure tracked. For this procedure, information—such as the manifestation of the defect, the location of the suspected defect, the person who found it, and the person who closed it—will be needed. Once each defect found is logged (and later closed), analysis can focus on how many defects have been found so far, what percentage of defects are still "open," and other issues for the project. Defect tracking is considered one of the best practices for managing a project [3].

Merely logging defects will not be sufficient for other desirable analyses. To understand the quality capability of the process in use, for example, defects found during acceptance and post-delivery need to be separated from other types of defects. To create the baseline that specifies what percentage of defects are caught where, and to compare the actual defects found with estimates, information about the phases at which defects are detected also needs to be recorded. If the phase in which each defect is detected is identified, then such analysis becomes possible.

This information is still not sufficient, however. One of the organization's objectives is to continually improve the process so that quality and productivity can be improved. One approach intended to yield quality and productivity improvement is to study the defect removal efficiency of various defect detection stages and then see where room for improvement exists. The defect removal efficiency of a defect detection stage, as defined in Chapter 5, is the ratio of the number of defects detected by that stage and the total number of defects present at the time of the stage's execution. If defect removal efficiencies are high, then the latency time of defects is low. A low latency time reduces the effort required for removing the defects—the effort to remove a defect increases exponentially with an increase in latency [2]. Clearly, one way to improve productivity is to improve defect removal efficiencies. For computing the defect removal efficiency, it is not sufficient to know where a defect is detected. We must also know the point at which a detected defect was "injected." In other words, for each defect logged, we should also provide information about the phase in which the defect was introduced in the system.

At Infosys, the defect control system (DCS)—a commercially available tool—is used in projects for logging and tracking defects. The DCS permits various types of analysis, so it is also used for defect analysis. For each project, the DCS is set up, allowing all project members access to the DCS data for the project. During the DCS setup, the type of information about a defect that will be logged in the project is specified. That is, a project, depending on its needs, customizes the information it will record. Infosys has specified some of the fields as mandatory for all projects. The various options and mandatory fields are shown in Table 13.2.

Table 13.2   Defect Data

Data	Description of the Data	Mandatory/Optional
Project code	Code of the project for which defects are captured	M
Description	Description of the defect	M
Module code	Module code	O
Program name	Name of program in which the defect was found	O
Stage detected	Stage in which the defect was detected	M
Stage injected	Stage at which the defect was injected/origin of defect	M
Type	Classification of the defect	M
Severity	Severity of the defect	M
Review type	Type of review	O
Status	Current status of the defect	M
Submitter	Name of the person who detected the defect	M
Owner	Name of the person who owns the defect	M
Submit date	Date on which the defect was submitted to the owner	M
Close date	Date on which the submitted defect was closed	M

The process of defect detection and removal proceeds as follows. A defect is found and recorded in the DCS by a submitter. The defect is then in the state "submitted," essentially implying that it has been logged along with information about it. The job of fixing the defect is then assigned to some person, who is generally the author of the document or code in which the defect is found. The project or module leader makes the assignment. The person who is assigned the defect does the debugging and fixes the reported defect, and the defect then enters the "fixed" state. A defect that is fixed is still not closed. Another person, typically the submitter, verifies the fixing of the defect. Once the defect fixing is verified, then the defect can be marked as "closed." In other words, the general life cycle of a defect has three states—submitted, fixed, and closed. A defect that is not closed is also called open. These states of a defect are shown in Figure 13.2.

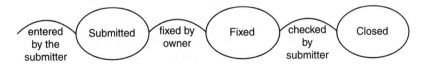

Figure 13.2   Life cycle of a defect

DCS can be customized for a project, though some of the fields have been specified as mandatory. In Table 13.2, the various information fields are described that can be entered for a defect and whether they are mandatory or optional. The mandatory fields must be filled for each defect.

Project code is the code of the project, *description* is the description of the defect, *module code* is the code of the module in which the defect is found, *program name* is the name of the program in the project in which the defect is found, *review type* describes the way in which review is being carried out (that is, one-person review or group review), *status* represents the state of defect at any point of time (open, closed, or fixed), *submitter* is the name of the person who submitted the defect after reviewing or testing, *owner* is the person who has the responsibility to correct the defect (typically, the author of the work product in which the defect was found), *date of submission* is the date on which the defect was submitted, and *close date* is the date on which the defect was closed. *Stage detected* is the stage in the life of the project in which the defect was detected; it is typically one of the review or testing stages. The various stages of detection and some sample defects for each stage are given in Table 13.3.

Stage injected represents the process stage in which the defect was injected. Determining this stage requires analysis of the defect. Whereas defect detection stages consist of the review and testing activities, defect injection stages include the stages that produce work products, such as design and coding. Based on the nature of the defect, some judgments can be made about when it might have been introduced. This information is captured in the stage injected field. Unlike the defect detection stage, which is known with certainty, the defect injection stage is more ambiguous—it is estimated from the nature of the defect and other related information about the defect. With stage injected and stage detected information about the defects, the defect removal efficiencies, percentage distributions, and other metrics can be computed.

Sometimes it is desirable to understand the nature of defects without reference to stages, but rather in terms of the defect category. Such a classification

Table 13.3   Defect Detection Stages

Stage Detected	Examples of Defects
Requirements specifications review	Incorrect or strong assumptions; incomplete external system interface specification; process flows not clear; requirements not traceable; ambiguity; incompleteness
Project plan review	Improper effort or schedule estimates; issues in risk assessment; improper manpower planning; incompleteness of plan
Configuration management plan review	Improper configuration management structure; problems in naming and directory structure; insufficient change management plans; access control problems
High-level design review	Incompleteness (that is, requirements not fully implemented); traceability not maintained; modularity; standards-related issues
Detailed design review	Logic problems; problems in handling all cases; standards-related issues
Unit test plan review	Standards-related issues; wrong test cases; proper test data not identified; insufficient test cases; some conditions not tested; improper testing criteria
Code review	Problems with coding standards, redundant code, logic, or style
Independent unit testing	Problems with logic, data handling, or input/output
Integration test plan review	Standards-related issues; wrong test cases; insufficient test cases; test cases not exercising the interaction between modules; insufficient test criteria
Integration testing	Interface errors; problems with logic or data flow across modules
System test plan review	Similar to integration test plan review
System testing	All types of defects
Acceptance testing	Problems with functionality, external interface, input/output, or performance

can help understand the distribution of defects across different categories. For this reason, the type of defect is also recorded. The types of defects possible, along with some examples for the types, are given in Table 13.4. A project may also define its own type classification.

Table 13.4 Defect Types

Defect Type	Example of Defects
Logic	Insufficient/incorrect errors in algorithms used; wrong conditions, test cases, or design documents
Standards	Problems with coding/documentation standards such as indentation, alignment, layout, modularity, comments, hard-coding, and misspelling
Redundant code	Same piece of code used in many programs or in the same program
User interface	Specified function keys not working; improper menu navigation
Performance	Poor processing speed; system crash because of file size; memory problems
Reusability	Inability to reuse the code
Design issue	Specific design-related matters
Memory management defects	Defects such as core dump, array overflow, illegal function call, system hangs, or memory overflow
Document defects	Defects found while reviewing documents such as the project plan, configuration management plan, or specifications
Consistency	Updating or deleting records in the same order throughout the system
Traceability	Traceability of program source to specifications
Portability	Code not independent of the platform

Finally, the severity of the defect is recorded. This information is important for project management. For example, if a defect is very severe, then a project leader will likely schedule it such that it gets fixed soon. Also, one might decide that minor or unimportant defects need not be fixed before software delivery, if there is some urgency. Hence classification of defects with respect to severity is very important for managing a project. It is also a standard practice in most software organizations. The classification used by Infosys is shown in Table 13.5.

Depending upon the information being entered for defects, various analyses are possible. A common analysis is the breakup of defects with respect to severity, owner, or module. Another popular form of analysis is to plot trends of open and closed defects with respect to modules, severity, or total defects. Analysis with respect to type is also possible. Some examples of analyses are given later in this chapter.

Table 13.5   Defect Severity

Severity Type	Explanation for Categorization
Critical	Defect may be very critical in terms of affecting the schedule, or it may be a show stopper—that is, it stops the user from using the system further.
Major	The same type of defect has occurred in many programs or modules. We need to correct everything. For example, coding standards are not followed in any program. Alternatively, the defect stops the user from proceeding in the normal way but a work-around exists.
Minor	This defect is an isolated defect or does not stop the user from proceeding, but causes inconvenience.
Cosmetic	A defect that in no way affects the performance of the software product—for example, aesthetic issues and grammatical errors in messages.

13.1.3   Size Measurement

Size is another fundamental metric, as many data are normalized with respect to size. For example, productivity is defined as size produced per unit effort. Similarly, many quality metrics are defined with respect to size—for example, delivered defects per unit size. This type of normalization is essential if data from past projects are to be used for other projects. Clearly, the total effort or total number of defects in a project cannot be used to predict effort or number of defects in another project, as there may not be any correlation between these measures for the two projects. When normalized with respect to size, however, they become "process characteristics," which can then be used for prediction and control. Hence, unless size measurements are made, using past data for predicting performance of projects (as is required for planning or quantitatively controlling a project) will not be possible. Also, without normalization with respect to some standard measure of size, it is impossible to benchmark performance for comparison purposes.

If the bottom-up estimation technique (discussed in Chapter 6) is used, size is frequently estimated in terms of number of programs of different complexities. Although this metric is useful for estimation, it does not permit a standard definition of productivity that can be meaningfully compared across projects. The same problem arises if lines of code (LOC) are used as a size measure; productivity does differ with the programming language. To normalize and employ one uniform size measure for the purposes of creating a baseline and comparing performance, function points are used as the size measure [1, 4].

Function points provide uniformity. The size of delivered software is generally measured in terms of LOC through the use of regular editors and line counters. This count is made when the project is completed and ready for delivery to the customer. From the size measure in LOC, size in function points is computed using published conversion tables [9].

13.2 Project Tracking

Before we discuss how projects are monitored and controlled using metrics data, let us first examine basic project tracking. Project tracking is an integral part of project management that is required at level 2 of the CMM. Basic project tracking does not require elaborate metrics data, as are required for advanced project tracking. Once a detailed project plan is made, in which all schedulable tasks are listed along with their start and end dates and the person assigned, at the very least the execution of the tasks must be tracked. That endeavor constitutes activities tracking. In addition, a project must track the unresolved issues that crop up. Although tracking by the project leader is essential, the status of the project should also be regularly reported to senior management—thus ensuring that senior management has some visibility into the project. This section discusses the basic mechanisms of project tracking employed at Infosys.

13.2.1   Activities Tracking

One of the first tasks in project tracking is to ensure that planned activities are getting done on time. As mentioned earlier, activities are usually scheduled using MSP. Hence MSP is used for activities tracking as well.

Every day (or more or less frequently), the project leader checks the status of the scheduled tasks and updates this status in the MSP. In addition, a weekly project meeting is usually held to discuss project schedule and other issues. Although MSP allows an activity to be specified as partially completed, for tracking purposes an activity is typically specified as 0% done until it is completed. Once the activity is finished, it is marked as 100% done. MSP features can then be used to determine which activities are lagging behind, what percentage of a task is done, what effects slippage will have on the execution of the overall project and so on.

13.2.2   Defect Tracking

Tracking of defects is another key point in tracking. Defect tracking was described earlier in the discussion of collection of defect data. As mentioned then, Infosys uses a DCS for tracking defects. If a defect is found in a review or some testing, it is entered in the DCS, along with information about the defect, for tracking purposes. When logged, the state of the defect is "open" or "submitted." The defect is then assigned to someone for fixing. Once corrected, the defect is marked as "fixed," even though it remains open. Finally, the submitter (or the project leader) checks whether the fix was satisfactory. If so, the defect is marked as "closed" and nothing further is done. In this way, each defect is logged and tracked to closure. At the end of the project, ideally no open defects should remain (or a conscious decision is taken to leave the defects uncorrected). At any time, the overall rate of defect arrival and rate of defect closure can be checked.

13.2.3   Issues Tracking

Many small jobs or clarifications inevitably come up during the course of the project. These problems are called issues. Managing issues is an important task for any manager, as they can be quite numerous and can potentially delay a project. For example, a clarification sought regarding a requirement from the customer (an issue) can delay many activities unless it is resolved. Many such issues have the potential to stop some activities of the project. Hence, it is important that issues are properly managed and tracked.

One method of issue tracking is to simply write the issues down and "check them off" in due course. In projects, however, the list of issues can become quite large. Formal methods are therefore useful for tracking them. For this purpose, projects usually open an "issues log."

In the issues log, issues are recorded as they arise, along with relevant information. When issues are closed, they are marked as closed. For the issues log, projects can use a spreadsheet, maintain a document, use some issue tracker, or use the defect tracking system (issues are "logged" as defects to be assigned and closed). If an automated tool is used, some simple queries become feasible. Table 13.6 provides part of the issue log for the WAR project to give an idea of the type of items that go into this log (the actual log contains the submit and close dates and some other information).

Table 13.6   An Example of an Issues Log

Issue Description	Comments/Closure Comments	Status
Integration with defect tracking system—Anything needed?		Open
Consultants—How do they enter WAR?		Open
MSP the only tool for scheduling?	Will be taken up for the next release—transferred to wish list.	Closed

Table 13.6   An Example of an Issues Log (*continued*)

Issue Description	Comments/Closure Comments	Status
Constraints—Default screen size is decided as 800 x 640. Is it OK?	Check in next meeting.	Open
Login screen—Is it a user-defined screen or a browser login screen? MIS to decide on the login screen.	It is browser login screen.	Closed
Should project be put as a line item?	No. It will make the data entry process very cumbersome.	Closed
Cancellation of WAR—Should it be a workflow?	No. Workflow will be too much overengineering.	Closed
Should we have default module code?	Yes. We will have a default module code.	Closed
Can the shortcut be put in a separate frame in the bottom so that the user need not scroll so much?	No. This shortcut will occupy most of the screen, so it is better to have it as a footer.	Closed
Rules for uploading data to be decided.	Yes. Done.	Closed
Filter for planned activities to be decided.	Yes. It is decided.	Closed
The text boxes for entering hours should be blank instead of appearing as zeros in the WAR entry screen.	Yes. All boxes will be shown blank.	Closed
Should we show only the project leader in the authorizer list in the entry screen?	No. People may submit WARs to someone other than their project leader.	Closed
WAR entry screen format—Can it be a setup parameter for each project?	No.	Closed
User ID is not shown anywhere and should be shown somewhere permanently.	Yes.	Closed
Should we specify which fields are mandatory in the WAR entry screen?	Yes. Mandatory fields will be shown with an asterisk.	Closed

The status of issues must be regularly tracked, particularly if all team members can enter issues. As mentioned earlier, unresolved issues pose a risk to the project. If issues remain open for too long, escalation channels need to be used to resolve them, as given in the project management plan (refer to Chapter 9).

13.2.4 Status Reports

Status reporting is the main mechanism for providing visibility to senior management about the project and seeking guidance, if needed. A status report is given by the project leader to his or her superior; it may also be sent to the customer. The frequency with which status reports are generated is generally weekly. The items typically included in a status report are as follows:

Customer complaints

Milestones achieved this week

Milestones missed this week and the reasons for them

Status Report for WAR 2.0 for the Week Ending dd-mm-yy

1. Customer Complaints
Nil.

2. Milestones Achieved and Missed

Task	Status	Remark	Delay
Group review of architecture design	Complete	Needs one more review after the sample application	—
Functional specification	Not complete	40% of work is complete	2 days

3. Milestones Planned for Next Two Weeks
Complete screen prototyping
Complete function specification
Complete milestone analysis report
Finish review of functional specification
Complete database design

4. Quality Assurance Activities

QA Activity	Defects Detected	Defects Closed Last Week	Defects Open
Architecture document review	59	46	13
Functional specifications review			
Database design review			

5. Issues

No.	Issue	Raised By	Action By	Status
1	Architecture Issues need to be resolved	Dev	Sastry MS	Open

6. Number of Requirement Change Requests
Nil.

Milestones planned for the next week

Issues requiring clarifications or attention

Escalation, if any

Estimated work versus available time by milestone

Number of requirement changes

Major changes from the plan

Clearly, the focus is on ensuring that the project continues to progress according to the plan and on resolving pending issues. The "comfort level" for a project may also be checked by seeing whether the available time matches the required effort. Visibility in requirement changes, which are a major source of effort overruns and schedule slippage, is also provided through status reports.

Most projects use a subset of these fields in their status reports—fields are selected based on the need for them. An example status report for the WAR project is given on page 274. This weekly status report focuses on what was done last week, what needs to be done, what open issues remain, what open defects persist, and so on.

13.3 Quantitative Monitoring and Control

A status report provides the mechanism for regular monitoring of the project. It focuses primarily on whether the schedule is being met. A key advantage of status reports is that they do not require much metrics data or analysis. For more advanced project tracking, additional metrics data must be available. This section discusses how Infosys performs metrics-based monitoring and control for its projects.

Because the main objective of metrics analysis for monitoring and control is to take corrective and preventive actions in a timely manner, such analysis should be done frequently. As a cost is associated with analysis and as corrective and preventive actions can be applied meaningfully only at certain points in the project's process, however, metrics-based reporting and control are best carried out at defined points, such as at project milestones or upon completion of a task. Analysis at milestones can provide a suitable granularity for this analysis, as long as the milestones are not too far apart. For this reason, Infosys defines project milestones separately from the customer-driven milestones, choosing them such that they are only a few weeks apart (refer to Chapter 9). For further strengthening of the monitoring and control activities, the analysis at milestones is augmented by analysis at some events (such as completion of some task). Generally, analysis at milestones is more general and reviews the overall project, whereas event-driven analysis focuses on evaluating the event that triggered the analysis.

13.3.1   Milestone Analysis

We have already discussed measurements for the basic metrics. Collecting data is merely the first step in deploying metrics. The next question that arises is how to analyze the data. One approach for analysis is to begin with the assumption that the project plan has been carefully derived and evaluated; if it can be followed, the project will succeed. It follows, therefore, that analysis should use the project plan and schedule as its baseline. In other words, analyze the plan versus the actual progress. This strategy is employed in the two common approaches for metrics-based tracking: cost-schedule-milestone chart and earned value method [2]. In the cost-schedule-milestone chart, cost (effort) and schedule are placed on the two axes. In the earned value method, the actual cost is tracked against the planned cost. Analyzing planned versus actual progress is considered a best practice for project management [3].

Given that the key parameters for the success of a project are effort, schedule, and quality, providing visibility of actual progress against the plan in all of these dimensions is desirable. In addition, because risks can have adverse effects on the outcome of the project and can change as the project progresses, they are a focus of milestone analysis.

Control limits have been defined for effort and schedule deviation (between the actual and estimated). These values are based on past data and are computed in the same manner as in the PCB. These limits were originally developed based on judgment and experience. Infosys's current limits are 35% for effort deviation and 15% for schedule. The control charts showing the deviation in schedule and effort are shown in Figures 13.3 and 13.4.

If the deviation at the milestone of the project exceeds these limits, then it may imply that the project will run into trouble and might not meet its objective; under time pressure, the project might therefore start taking undesirable shortcuts. This situation calls for understanding the reasons for variation, followed by corrective and preventive actions, if necessary. Some guidelines for analysis and possible control actions are discussed in Table 13.7.

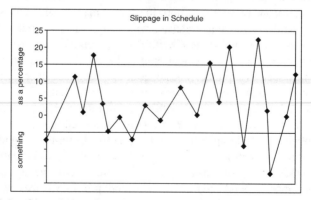

Figure 13.3   Control chart for schedule deviation

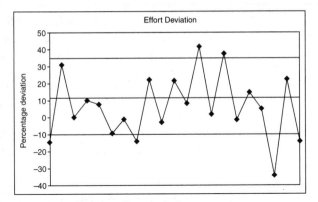

Figure 13.4   Control chart for effort deviation

Table 13.7   Guidelines for Effort/Schedule Performance

Possible Reason	Actions to Consider
If Actual Is Less Than Estimate by More Than the Allowable Limit	
Estimates for programs were too high or Project team has more domain knowledge or experience than expected	Reestimate for future modules Release resources
The tasks so far have not been thoroughly performed	Review tasks done so far and schedule reviews for work products not reviewed Examine issues log
If Actual Is More Than Estimate by More Than the Allowable Limit	
Low domain knowledge Low software/coding experience of author New technology area	Schedule training Reassign to leverage existing experience Reestimate or request resources Negotiate delivery dates
Estimates were too aggressive	Identify main components for extra effort, and revise estimate for future activities Request resources Negotiate to scale down project objectives
Resource optimization is low	Reschedule and reprioritize tasks, and identify and eliminate "waiting times"
Nonavailability of a critical resource	Escalate the issue Get a backup resource Reschedule, keeping critical resource(s) in mind
Too much rework due to poor quality of output of some earlier phases	Identify sources of problems and rectify them Change project schedule

The pattern of effort deviation can also be useful for analysis. If the effort deviation has been consistently increasing from milestone to milestone, then even though it remains below the threshold, some action might be warranted. Likewise, if some control actions are taken and a reduction is observed in the deviation percentage in the next milestone, then it suggests that the actions are having the desired effect. On the other hand, if the effort deviation increases even more after the actions are taken, then it will imply that the previous actions are not working well and "more drastic" actions might be needed. The guidelines for analysis and actions when the schedule and effort deviation crosses the specified limits appear in Table 13.7.

Table 13.7 includes suggestions for both types of variation—estimated effort too low or estimated effort too high. Some reasons for why it might be too low or too high are given, along with possible control actions. For example, if the estimate is too low, then the possible reasons are that the estimate was too aggressive, resource utilization is low (that is, there is wastage in the project), a critical resource is not available, or team members have a low expertise level. For each reason, some control actions have been suggested. For example, if the estimates were too aggressive, then one might revise the estimates, request resources, or try to scale down the project. Most of the items in Table 13.7 are self-explanatory.

For monitoring the third dimension—quality—two particular metrics are monitored: defects and number of reviews. Defects are assessed in the same way as schedule and effort. That is, the defect levels for various stages are predicted in the project plan. Using these levels and the actual number of defects found, an actual versus estimated analysis is prepared. If the deviation exceeds the threshold set for the project, then causes for the deviation have to be analyzed, based on the decision made on what actions to take to bring the project back under control. Some guidelines relating to possible reasons and possible control actions are given in Table 13.8. Guidelines for evaluating reviews were discussed in Chapter 12.

The second metric monitored is the number of reviews conducted. As the time pressures mount, there can be a tendency to "skip" the planned reviews. Because these reviews are an important part of the quality plan developed to achieve the project's quality goal, their satisfactory execution is essential. The milestone report should therefore indicate which reviews were planned and which were actually executed. The monitoring of reviews was discussed in Chapter 12.

Finally, risks are monitored at milestones. As discussed in Chapter 8, risks for a project are not static—risk perceptions change with the course of time and as risk mitigation steps are executed. Thus, it is important to take stock of risks and note the effects of risk mitigation steps taken so far. For this reason, the current risk perception, along with the status of current risk mitigation steps, is reported in the milestone analysis report. Clearly, if risk exposure due to some

Table 13.8 Guidelines for Testing Performance

Possible Reason	Actions to Consider
If Actual Number of Defects Found Is Less Than the Estimate	
Work product is of high quality	Identify reason and see whether there are possible lessons for the project or the process
Inadequate testing	Check the effort spent on testing; review the test plan and enhance it Schedule further testing
Very thorough execution of earlier quality control activities	Examine all review and testing records for the project Check whether there are possible lessons for the project on the process
Defect estimates are too high	Identify cause and correct estimates
If Actual Number of Defects Found Is Less Than the Estimate	
Inadequate execution of quality control activities so far or Insufficient reviews and unit tests planned	Examine all testing and review records Schedule reviews of critical modules before continuing with testing Enhance test plan and schedule further testing Review estimates and plans for acceptance
Defect estimates are too low	Identify cause and correct estimates

risk has not been reduced, then it implies that the risk mitigation steps are not having the desired effect. The risk and its mitigation steps therefore need to be evaluated.

An important risk mitigation step is training, which is suggested to counter many types of risks. Training is also an important component in any project involving new technology or new people. Unfortunately, its monitoring tends to "slip through the cracks" because the focus is on effort, schedule, quality, risks, and other factors. On the other hand, training does not need to be monitored regularly. Hence, at milestones, the project-related training planned and actually executed is reported.

A milestone analysis template has been provided that captures all of the elements discussed here. A sample milestone analysis report, using the standard template, is given on page 281. The senior management also has access to milestone analyses.

13.3.2 Event-Driven Analysis

Focused metrics analysis is performed after the completion of some tasks. This analysis evaluates whether the task was performed properly and determines whether any corrective action should be taken for this task (and preventive action for similar tasks in the rest of the project). Event-driven analysis can provide a finer granularity of control. At Infosys, event-driven analysis is mostly done for reviews and unit testing. Monitoring and control of reviews were discussed in Chapter 12. This chapter discusses analysis and control for unit testing.

The approach for unit testing is similar to that used for monitoring reviews. The main performance characteristic that is monitored is the density of defects detected in unit testing. From the past data on unit testing, the control limits (that is, the range of acceptable density) are obtained. At the end of each unit test, or at the end of unit testing of a few units, the defect density is checked against the range. If it falls outside the limits, then some corrective or preventive actions may have to be taken. The guidelines given earlier for testing can be used when deciding which actions are needed (for analysis, supporting information about effort spent on the task, effort expended on previous tasks, and defects found may be utilized). The control chart for defect density for unit testing of one programming language is shown in Figure 13.5.

Monitoring and controlling reviews provide control for some of the major tasks, such as high-level design and system test planning. Similarly, as milestones usually mark the end of each major phase, the performance of system testing is monitored through milestone analysis. By evaluating unit testing and reviews, a finer level of control is brought in the coding phase.

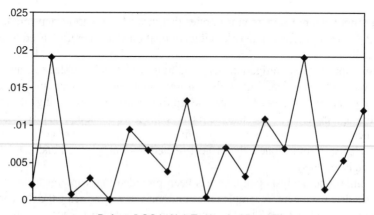

Defects/LOC in Unit Testing for Visual Basic

Figure 13.5 Control chart for unit testing

13.3.3   A Milestone Analysis for the WAR Project

This section includes a milestone analysis report of the WAR project. This analysis was performed when the functional specification was done and is the first milestone in the project. It reveals a considerable slippage in schedule and effort in this early phase. Although this slippage could be an early warning signal for the project, in this case it was felt that the culprit was a failure to account for the effort needed for prototyping while planning. This failure arose largely because data for requirements specification from the PCB were used; these data were derived mostly from projects that did not use prototyping. Nevertheless, the schedule was renegotiated, and a backup resource was assigned.

On the quality front, the report indicates that group reviews are taking place as planned, and all defect levels are within the expected range. Hence, no special actions are needed. The project reevaluated the risks and developed a modified mitigation strategy, based on experience so far.

The report also indicates that the training activities are progressing as planned, although they are consuming more effort than planned.

Milestone Analysis for WAR 2.0

1. Milestone Description
   End of functional specifications.

2. Effort and Schedule

	Schedule			Effort		
Milestone	Estimated	Actual	Deviation	Estimated	Actual	Deviation (%)
End of Functional Specifications	Jan 15	Jan 29	2 weeks	14 person-days	39 person-days	178%

Reasons for Slippage

- Cost of prototyping was not estimated properly as the standard figures from the PCB do not account for prototyping.
- Three cycles of prototype review and rework were done.
- The user group frequently postponed the reviews.
- This extra effort does not reflect the fact that the effort will proportionately increase for later phases. In reality, it should reduce the effort somewhat in later phases as fewer defects in requirements and fewer change requests are expected. Hence the project will likely have only a limited effort overrun.
- The schedule slippage is not likely to be made up—it is likely to be reflected in the final delivery date. The duration of the later stages is expected to remain mostly unchanged.

(continued)

Actions Taken

- The schedule will be changed.
- A backup resource will be assigned and utilized, if needed, for a limited duration.

3. Defects

QC Activity	Estimated Effort	Actual Effort	Size	Estimated Number of Defects	Actual Defects
PMP review	24 hours	24.5 hours	25 pages	3–7 major, 9–18 minor	6 major, 15 minor
Requirements review	27 hours	29 hours	16 pages	1–4 major, 8–24 minor	10 (3 cosmetic, 6 minor, 1 major)
Functional specifications	34 hours	30 hours	45 pages	22–68 minor, 4–12 major	62 (21 cosmetic, 29 minor, 12 major)

Notes

Most defect rates are consistent with the review capability baseline, so no action needs to be taken on this front.

4. Risks

The risk perception is as planned before, except that a change is planned in the risk mitigation strategy for one of the risks.

Risk (Priority)	Current Mitigation Plan	Status	Fresh Mitigation Step
Availability of functional/ technical group for reviews (priority: 1)	Inform group of possible review dates at least one month in advance	With people traveling, it is becoming difficult to coordinate the reviews despite the advance notice	Identify people who will be present for at least the next 3 to 4 months

5. Training Activities

Training Area	Duration	Status
Technical		
HTML, CGI	1 week—on the job for 1 person	Completed
Netscape Enterprise Server	2 days—on the job for 1 person	Completed
Java/C++/object-oriented design	1 week—mentoring for 1 person	Completed

Training Area	Duration		Status
Process-Related			
CMM-level 4 process	2 days—mentoring		Completed
VSS	1 day—on the job		Completed
Standards discussion	1 day—on the job		Completed

6. Group Reviews

Reviews Planned	Status	Type of Review
Project plan	Done	Group review
Requirements specifications document	Done	Group review
Functional specifications	Done	Group review

7. Other Issues
None.

13.4 Defect Analysis and Prevention

The metrics analysis performed during a project is primarily intended to maintain good control on the project. These analyses can be complemented by focused defect analysis that will help understand the nature of defects and prevent them in future. Institutionalized defect prevention is one of the key requirements of level 5 of the CMM. Nevertheless, some forms of defect prevention are done in all organizations, regardless of their maturity level. In a sense, the goal of all standards, methodologies, rules, and so on is to prevent defects. When actual data are available, however, more effective defect prevention becomes possible through defect data analysis [5, 6].

Defects analysis can be done at the organization level as well as at the project level. Organization-level analysis of defects can lead to enhancements of organization-wide checklists, processes, or training. The idea behind such analyses is that one learns from defects found in projects and improves the organization-wide processes for future projects. Defects analysis at the project level, on the other hand, aims to learn from defects found so far on the project and prevent defects in the rest of the project. In this section, we discuss only project-level analysis.

Defect prevention activity is intended to improve quality and improve productivity. It is now generally accepted that some defects present in the system will not be detected by the various quality control activities and will inevitably find their way in the final system. Consequently, it is generally believed that the higher the number of defects introduced in the software during the process of software building, the higher the number of residual defects that will remain in the final delivered system.

This point can be stated in another way. The overall defect removal efficiency of a process is the percentage of total defects that are removed by the various quality control activities before the software is delivered. The total number of defects in a system can be approximated as the sum of the defects found by the various quality control activities and the defects found during acceptance, installation, and a fixed period (say six months) after delivery to the customer. Thus, if the total number of defects caught (and removed) by the various in-process quality control activities is 970, and 30 defects are found after the software is delivered, then the overall defect removal efficiency of the process is 97%. For a stable process, the defect removal efficiency is generally stable as well. Hence, the greater the total number of defects in the system, the greater the number of defects in the delivered system. In other words, the higher the defect injection rate, the poorer the quality. Clearly, for a given process and its removal efficiency rate, the quality of the final delivered software can be improved if fewer defects are introduced while building the software. This recognition serves as the quality motivation for defect prevention.

Defect prevention also has productivity benefits. As discussed in Chapter 7, the basic defect cycle during the building of software is that developers introduce defects and later identify the introduced defects and remove them. In other words, something is introduced that is later removed. Clearly, this defect injection and removal cycle is a waste of effort—it adds no value to the software. In this cycle, we introduce something only to put in more effort to remove it (and we hope we remove all of the errors). It therefore makes sense not to introduce defects in the first place—then the effort required to identify and remove them will not be needed. In other words, if we inject fewer defects, fewer defects must be removed; the effort required to remove defects, in turn, will be reduced, thereby increasing productivity. This concept serves as the cost motivation for defect prevention.

For defect prevention activities in a project, analysis of defects found during a phase will generally have greater relevance for finding defects during the rest of that phase. For example, defects analysis can be done during the build phase after some modules have been built and sufficient defect data are available for analysis. The results of this analysis can prove useful in the remainder of the build phase. At a minimum, defects analysis with respect to severity and type is recommended. If this analysis reveals that some defect type is dominant, then the process can be improved to prevent such defects. Figure 13.6 illustrates a defect analysis with respect to severity and type for one of Infosys's projects.

As can be seen in Figure 13.6, the user interface errors are the most numerous in this project. This observation led to the development of user interface standards, which were then used for the rest of the project (defect analysis at a later milestone can be used to check whether the methods achieved the desired results).

Other analyses are also possible, depending on the project characteristics. For example, in one project that was in the maintenance phase, a distribution of defects with respect to modules in the system was calculated. Figure 13.7 depicts the results of this analysis.

This analysis clearly shows that more defects are being found in one particular module (UDMM). Later analysis, however, revealed that the particular module was also the largest and most complex. Hence the greater number of defects was to be expected, and no action was taken.

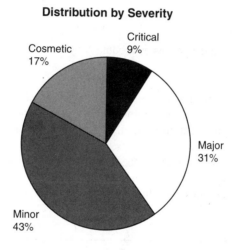

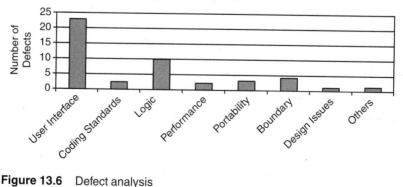

Figure 13.6 Defect analysis

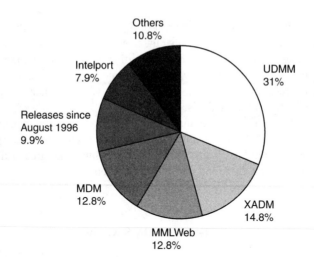

Figure 13.7   Defect analysis by module

Another useful analysis assesses the defect arrival trend and closure trend. This activity is carried out primarily for project control purposes and has little relevance in defect prevention. These trends for one project are shown in Figure 13.8.

According to this analysis, the gap between the total defects and the total closed defects is gradually increasing, although the increase is not too alarming. In the project, this visibility prompted a change in the project schedule—

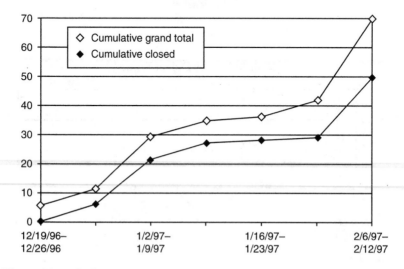

Figure 13.8   Defect arrival and closure trends

development activity was slowed and resources were assigned to defect fixing such that the number of open defects was brought down.

Another type of analysis examines the defect arrival rate, which can be used to estimate the reliability of the system and the amount of system testing needed to reach some desired reliability. Many software reliability models have been developed [10, 11]. One of the simplest tracks the defect arrival rate during system testing. The information about a defect that is captured is sufficient to support this type of analysis because the submission date of the defect is also recorded. Such an analysis is meaningful only for large projects with large system testing efforts. The defect rate analysis of one large project is shown in Figure 13.9. This arrival rate pattern can be used to estimate how much more testing is needed before the product can be released.

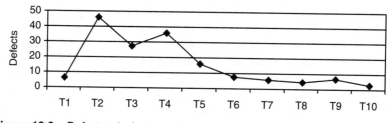

Figure 13.9   Defect arrival rate analysis

13.5 Summary

Effective monitoring of the progress of a project and application of the proper controls as and when needed are essential components of project management. A carefully made project plan is still just a plan that has to be executed. And when a plan is executed, frequently things do not work out as intended, either due to limitations of the planning itself or due to unplanned situations that arise. In any case, project monitoring is needed to check whether the project is progressing as planned. If it is not progressing along the desired path, then control actions have to be applied to the project to ensure that the project still meets its objectives. These actions are based on the information obtained in monitoring. In this chapter, we discussed how Infosys handles project monitoring and what guidelines exist for controlling a project that deviates from the planned course.

The basic project tracking involves tracking the completion of activities scheduled in the project plan, tracking the defects found during development, and tracking the issues that come up during the course of the project execution. Activities tracking is generally done via Microsoft Project, which is used for scheduling project tasks. Defects are logged and tracked to closure through a defect control system (DCS); issues are managed through some tracking tool.

The basic tracking mechanisms do not need elaborate metrics and hence can be performed even when metrics systems are lacking. If metrics have been deployed, however, then advanced monitoring can be performed by making measurements and then analyzing them. The key raw data for a metrics-based analysis include information on effort, schedule, defect, and size. Data on effort are collected through the weekly activities report (WAR) system. Defect data are recorded through the DCS. Size is measured at the end of the project and then converted to function points for uniformity.

The metrics data collected are used for project monitoring through milestone and event-driven analysis. At project milestones, all major parameters of interest—schedule, effort, and quality—are analyzed. The primary analysis method is to compare the actual values for these parameters (as found through metrics data collection) with the estimated values. If deviations are within the "threshold" values for the project, then it is assumed that the project is progressing as planned. If the deviation exceeds the threshold, then the reasons for deviation must be understood and actions taken to improve the situation. Guidelines have been provided for understanding the reasons and the possible actions that can be taken for deviations. An actual milestone report was also presented in this chapter to illustrate the various concepts. Event-driven analysis occurs at the completion of some task—generally, a review or test. At Infosys, acceptable ranges for some parameters have been established based on past data. If the data are out of range, some action is taken.

Finally, defect analysis and prevention were discussed. Although institutionalized defect prevention is an advanced activity that is stressed in the level 5 of the CMM, some defect prevention occurs at all levels. With defect data, defect prevention can be done in a more scientific manner during the course of the project. As such defect analysis should be performed while the project is executing, it is viewed as a part of project monitoring. This chapter presented some examples of how defect data of a project can be used to bolster defect prevention in the rest of the project.

References

[1] A. J. Albrecht and J. R. Gaffney. Software function, source lines of code, and development effort prediction: A software science validation. *IEEE Transactions on Software Engineering,* 9(6):639–648, 1983.

[2] B. Boehm. *Software Engineering Economics.* Prentice Hall, 1981.

[3] N. Brown. Industrial-strength management strategies. *IEEE Software,* pp. 94–103, July 1996.

[4] D. Garmus and D. Herron. *Measuring the Software Process, a Practical Guide to Functional Measurements.* Yourdon Press Computing Series, 1996.

[5] R. Grady and D. Caswell. *Software Metrics: Establishing a Company-wide Program.* Prentice Hall, 1987.

[6] R. Grady. *Practical Software Metrics for Project Management and Process Improvement.* Prentice Hall PTR, 1992.

[7] P. Hsia. Making software development visible. *IEEE Software,* pp. 23–26, May 1996.

[8] W. Humphrey. *Managing the Software Process.* Addison-Wesley, 1989.

[9] C. Jones. *Applied Software Measurement—Assuring Productivity and Quality,* second edition. McGraw Hill, 1996.

[10] S. H. Kan. *Metrics and Models in Software Quality Engineering.* Addison-Wesley, 1995.

[11] J. D. Musa, A. Iannino, and K. Okumoto. *Software Reliability—Measurement, Prediction, Application.* McGraw Hill, 1987.

[12] L. H. Putnam and W. Myers. *Industrial Strength Software—Effective Management Using Measurement.* IEEE Computer Society Press, 1997.

[13] D. B. Simmons, N. C. Ellis, H. Fujihara, and W. Kuo. *Software Measurement—A Visualization Toolkit.* Prentice Hall PTR, 1998.

[14] D. P. Youll. *Making Software Development Visible—Effective Project Control.* John Wiley and Sons, 1990.

14

Project Audits

In a process-oriented approach for software development, two key tasks are process definition and process implementation. The process definition activities deal with identifying and specifying processes that, if followed, will give good performance with respect to quality and productivity. The process implementation activities deal with implementing the defined processes—that is, ensuring that the defined processes are followed in the project. Unless they are followed properly, the defined processes are of little value. Unless the projects adhere to the standard processes, one cannot even speak of the "capability" of the process or improving "the" process, as no standard process exists. Hence, for a process-oriented approach, it is absolutely essential that defined processes be followed in all projects.

Traditionally, the process definition aspect of the process-oriented approach has attracted a great deal of attention. The implied assumption has been that once the process is defined, following the process should not be a problem. This assumption is valid in production engineering, as the defined process is frequently built into the production line. This tactic ensures that the defined process is followed automatically and not much else is needed to enforce process compliance.

In software, however, the situation is quite different. The defined processes are not executed through the aid of assembly lines, but mostly executed by humans. In other words, the defined processes must be followed by people working on the projects. To ensure that they are employed correctly, training on the processes must be provided to the people who have to deploy the processes. Providing training to people is not the end of the process implementation task— it is merely the beginning. In fact, following a process may be difficult even when the processes are clearly defined and people have been trained.

A few reasons explain this difficulty. For example, humans tend to take shortcuts or expedient measures, particularly under deadline pressures (which is very common in software projects). The processes in an organization are generally defined based on past experience such that optimal quality and productivity can be obtained in projects. Nevertheless, the rationale for some process steps may not always be clear to a person or a project team with little experience. Frequently, people without sufficient experience deem process steps to be "unnecessary bureaucracy" that can be "skipped" to "speed up" the process. For example, a new project leader might not see why he or she needs to document the design clearly when he or she "knows" the design and can quickly assign different parts to the team members for coding. Similarly, an inexperienced person might not understand why a test plan must be developed that lists all test cases for the programs rather than just sitting at the terminal and trying different test cases. Only when the people "get burned" do they realize the importance of many of the steps—but this realization comes too late to save the project. Only in the end, when design defects are detected and must be removed, resulting in long nights in front of the terminals, will the skeptic recognize the value of documenting the design clearly and getting it reviewed.

Taking shortcuts or skipping process steps need not always lead to project failures. Nevertheless, a project could potentially fail if the processes are not followed properly. Just because the risk does not materialize on a particular project in which some steps were skipped does not mean that the process steps are "unnecessary." Truly appreciating this risk is difficult to do; even many experienced persons are unable to understand it well.

An analogy may help explain this concept. Traffic rules have been instituted to provide optimal movement of the traffic. Just because a rash driver fails to stop at a stop sign and jumps a red light but nevertheless reaches home without an accident, it does not mean that a stop sign or a traffic light is unnecessary. The driver took a risk of getting into an accident by deciding to "skip" the process steps of stopping at a stop sign and a red light, even though the risk did not materialize during this trip. Hence taking shortcuts and having everything work out well in the end for a project does not imply that the skipped steps have no value. This point is generally appreciated in the case of the traffic example— the person who skipped the light is likely to be admonished by friends and relatives and might feel that his or her actions were not right. In software, however, the risk of not following the process is rarely appreciated—perhaps because the consequences are not as gruesome as those for not following the driving rules. As a result, even people with experience tend to take shortcuts, especially when they have not been hurt by this choice in the past.

Another reason why process implementation requires a fair amount of effort is that people generally resist changes. In software, any change of process requires that people change their way of working. Change requires effort and relearning, and it tends to threaten people and the "comfort zone" they have created. Thus, change is resisted. Programmers also sometimes reject processes because their very nature and objectives tend to restrict the degrees of freedom available to people in the project.

Finally, a much simpler reason for not following processes also exists. People make mistakes! Any process specification is likely to have some ambiguities and scope for interpretation simply because it is defined in a natural language like English. Furthermore, if all explanations are included with examples and other expository material, then the process description might become very large. Hence, in the interest of brevity, a terse language might be used, which could leave room for different interpretations. Just having a process specification therefore does not imply that following the process will be easy, even if the person is willing to adhere to it. The people following the process might make mistakes because they do not understand the expectations clearly.

Thus one cannot assume that processes will be followed automatically just because they have been clearly defined and explained. An active effort is needed to ensure compliance to the defined processes. One method is to provide assistance (by the SEPG) in helping people actually implement the processes. Although the availability of help will definitely enhance compliance, it may not be sufficient because such assistance usually takes the form of "advice" or "suggestions," which may or may not be followed by the project personnel. In addition, providing too much assistance or "hand holding" is not a long-term solution for ensuring that personnel can understand and follow the processes. Instead, a formal method is needed that will regularly check for compliance and ensure that proper actions are taken where deviations arise. Audits aim to fulfill this need. Such audits are therefore an indispensable tool for process implementation.

The basic objective of audits is to ensure compliance to the defined process. To achieve this objective, the audit mechanism should produce a reasonable confidence that processes are being followed by the projects in the organization. Meeting this goal clearly requires that a project should either be audited or at least have the possibility of being audited while it is executing. Although they are process implementation activities, audits are performed on a project during its execution. Hence, we cover them in Part III of this book.

Audits are an essential part of software quality assurance [1]. The quality control activities in the life cycle of software development focus on testing and reviewing. They are not sufficient by themselves, however, as the process being used in the project has great influence over the final quality delivered. Hence the process of the project must be closely monitored. Audits are also an important requirement of the ISO 9000 quality system [2, 3, 4, 5].

In the CMM, the Software Quality Assurance KPA of level 2 can be supported through audits. In addition, for many other KPAs, some of the key practices under "verifying implementation" require independent auditing of the project's process activities. An organization can organize its audits in various ways. The rest of this chapter describes the audit mechanism employed by Infosys.

14.1 Audit Process

Auditing is a systematic and independent examination of various activities, intended to determine compliance with the quality system of an organization (the quality system is a set of documents that contains the definitions of all processes). Although ensuring and encouraging compliance constitute the basic goal of audits, the audit process focuses on the implementation of processes in an organization, so the information it generates becomes very useful for analyzing the processes. Another goal of audits is therefore to determine the effectiveness of the processes and to identify areas of improvement.

Audits can be either external or internal. Auditors who come from outside the organization under scrutiny do external audits. External auditing is generally employed when an organization is being assessed for some type of certification regarding implementation of some standards (for example, ISO 9000). Hence external auditing is conducted primarily for certification purposes and generally uses some external standard against which compliance is checked. Internal auditing, on the other hand, is conducted by the organization itself using people from within the organization. Its primary goal is to ensure compliance with the organization's processes and aid in process improvement. As internal audits remain under the control of the organization, we restrict our attention to them in this chapter.

To ensure a reasonable degree of compliance with the defined process, audits must be done regularly. They cannot be performed, for example, once every year or two; in such a case, only the projects around the audit time would be checked and the tendency would be to ensure compliance only at the audit time.

In addition, no project should be outside the purview of audits, as then the projects outside the reach of the auditors might slowly degenerate in their use of the organization's processes. There are two ways in which all projects can be brought under the purview of audits: all projects can be audited, or some projects can be audited but with projects being selected randomly (or with some other strategy). The latter option essentially uses the sampling approach. It is also effective even though all projects are not audited, because the "fear" of getting audited will ensure some degree of compliance.

Audits also have to be formal, with a formal notice of noncompliance being issued and later tracked to satisfactory closure. Formality ensures that "personal equations" do not play a major role and that senior management gains visibility into process compliance through the summary reports of audits.

Who should the auditors be? In internal auditing, the auditors will be people from within the organization. Ideally, they should understand the processes of the organization and their importance, and have the necessary maturity and stature to be able to assess the implementation on a project objectively. The auditors will also need to be trained in the process of auditing. They could be personnel whose primary job consists of auditing and related activities, as is frequently done in financial systems. In software, this pool of potential auditors might consist of the members of the SEPG.

At Infosys, other project personnel perform the audit of a project. That is, SEPG members do not automatically play the role of auditors. Instead, SEPG trains people to become auditors. Trained personnel (who could include SEPG people) do the actual audit. This strategy was chosen so as to make audits a means for exchanging ideas among projects—people from one project can see how another project is functioning and can even give some advice based on experience from their own project. Furthermore, once people become "law-keepers," they generally develop a respect and appreciation for the "law." That is, this means ensures that not only are audits done, but people also receive training in audits and processes and develop a respect for processes, which helps in furthering process compliance.

Next, we discuss how audits are actually conducted at Infosys. The audit activity has three main components: planning, auditing, and followup.

14.1.1   Planning

If any activity is to be successful, careful planning is essential. This idea is also true with audits. Before audits are actually conducted, they must be carefully planned if the desired results are to be achieved. Planning for audits operates at three levels: a strategy, a high-level plan, and a detailed schedule.

The audit strategy defines how audits will be scheduled and planned so as to monitor compliance and the effectiveness of processes. It defines the objectives of the audit and provides the direction for audits. The corporate level audit strategy at Infosys has three elements:

1. Audits are conducted monthly.

2. During an audit, a sample of the projects is selected for audits, but the projects selected are not known before the month of the audit.

3. Each month has some focus area for the audit, which will be examined in detail during the audit.

Monthly scheduling ensures that audits occur quite frequently. A sampling technique is used for selecting projects, although projects are generally not selected fully at random. If feedback from any quarter suggests that some project might be having some problems, then the project might be selected for auditing. This feedback might come from the customer, the senior manager for the project, or the quality advisor who is associated with the project and is helping the project implement the processes. On average, in a given month

10% to 20% of ongoing projects are audited. If the life of a project is less than a year, this sampling rate and audit frequency ensure that there is a very high chance that a project will be audited at least once during its life.

Having a focus area has many advantages. It does not mean that other aspects of the project will not be examined. Rather, it just implies that some aspect of the project will be examined in more detail. The focus area "declares" the importance of the topic to the projects, which encourages projects to do an internal review of their own processes in that area. By focusing attention and then changing the focus each month, different aspects of the process are "tightened" each month in a project. Also, the existence of focus areas encourages more in-depth auditing, which is not easily achievable with a general audit. Finally, focus areas offer a powerful tool for "reorienting" the projects to new processes, if needed, and conveying the priorities of the management and the SEPG. For example, when processes change, a focus area can target the changed aspects of the process, thereby honing in on these characteristics. Focus areas can also be used to implement newer models or frameworks. For example, if the CMM is to be implemented, an easy way to check whether it is indeed being applied to projects is to designate different KPAs as the focus areas and to use some of the key practices as the checklist for audits.

The audit plan is an implementation of the audit strategy for a specific period (6 or 12 months). This plan specifies how the strategy will be implemented through the mechanisms available to auditing—selection of focus areas, selection of projects, selection of auditors, and so on. In the absence of any clear strategy, the plan aims to cover the entire organization and all aspects of the processes over a period of about one year. Typically, the plan specifies

- The focus area for the month and the relevant processes corresponding to the focus area
- The type of projects to be examined

Table 14.1 provides an audit plan for six months. This plan covers some of the key areas for projects that are closely related to the CMM.

An audit schedule is set every month; it specifies the actual audits to be carried out that month. The schedule uses the audit plan as one of its inputs. During this phase, some projects that satisfy the criteria in the plan are selected for audit. For each audit, two auditors from the pool of auditors are named, along with a backup auditor (the pool of auditors is the set of people who have been trained in conducting audits). The date of the audit is specified as well. An audit checklist is prepared that indicates the questions to be asked or the documents to be examined during the audit. This checklist is given to the auditors. It serves as a guide for them and ensures that audit is not cursory but has sufficient depth. Over a period of time, "standard" checklists are built for many focus areas that can be reused.

Table 14.1   The Audit Plan

Month	Focus Area	Projects to Be Audited
July 1997	Project management (project planning and initiation; project execution and tracking; project reporting)	Some projects in planning stage Some projects in later stages Some projects that were audited earlier
August 1997	Configuration management; software quality assurance	Projects should not be in the start of the LC Some projects in coding stage Some in the last stages of LC
September 1997	Requirements management	Some in requirements stage Some in later stages Some close to delivery
October 1997	Integrated software management; software product engineering	Projects in the middle or later stages of their LC
November 1997	Quantitative process management; software quality management	Some in the planning stages Some in the middle Some toward the end
December 1997	Repeat the required focus area after doing audit analysis	Some projects should be "repeated" Some should be new

14.1.2   Auditing

A team of two people normally conducts the internal audit. The audit team specified in the schedule consists of three auditors, one of whom is a "stand-by," to be called upon if one of the primary auditors cannot participate. A reminder is sent to the auditors and the project leader whose project is to be audited one day before the audit begins.

On the day of the audit, the auditors first meet with the quality advisor associated with the project to get some views on the use of processes in that project. The team then plans out its audit strategy—what questions they will ask, who they will interview, and what artifacts they will need. This rough plan provides guidance to the audit team, preventing conflicts between the team members themselves. The actual evaluation and the questions asked also depend on the information gathered during the audit.

In the actual audit, the auditors focus on whether the defined process is being followed in the project, paying more attention to the processes in the focus area. Checking is done by asking questions about how some activity is done and by looking at the evidence or outputs of these activities. For questions, the checklist may be used. As one would like to reduce the effort spent on auditing (auditing consumes not only the effort of the auditors, but also the time of the auditees), a checklist for a focus area highlights the key concerns in that area. Such checklists are derived from the approved processes and try to maximize the returns from an audit by concentrating on the key aspects rather than the less important or peripheral issues of the project. Sample checklists for two focus areas are given below.

Project Planning Checklist
- Is the project plan documented in the standard project plan template?
- Has the project plan been group-reviewed?
- Has the project plan been approved and baselined and is it under configuration management?
- Is there a signed contract?
- Have the commitments to the customer or other groups been reviewed?
- Is there an estimated effort for the project that is based on historical data?
- Have the effort estimates and the schedule been reviewed?
- Has the quality plan been reviewed?
- Is the life cycle used in the project identified and documented?
- Are personnel identified and responsibility for each work element (such as planning, requirements, design, and code) defined and tracked?
- Are reestimation triggers such as scope changes and required corrective actions defined?
- Are deliverables to the customer, including user documentation, clearly identified?
- Are risks and risk mitigation plans identified and properly documented?
- Are reviews, progress reporting, tracking, and approval mechanisms identified?

Requirements Management Checklist
- Is there a requirements document that includes technical and nontechnical requirements?
- Have the requirements been reviewed and are review records available?
- Has the requirements document been signed off by the customer and other affected groups?
- Are changes to requirements logged?
- Have changes to requirements been reviewed/discussed with the team and other affected groups?
- Has traceability to changed requirements been established in other work products, such as the design, system test plan, and acceptance test plan?
- Have requirements change thresholds been negotiated with the customer?
- Is the status of changed requirements available and maintained properly?
- Are the acceptance criteria defined and signed off by the customer?
- Is there a record of the reestimation of size, effort, and critical computer resources?

The audit is considered complete when the audit team has asked all questions and looked at whatever artifacts they want. A noncompliance report (NCR) is issued if the evidence suggests that the organization-wide processes or the processes authorized for the project are not being followed, or if some weaknesses in the project are identified that might lead to loss of control. The questions and the checklist aid in unearthing noncompliance. A key aspect of auditing (and one that is stressed in training) is that the procedure seeks to audit the compliance to the process and not people. This idea is fundamental to the entire process-oriented approach—the focus should always remain on the process and process improvement, and problems found in a project should be attributed to process factors and not people. The NCRs clearly indicates the type of deviation found.

Although identifying noncompliance is the goal of audits (and the analysis of audit results is utilized for evaluating the effectiveness of processes), when two software professionals evaluate a project, they are likely to develop some ideas regarding the technical or management aspects of the project that might be useful in improving the project. These issues often do not constitute noncompliance, but one would not like to lose them. Such observations are therefore recorded as the auditors' suggestions to the project on a separate form. The project leader and project personnel can then decide whether the suggestions will be implemented. The audit reports, including NCRs and suggestions, have to be sent to the coordinator of audits, who is a member of the SEPG, within three days of conducting an audit.

14.1.3 Follow-up

The submission of the NCR is not the end of the auditing activity. As the audit's basic purpose is to ensure that projects deploy the organization's approved processes, these reports should be used to make the necessary changes in the project such that any issue raised in the NCR is satisfactorily addressed. This step is called a "corrective action." For each NCR, some corrective action must be taken. Once taken, it is recorded on the NCR form itself (the NCR form is created in duplicate—one copy is kept by the audit coordinator and the other is sent to the project on which the NCR was issued). The form, along with the corrective action, is then returned to the audit coordinator.

To ensure that the issue raised in the NCR was satisfactorily resolved, the audit coordinator gets the action approved by the auditors. If these personnel are not available, then the quality advisor for the project or the audit coordinator may approve the action. Once the action is approved, the NCR is considered "closed."

Table 14.2 gives an example of an NCR and its corrective action. This NCR specifies the project, date, and the severity of the noncompliance. The severity indicates both the seriousness of the issue and its consequences (major or minor). Some project personnel usually take the corrective action. In this case,

Table 14.2   A Noncompliance Report with Corrective Action

Infosys	
Page..... of	**Nonconformity Report**

Project/Dept.: Projyyy	**Date:** 21 Oct 97
QSD Ref.: Req. chg. Process	**Severity:** Serious

Nonconformity

Requirement changes in the development project are not being tracked/recorded. For example, five programs were sent for modification, but the mails pertaining to those changes were not logged.

Corrective Action:	**Action by:** PL
	Action Date: 10 Dec 97

A spreadsheet will be created in which all changes, along with their impact analysis, will be recorded.

Preventive Action:	**Action by:**
	Action Date:

Auditor
Auditee

Follow-up Action:
Done.

Closed by:	**Recommendation:**
Closed	

the issue raised concerned requirements changes, which are handled generally by the project leader. The corrective action was therefore instituted by the project leader. The date on which the corrective action took place is also mentioned.

Sometimes, the issue is likely to recur later, either in the same project or in other projects. In such a situation, besides taking a corrective action, the project may need to take some preventive action to ensure that a similar problem does not crop up in the rest of the project. Similarly, an audit may reveal some weaknesses in the processes. In such a situation, the process specification itself might need to be modified (by the SEPG) to prevent the problem from occurring in other projects. Hence preventive actions might need to be taken in some situations. The NCR includes a section in which to record the preventive actions taken and who took them. An example of an NCR that required both corrective and preventive action is shown in Table 14.3. The preventive action for this NCR is to upgrade a checklist to ensure that a similar problem does not happen in the future.

At Infosys, an NCR must be closed within 60 days of the audit. Generally, the audit coordinator sends a reminder at the end of one month and another a week before the time limit expires. The NCRs whose "age" is more than 60 days are reported to the senior management for the project. This kind of formal followup ensures that audit reports are taken seriously and that the issues raised are addressed properly.

Table 14.3   A Noncompliance Report with Preventive Action

Infosys	
Page..... of	**Nonconformity Report**

Project/Dept.:	**Date:** 15 Dec 97
ISO 9001 Clause:	
QSD Ref.:	**Severity: Serious**/Minor

Nonconformity

When a review finds no defects, no evidence exists to show that the review was done.

Corrective Action:	**Action by:** PL
	Action Date: 28 Dec 97

Reviewed documents will be marked as **"reviewed"** with reviewer's signature.

Preventive Action:	**Action by:** Manager—SEPG
	Action Date: 31 Jan 98

The review checklist will be enhanced to ensure that some review record is created even if no defects are found during the review.

Auditor
Auditee
(Signature)
(Signature)

Follow-up Action:
Done.

Closed by:	**Recommendation:**
Closed	
(Signature)	

14.2 Audit Analysis

The audit report for a project provides information about the state of the process implementation on that project. An individual audit report has limited value in assessing the processes. Over a period of time, as most projects undergo audits, however, the reports from the different projects together offer valuable data about the state of the implementation of the processes across the organization. These data can be very useful in analyzing the effectiveness of the processes and scopes for improvement. For this purpose, the audit reports are periodically analyzed. The basic objective of this analysis is to study audit trends so as to identify areas for process improvement.

To illuminate the trends, summaries are produced for items such as the number of audits scheduled versus the number conducted, the total number of NCRs given, the age distribution for NCRs when they were closed (for example, how many are closed within 30 days, how many between 30 days and 60 days, and how many beyond the 60-day limit), and the distribution of NCRs by severity. These summaries yield information about the health of the audit system and the seriousness with which audits are being conducted. In other words, these types of analysis provide some visibility into the implementation of the audit process itself.

The identification of areas for process improvement is primarily done by analyzing the nature of NCRs. The basic approach is to classify the NCRs into different categories, then to search for trends. In contrast, if some problem occurs in very few projects, then it could be considered as a problem of implementing the process on those projects. If a problem occurs commonly, however, then it should not be viewed as a problem of the projects but as a problem with the process at the organization level. Hence, by analyzing the NCRs, potential areas for process improvement can be identified.

For example, the results of an analysis of the NCRs in Figure 14.1 clearly show that the bulk of the NCRs are in the project management area. This analysis clearly suggests that project management is a potential area for process improvement. To take steps for improving the processes, however, a better understanding is needed regarding which aspect of project management is home to the weak areas, as project management involves many activities and their corresponding processes. To gain further insight, the project management NCRs were further broken down into different areas under project management. The results are shown in Figure 14.2.

As can be seen from the pie chart in Figure 14.2, the greatest number of NCRs are in "project process not documented." This area can be considered the primary target for improvement of the management processes. Once an improvement area is identified, a better understanding is developed by studying the details of the NCRs under this category. This analysis will then lead to actions needed to improve the process. In the case depicted in Figure 14.2, the

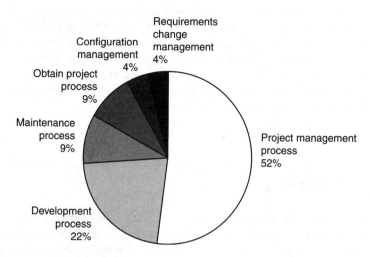

Figure 14.1   NCR analysis

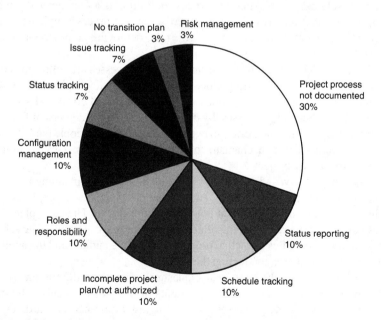

Figure 14.2   Analysis of project management NCRs

improvement action was to upgrade the project management plan template to include a section on process definition. As this template is used by most projects for recording the plan, this change "forced" project leaders to explicitly state the processes they planned to use in their projects.

Note that the process improvement activity itself is outside the audit process and forms a part of process management, which was discussed in Chapter 1. Nevertheless, the audit analysis provides one possible "trigger" for process improvement. This analysis is done by the SEPG (the audit coordinator) and the results are periodically reported to senior management, which also helps in preserving the formality of the audit process.

14.3 Summary

Two assumptions must hold true in a process-oriented approach to software development: the processes must be clearly specified, and they must be properly implemented. Often, the process definition activity is considered the central and most important activity for having a process-based approach. This idea comes from the belief that once processes are defined, following them should be a relatively easy task. Although process definition is an intellectually more complex task that requires technical expertise, in fact process implementation frequently consumes the maximum effort in deploying a process-oriented approach.

Many reasons explain why ensuring that the processes are followed across the organization is not a straightforward activity. First, people tend to take shortcuts, believing that such actions will lead to reduced effort and schedule for the project. Second, processes, by definition, restrict the degrees of freedom of project personnel, which often spawns resistance. Third, people tend to make mistakes. Audits are a mechanism to help ensure that processes are implemented properly on projects.

Like any activity, audits require careful planning. Audit planning has three elements: a strategy, an audit plan, and a schedule. The strategy explains how audits will be conducted and what goals they will achieve. The audit plan indicates how this strategy can be implemented in the next year or two. The schedule for a month specifies the actual projects that will be audited and the auditors who are responsible for conducting the audit.

During the audit, the auditors ask questions about how different activities are done in the project and check the outputs of the project to ensure that the project is following the processes and complying with other standards of the organization. If any noncompliance is found, a noncompliance report (NCR) is issued. In the last phase of the audit process, the NCRs are followed up. The project for which an NCR has been issued must take a corrective action to remove the problem and report the action taken. If the auditors (or the SEPG) are satisfied with the action taken, the NCR is considered closed. Sometimes, preventive actions might also be needed to ensure that the same problem does not recur in the future.

Although an NCR gives an indication of the state of the processes on a particular project, the set of NCRs gathered over a period of time can give insight into the state of processes across the organization as a whole. Hence the NCR data across projects are a useful source when evaluating the effectiveness of the processes and can reveal some areas for improvement. The NCR data are therefore analyzed periodically. Each NCR is classified and then analysis is done regarding the distribution of NCRs across different categories. The categories with a high incidence of NCRs represent potential areas for improvement. Further analysis is done to understand the exact nature of the problem, based on which some improvement may be effected. In this manner, audits also become a source of process analysis and improvement.

References

[1] W. Humphrey. *Managing the Software Process.* Addison-Wesley, 1989.
[2] International Standards Organization. *ISO 9001, Quality Systems—Model for Quality Assurance in Design/Development, Production, Installation, and Services.* 1987.
[3] International Standards Organization. *ISO 9000-3: Guidelines for the Application of ISO 9001 to the Development, Supply and Maintenance of Software.* 1991.
[4] O. Oskarsson and R. L. Glass. *An ISO 9000 Approach to Building Quality Software.* Prentice Hall PTR, 1996.
[5] U.K. Department of Trade and Industry and British Computer Society. *TickIT: A Guide to Software Quality Management System Construction and Certification Using EN29001.* 1992.

15

Project Closure

When does a project end? Does it end when the software has been delivered to the customer and acceptance-tested? Although successful delivery might indeed mark the end of an individual project, it is not so for the organization that is in the business of executing projects. An organization also needs to improve its productivity and quality. One improvement paradigm is to learn from past successes and failures so that successes can be repeated or improved and failures can be avoided. From the organization's point of view, the implementation of this paradigm requires that a project should not be considered as complete only with a successful delivery—the experience in the project should also be captured to help the organization learn. This goal is achieved through project closure analysis, also called post-project analysis or postmortem analysis [2, 4, 5, 6].

Learning from past projects is a key theme in the CMM and is necessary for level 3 (in the Organization Process Focus and Integrated Software Management KPAs). In addition, closure analysis is essential for populating the process database (PDB) and for creating the process capability baseline (PCB), which in turn are necessary for the Organization Process Focus and Organization Process Definition KPAs of level 3 and the Quantitative Process Management and Software Quality Management KPAs of level 4.

It has been argued that a project closure or postmortem analysis is a golden opportunity for process improvement that should not be missed [4, 5]. Indeed, this exercise is considered a best practice of software engineering [3]. One step in the quality improvement paradigm of the experience factory [1] is to analyze the data at the end of each project to evaluate current practices, determine problems, and so on.

Nevertheless, a postmortem analysis is not a "standard" activity. Some statistics about what percentage of organizations perform a postmortem analysis, when they do it, who is involved, and more are given in [7]. Although many human and process implementation issues exist when postmortem analysis is performed, this chapter will focus on the contents of a project closure analysis report.

Besides closure analysis, archiving should also be done before project closure. Archiving is pursued for various reasons, including legal reasons. This chapter therefore briefly discusses closure analysis and archiving at Infosys, then gives the project closure analysis report for the WAR project.

15.1 Project Closure Analysis

As noted earlier, project closure analysis is the key to learning from the past so as to provide future improvement. To achieve this goal, it must be done carefully in a fear-free atmosphere such that lessons learned can be captured and used to improve the process and future projects. Before we describe the details of the closure analysis report, we will briefly discuss the role of closure analysis and its implementation.

15.1.1 Role of Closure Analysis

The objective of a postmortem or closure analysis is "to determine what went right, what went wrong, what worked, what did not, and how it could be made better the next time" [4]. Relevant information needs to be collected from the project, primarily for use by future projects. That is, the purpose of having an identified completion analysis activity, rather than just saying, "the project is done," is clearly not to help this project, but to improve the organization by leveraging the "lessons learned" in the project. This type of learning can be effectively supported by analysis of data collected in earlier projects. Data analysis of completed projects is also needed to understand the performance of the process on this project, which in turn is needed to determine the process capability.

As noted earlier, the data obtained during the closure analysis is used to populate the PDB. The data from the PDB may be used directly by subsequent projects for planning purposes. This information is also used in computing the process capability, which is used by projects in planning, and for analyzing trends. This role is depicted graphically in Figure 15.1.

In earlier chapters, we discussed the types of data generally collected in a project and the collection methods. The amount of raw data collected in a project could be quite large. For example, a project involving 5 people and lasting for 25 weeks will have 125 WAR entries and is likely to have data for about 400 defects, data on many change requests, various outputs, and so on. Clearly, these data will be of limited use unless they are analyzed and presented within a proper framework and at a suitable level of abstraction. Closure analysis aims to accomplish this goal.

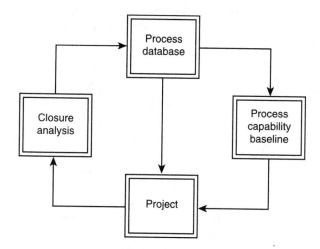

Figure 15.1   Role of closure analysis

After data analysis and extraction of all lessons learned from the analyses, the results should be packaged in a manner such that they can be used by others (packaging is the last step in the quality improvement paradigm [1]). Furthermore, to leverage this information, project processes have to be constructed such that their execution requires the use of data in an effective manner. It can be argued, however, that even if others do not learn from the packaged information, the project personnel for the recently finished project will have consolidated their experience and will carry the lessons learned from the analysis into future projects [4]. In other words, a closure analysis is useful even if others do not directly gain from it.

15.1.2   Performing Closure Analysis

Although a postmortem analysis can prove very useful for process improvement and understanding, it is frequently not done. A process for performing these analyses has been given in [5]. Here we briefly describe how closure analysis takes place at Infosys.

The closure analysis is carried out by the quality advisor from the SEPG associated with the project, in conjunction with the project leader and other project members. A template for the analysis report has been defined. The person carrying out the closure analysis must fill out this template properly, using mostly the metrics data for the project (which keeps the focus on objective information, as suggested in [5]).

As discussed earlier, the effort data for the project are available from the WAR database. The defect data can be gathered from the defect control system.

Size data are obtained from the project. Planning data appear in the project management plan. These data constitute the main information needed for metrics analysis.

The data analysis is first done by the quality advisor, who develops an initial interpretation of analysis results. A meeting is then held among the quality advisor, the project leader, and other project members. The initial report serves as the basis of discussion. Further points and observations that come up are noted. This meeting yields the basis of the final closure analysis report.

The final report is prepared by the quality advisor and submitted to the SEPG head, the project leader (who gives it to the project team members), and the business manager of the project leader. The report is also entered in the PDB, as discussed earlier in Chapter 5. In other words, the closure analysis report is published, which helps in recycling this information [5]. Once the SEPG head approves the closure analysis report, the data in the PDB also become "available" for process capability analysis.

15.1.3   Closure Analysis Report

In this section, we briefly discuss the major elements in a project closure analysis report at Infosys; later, we give the closure report of the WAR project (Section 15.3). The contents of this analysis report form a superset of data that is put in the PDB. Only those metrics data that are needed frequently by projects and whose use is required by the current processes are included in the PDB. In the analysis report, however, other data that might shed some light on process performance or help to understand the process better may also captured.

General and Process-Related Information.   The closure report first gives some general information about the project, overall productivity achieved and quality delivered, process used and process deviations, estimated and actual start and end dates for the project, tools used, and so on. A brief description regarding the experience with tools might also be included (detailed "experience reports" are put into the Body of Knowledge [BOK] system). The information about tools can be used by other projects to decide whether use of the tool is warranted. It can also be examined to identify tools that have good advantages and to propagate their use throughout the rest of the organization.

Risk Management.   The risks initially anticipated for the project are given in the risk management section, along with the risk mitigation steps planned. In addition, the top risks as viewed in the post-project analysis are listed (they are the real risks for the project). This information can be used by later projects and can be used to update risk management guidelines. Notes may also be provided on effectiveness of the mitigation steps employed.

Size. As discussed in Chapter 6, many projects use the bottom-up method for estimation. In this method, the size of the software is estimated in terms of number of simple, medium, or complex modules. Hence the size in terms of number of simple/medium/complex programs is captured, along with the criteria used for classification (different projects may use different criteria for classification). Data on both the estimated size and the actual size are included.

For normalization purposes, the productivity of a project is measured in terms of function points (FP) per person-month. Although FP can be counted by studying the functionality of the system, at closure time it is computed from the measured size in lines of code (LOC). If multiple languages are used, we simply add the sizes (in FP) of the modules in different languages. Strictly speaking, function points are not an additive measure like lines of code. Because we are measuring only the size of the complete system in FP, however, this approach is equivalent to converting all LOC counts into an LOC count of some "universal" language and then converting that size into FP. Furthermore, due to the inherent limitations in software metrics and use of those metrics, some inaccuracies are acceptable, provided that the methods are used consistently. The size in FP is also captured in the closure analysis report.

Effort. Total estimated effort and actual effort in person-hours are recorded in the closure analysis report. The total estimated effort is obtained from the project management plan. The total actual effort is the sum of the total effort reported in all WARs submitted by the project members, including the project leader. If the deviation between the actual and estimated values is large, reasons for this variation are recorded as well.

For each of the major steps in the process, the total actual effort and estimated effort for the stage are captured, too. This information can be useful for a project in planning, and it is a key input in forming the PCB. For a stage, where possible, the effort for doing the task, doing the review, and doing the rework is separated. The WAR codes described earlier in the book permit separating the effort in this manner. The distribution of effort in different phases can then be computed and recorded in the closure analysis report. The separation of effort between task, review, and rework aids in identifying the scope for productivity improvement.

The cost of quality for the project may also be computed. It measures the cost of all activities that directly contributed to achieving quality. The cost of quality can be defined in many ways; here it is defined as the percentage of the total effort spent in review, testing, rework to remove defects, and project-specific training (which is done primarily to prevent defects). Although the cost of quality is not currently part of Infosys's officially published PCB, later, when there is a better understanding of the cost of quality in projects, it is likely to become a part of the process capability. Some indications suggest that the cost of quality should be less than 30% to 40% in properly managed projects.

Defects.   A summary of the defects found during the project is given in the defects part of the closure analysis report. The information recorded for each defect includes stage injected, stage detected, severity, program and module in which the defect was found, and more. These data are marked by a considerable amount of detail, which permits different types of analyses. In the closure analysis report, defects may be analyzed with respect to severity (percentage of defects that were major, minor, or cosmetic), stage detected (percentage of total detected defects detected by which activity), stage injected (which activity introduces what percentage of total defects), and so on. As we have seen, information on defect distribution, when coupled with the defect injection rate, is useful for defect prediction. The data on defect distribution and introduction are also used for computing the PCB.

When the information about the stage injected and stage detected for defects is given, then defect removal efficiencies of various quality assurance stages can be computed. The defect removal efficiency of a defect removal task is defined as the percentage of total defects that existed at the time of execution of the task and that are detected by the execution of the task. Although the defect removal efficiency is not currently included in Infosys's PCB, it provides a very useful insight for improving the quality of the process. Such data can be effectively employed to determine which quality activities need improvement. For example, if the effectiveness of design review is only 60%, then we know that it is an area ripe for process improvement. Once this potential for improvement is identified, the current design review method can be studied to determine ways to boost its effectiveness. The study may reveal that the effectiveness of reviews can be enhanced by making the design review more formal, by improving the review checklist based on analysis of defects that slip by the design review, by improving the standards for design specification, and so on. Other analyses of defect data may also be included. Sometimes, a separate analysis of the review data may be performed. Analysis of estimated defect levels and actual defects found is also done.

Causal Analysis.   Once the project has finished, the performance of the overall process on this project is known. We also know the capability of the overall process. If the performance of the process on this project is out of the range given in the capability baseline, then there is a good chance that the variability has an assignable cause. Causal analysis involves looking at large variations and then identifying the causes for them. Standard causal analysis techniques like the fishbone diagram and Pareto charts may be used for this purpose. Frequently, the cause can be determined through discussion and brainstorming.

Once the causes are identified, we must decide whether some of them can lead to process improvements or can form some "lessons learned." In the former case, suitable actions must be taken to modify the process, as discussed in Chapter 1. The lessons learned may be captured using the BOK system discussed in Chapter 5.

Process Assets.   Besides the metrics data, other artifacts are produced during a project that are potentially useful for future projects. These artifacts are called process assets. In Chapter 5, we discussed how process assets are organized for use in projects. The process assets from projects that are made available to other projects are collected at project closure. These artifacts are then put into the system with links from the PDB entry for the project.

Whereas the assets are typically artifacts or outputs from a project that might be useful to other projects, any knowledge acquired or lessons learned in the project that might be useful to other projects are put in the BOK system. The entries in the BOK system consist of articles that are written by team personnel after the project ends, based on their experience. As such articles have to be written, they cannot be "collected" in the closure meeting. BOK submissions therefore take place asynchronously; that is, people submit articles as and when they have something ready. The entries that a project should aim to submit may, however, be decided in the project closure analysis meeting.

15.2 Archiving

Every time a software version is released, it is imperative that the source code be archived along with relevant documents for future use. When a project is being executed for a client, then the reason for archiving is primarily legal. Archiving also provides a long-term backup. In addition, archives may sometimes be needed by future projects that seek to reuse those parts of the project not captured as process assets. Consequently, archiving needs to be done methodically, ensuring safety, security, and availability.

At Infosys, on project completion two copies of the software and related documents are made; these copies are maintained in different places. For a project, all documents, records, sources, and other relevant information have to be archived. The list of documents and artifacts that are archived is given below. It also includes the most important documents in a project.

Project Initiation: Proposal, contract documents, review records

Requirements Specification: Data flow diagrams, entity relationship diagrams, data dictionary, customer's requirements document, any other analysis document, review records

Plan Documents: Project plan, configuration management plan, installation and acceptance plans, maintenance plan, review records

High-Level Design: Database design, functional design, environmental architecture design, test case design and checklists, project standards, review records

Program Specifications: Flowcharts/structure charts, pseudocode, program specification documents, review records

Source Code: Programs, copybooks, database definitions, include files, JCLs, batch files, files required to create development environment (script files, login files), utilities

Testing-Related Files: Simulators, test data, stubs, dummy programs, test case design, test results

Acceptance: Procedures for replication, delivery, installation and acceptance; acceptance records

Manuals: User manual, operations guide, installation manual, command reference manual, any other manuals

Configuration Management and Technical Support: Procedures used in customization of the development environment, any other documents of interest

Infosys's archiving policy states that all project records must be kept for a period of two years from the date of project completion. Contracts, proposals, and related correspondence with the customer are stored for even longer. The archiving is usually done on floppies or tapes, which are properly labeled and clearly identify the project name, code, version number, date of archiving, and so on. These items are maintained by the company librarian.

The librarian is responsible for maintaining the archival catalog, ensuring the safety of the archives, and periodically checking the physical existence of floppies and tapes that have been archived against the catalog entries. On receiving archival documents from a project, the librarian checks all of the documents and archival media, allocates a new catalog number, fills in the archival form, allocates the location for the documents and the archival media, and then archives them.

15.3 Closure Analysis Report for WAR 2.0

The closure analysis report of the WAR project is given in this section (it has been edited and portions containing general information, graphical representations, and other data have been omitted). The report gives the overall productivity of the project and the quality delivered. These values are computed from the data given later in the report—actual effort number of defects found during acceptance testing, and size. From these data, the productivity is computed as total actual effort divided by size; the quality is computed as the number of acceptance defects divided by size. Later, when the number of defects found during the warranty period becomes available, these findings may be modified. According to the closure ananlysis report, the quality of the WAR software delivered was 0.095 defect/FP, and the productivity achieved was about 25 FP/person-month—both poorer than the company norms. Reasons for this discrepancy are also included. The actual and estimated duration of the project are provided as well. As can be seen, this project was not delivered on schedule.

For risk management, the risks that were originally identified in the start of the project, as well as the real risks that the project leader and SEPG feel existed for the project, are given. The real risks, as perceived in hindsight, appear in the list of risks that were identified in the start, although their order is different. Experience with the mitigation steps followed has also been captured. This experience can help plan for risk mitigation in future. For example, the experience in this project suggests that developing a proof-of-concept application was an effective deterrent against the "new technology" risk. This information, once recorded and made available to other projects through the PDB, becomes very useful for other projects that involve new technology areas. Similarly, for performance risk, the experience with this project shows that caching at different levels was very effective.

The estimated and actual size in terms of number of programs of different complexity is recorded in this report. The estimated size was very close to the actual size. This closeness is due to the nature of the estimation approach—it requires a fairly detailed understanding of the programs included in an application. The size of the final output system is also given in LOC, along with the language. For the WAR system, the size was about 14 KLOC of Visual Basic 5 code, which translates to about 483 FP. This size figure was used to compute the productivity and quality for the project.

Next, the estimated and actual effort for the project is given in the closure analysis report. For this project, the actual effort was about 23% more than the estimated effort; although a substantial discrepancy, this deviation is within manageable limits (and within the limits set by the project). The distribution of the estimated and actual effort among various activities is given as well. From this information, we can see that the effort in requirements analysis was substantially more than estimated, due to the fact that prototyping was performed in this project. The build effort was lower than estimated, perhaps because unit testing was omitted. This reason also likely explains why the acceptance cost was high. From the detailed distribution of effort, the cost of quality has been computed for the project. It is defined as the percentage cost of all activities that were related to prevention or removal of defects. The cost of quality in this project is about 38%. Some observations regarding the effort distribution are also recorded.

After the effort analysis, analysis of defects is included. The distribution of defects among the various defect detection stages is given—the data from projects is subsequently used for PCB computation. As the stage injected and stage detected for defects are known, we can compute defect removal efficiencies for different stages. In this project, the removal efficiency was 80% for requirements review, 72% for design review, 42% for code review, and 68% for system testing (as we know only the defects that are found prior to acceptance testing, the removal efficiency is 100% for acceptance testing at this point). Except for requirements review and possibly design review, these removal efficiencies are low. To achieve an overall defect removal efficiency of 92% to 98%, the defect removal efficiency should be at least 60% for system testing, which usually detects 20% to 30% of defects (as given in the PCB). Similarly, for code review and unit testing, the efficiency should exceed 70%, if it is to detect half of the total number of defects. The low removal efficiencies in these two stages are largely due to insufficient unit testing, as recorded in the causal analysis section of the closure analysis report.

The defects distribution with respect to severity and defect type has also been computed. The actual number of defects detected by various activities and the estimated number of defects are given. Although the total number of defects found and the total number of estimated defects are similar, the actual numbers for different stages show considerable deviation from their corresponding estimated values. A higher number of defects was detected during requirements and design review, perhaps because prototyping was used and prototyping review revealed many more errors than is the case under normal situations (in which no prototyping is done). The actual number of code reviews and unit tests is much lower than expected, largely because unit testing was skipped. This fact likely explains the higher number of defects found during system testing and acceptance testing.

Finally, a causal analysis provides the possible process reasons for the situations in which the planned goals were not met. These reasons serve as the summary for lessons learned from this project's process usage. The process assets that have been submitted are also recorded.

Closure Report for WAR 2.0

1. General Information

Productivity	Total actual effort: 3,580 person-hours = approximately 420 person-days = approximately 19 person-months Size = 483 FP Productivity = approximately 25 FP/person-month
Quality	Acceptance defects = 45 Quality = 0.095 defect/FP
Number of Customer Complaints	Nil

2. Project Duration

	Estimated	Actual	Delay
Start Date	21-Oct-1997	21-Oct-1997	None
End Date	10-June-1998	10-Aug-1998	2 months (27%)

3. Process Details

Process Tailoring	Unit testing was not done although it was planned; it is a required step in the process. Prototyping was done although it was not originally planned. A proof-of-concept step was added in the process. A step was added in the design phase to evaluate transaction servers.

4. Tools Used

Notes on Tools Used	External tools: VSS, Netscape Enterprise Server, SQL Server 6.5 In-house tools: BugsBunny, WAR-MSP, MS Project

5. Risk Management

Risks identified at the start of the project:

Risk 1	Availability of functional/technical group for reviews
Risk 2	Requirement changes
Risk 3	Working on new technology
Risk 4	Change in customer coordinator
Risk 5	Meeting performance requirements
Risk 6	Acceptance criteria not available

Risks encountered during the project:

Risk 1	Working on new technology
Risk 2	Availability of functional/technical group for reviews
Risk 3	Meeting performance requirements

Notes on Risk Mitigation

Risk 1:	Developing proof-of-concept application was very effective
Risk 2:	Remained as a risk
Risk 3:	Design enhancements that employed caching for master data in the transaction server and generation of static HTML in the Web server instead of CGIs were very effective

6. Size

	Estimated	Actual
Number of Simple Units	4	4
Number of Medium Units	10	11
Number of Complex Units	5	5

(continued)

Notes on Estimation

Simple: Programs with minimum business logic, not more than 2–3 table access, less data display (build effort—4 days)

Medium: Programs with moderate business logic, 2–4 table access, moderate data display (build effort—6 days)

Complex: Programs with complex business logic, more than 4 table access, large data display (build effort—12 days)

Final System Size in FP

The size of the final source is measured in LOC. It is normalized to FP by using the published conversion tables. For Visual Basic 5, the published tables suggest that 29 LOC equals 1 FP

Output Language	Size in KLOC	Size in FP
Visual Basic 5	14.01 KLOC	483 FP

7. Effort

Peak Team Size	4
Estimated Effort	340 person-days = 2,890 person-hours (340 x 8.5)
Actual Effort	3,580 person-hours = approximately 420 person-days (3,580/8.5) = approximately 19 person-months (420/22)
Effort Billed	NA

Distribution Over Life-Cycle Stages

Stage	Task	Review	Rework	Total
Requirements analysis	153.25	40.25	139	332.5
High-level design	240	54.25	32.75	327
Detailed design	286.5	42	12	340.5
Coding (build)	969.75	19.5	161.25	1,150.5
(Independent) Unit testing	0	0	0	0
Integration testing	0	0	0	0
System testing	231	0	0	231
Installation, acceptance testing, and warranty	236	0	0	236
Project management	269.5	0	0	269.5
Configuration management	53.5	7	0	60.5
Project-specific training	377.5	0	0	377.5
Other	254	0	0	254
Total	**3,071**	**163**	**345**	**3,579**

Cost of Quality

$$COQ = \frac{\text{Review effort + rework effort + test effort + training effort}}{\text{total effort}} \times 100$$

$$= (163 + 345 + 231 + 236 + 377.5)/3,579 \times 100$$
$$= 37.8\%$$

Effort Distribution

Stage	Estimated		Actual		Percent Deviation (%)
	Percentage of Effort (%)	Effort (Person-Days)	Percentage of Effort (%)	Effort (Person-Days)	
Requirements analysis	4	14	9	39	178
Design	20	68	19	79	15
Build	40	136	32	135	0
Testing	10	34	6	27	−20
Acceptance	4	14	7	27	93
Project management	8	27	9	39	45
Training	5	17	11	44	160
Others	9	30	7	30	0
Total	100	340	100	420	23

8. Defects

Defect Distribution

Stage Defected	Estimated		Actual		Percent Deviation (%)
	Number of Defects	Percentage of Total Estimated Defects (%)	Number of Defects	Percentage of Total Defects Found (%)	
Requirements specifications review	102	30	12	3.3	41
Design review			132	36.2	
Code review	170	50	90	24.6	−47
System testing	41	12	86	23.6	110
Acceptance testing	27	8	45	12.3	66
Total	340	100	365	100	7

(continued)

Defect Removal Efficiencies

Defects Detection Stage	Defects Injection Stage				Defect Removal Efficiency (Not Considering the Defects in Other Category)
	Require-ments	Design	Build	Other	
Requirements review	12			0	80% (12/(12 + 3))
Design review	0	131		1	72% (131/(131 + 17 + 9 + 25))
Code review	0	17	73	0	42% (90/(90 + 85 + 40))
System testing	0	9	76	1	68% (85/(85 + 40))
Acceptance testing	3	22	15	5	100%

Overall defect removal efficiency = 320/365 = 0.87

Distribution by Severity

SI #	Severity	Number of Defects	Percentage of Total Defects
1	Cosmetic	91	24.9
2	Minor	75	20.5
3	Major	48	13.2
4	Fatal	10	2.8
5	Other	141	38.6
	Total	**365**	**100.0**

Distribution by Defect Type

SI #	Defect Type	Number of Defects	Percentage of Total Defects
1	Design issues	94	25.8
2	Hard-code	4	1.2
3	Initialize	5	1.4
4	Issue	27	7.2
5	Logic	72	19.8
6	Standards	6	1.6
7	User interface	118	32.3
8	Other	39	10.7
	Total	**365**	**100**

9. Causal Analysis

The major deviations in the process performance from expected are listed here along with the possible reasons for the deviation.

Deviation	Reason for Deviations
Delivered quality = 0.095 defect/FP (PCB range = 0.01–0.075) Overall DRE = 0.87 (PCB range: 90%–95%)	Code reviews not effective; proper control not applied. No unit testing done. Only one milestone analysis done.
Estimated schedule = 7.5 months Actual duration = 9.5 months Slippage: 27% (acceptable limit: 15%)	Prototype reviews took more time than expected. More than planned research needed to understand the new technology, which included building a proof-of-concept application. Duration of later stages was as planned; slippage occured in the early stages due to the above reasons.
Actual productivity = 25 FP/ person-month Range in PCB = (20–60 FP/ person-month)	Higher productivity could not be achieved because the project used new technology; as a result, there was considerable training effort and loss due to the learning curve.
Effort spent during acceptance phase much more (almost 100%) than estimated effort	More rework had to be done during this phase.
Percentage of defects removed during requirements/design stage higher than PCB norms	Use of prototyping.
Percentage of defects removed during code review/unit testing low	Unit testing not performed. Proper controls not applied for reviews.
User interface type defects accounted for one-third of total defects	Could have been reduced with better user interface standards.

Overall Conclusions

The quality of the delivered system could have been improved if deviations in the later stages of the process were not present. If unit testing and integration testing were done and all code reviews were conducted as planned, then the quality would have been better than the norms. Furthermore, additional milestone analyses at the later stages could have helped in keeping schedule slippage and effort deviation in check by highlighting the process deviations and their effects.

(continued)

The facts that requirement changes did not happen later in the LC and that very few defects at later stages could be tracked back to requirements indicate that the requirements gathering was very effective. This efficiency was possible because of the close interaction of the user group and the development team as well as the use of prototyping. Overall, prototyping could have provided rich dividends in quality and even productivity, but these potential gains were not realized due to "process shortcuts" in later stages.

10. Process Assets Submitted

- Project plan and schedule of the project

- Architecture and design document

- Documents relating to the evaluation of various transaction servers

- Some components used in the project

15.4 Summary

A project does not end with the delivery and installation of the software—it has to be used for learning before it is closed. Learning from experience is a key requirement at level 3 of the CMM, and a metrics analysis program is expected at level 4. Learning from the organization's past experience has to be properly planned and carried out. Project closure analysis is one method to achieve this goal.

The main focus of the project closure analysis at Infosys is the metrics analysis. In this phase, the metrics data collected in the project are analyzed. The results of the analysis are then used to understand the performance of the process and causes for any deviations from organizational norms. A typical metrics analysis report indicates the quality delivered in the project, the productivity achieved in the project, the distribution of effort, the distribution of defects, the defect removal efficiency of various quality activities, the cost of quality, the risks and effectiveness of risk mitigation, notes on planning and effectiveness of planning, and so on. If the performance of the process on this project is very different from past experience, then a causal analysis is performed to determine the cause of the variation. These causes can serve as a source of process improvement initiatives.

In addition to the metrics-based analysis, most of the project artifacts are archived. Process assets from a project are also collected during project closure, especially documents that may be useful for other projects. They can help other projects in terms of planning and execution. In addition, other forms of experience (such as how to do some activity or how to use some technology) that are not reflected in the project documents but that may prove useful for others to avoid "reinventing the wheel" are captured through the Body of Knowledge (BOK) system.

References

[1] V. R. Basili and H. D. Rombach. The experience factory. In *The Encyclopedia of Software Engineering.* John Wiley and Sons, 1994.
[2] S. Brady and T. DeMarco. Management-aided software engineering. *IEEE Software,* pp. 25–32, Nov. 1994.
[3] K. Caputo. *CMM Implementation Guide: Choreographing Software Process Improvement.* Addison-Wesley, 1998.
[4] E. J. Chikofsky. Changing your endgame strategy. *IEEE Software,* pp. 87–112, Nov. 1990.
[5] B. Collier, T. DeMarco, and P. Fearey. A defined process for project post-mortem review. *IEEE Software,* pp. 65–72, July 1996.
[6] R. Grady. *Successful Software Process Improvement.* Prentice Hall PTR, 1997.
[7] K. Kumar. Post implementation evaluation of computer-based information systems: Current practices. *Communications of the ACM,* pp. 203–212, Feb. 1990.

Appendix A

From ISO 9000 to CMM

A large number of software-developing organizations in the world are ISO 9001 certified. Many of these companies are now considering adopting the SEI's Capability Maturity Model (CMM) [2, 7], which provides a basis for process management and improvement [3]. In this transition from ISO 9001 to CMM, processes have to be enhanced to suit the CMM (while preserving ISO 9001). This appendix discusses the typical enhancements that might be needed by an ISO organization when moving to higher levels of maturity in the CMM framework, based on Infosys's experience in successfully transitioning from ISO to level 4 of the CMM. Although this work has its origins in Infosys's experience of successfully implementing CMM level 4, for the sake of generality, the discussion here focuses on the general issue of an ISO organization moving to higher levels of CMM.

ISO 9001 is a standard that has 20 clauses, which are meant for service organizations [4]. This standard has been interpreted for a software organization in ISO 9000-3 [5], and further guidelines and elaboration have been given in the TickIT guidelines [9]. ISO certification process is binary—an organization is either ISO certified or it is not. If an organization is ISO certified, then its processes must satisfy the 20 clauses. CMM, on the other hand, gives a framework for process improvement. It categorizes software processes in five levels of maturity—from initial (level 1) to optimizing (level 5). A software organization can be at any of these levels. Another key difference between ISO and CMM is that ISO is general and is written from the customer's and external auditor's perspective. On the other hand, CMM is software-specific, which provides a roadmap for internal process improvement.

This appendix is adapted from "Moving from ISO to Higher Levels of the CMM," by P. Jalote, which was presented in SEPG 1999, Atlanta. The full paper is available in the CD-ROM *Proceedings of the SEPG99,* Software Engineering Institute, 1999.

Comparisons have been made between the ISO 9001 model and the CMM [1, 6, 8]. They tend to be comparisons between the models themselves, however, and often involve a clause-by-clause or KPA-by-KPA (key practice area) analysis. These studies, although useful, provide little guidance to an organization in moving from ISO 9001 to CMM, a transition that focuses on the implementation of these models. What an ISO organization really needs is the likely "gaps" in its processes with respect to the CMM. In other words, an organization that wants to move from ISO to CMM can really benefit if it can easily find what is missing in its processes with respect to CMM.

One difficulty in defining the gaps is defining an implementation for a model, as a model renders itself to many possible implementations. Although a model may be implemented in various ways, all implementations are nevertheless likely to have certain properties. In this appendix, we attempt to compare the processes of a "typical" ISO 9001 software organization with the processes required in a software organization at CMM level 2, 3, or 4. The result is the set of gaps that are likely to exist in the processes of an organization that has an ISO-compliant quality system. This information will be very helpful to an ISO organization in its journey toward the CMM model.

In this appendix, we will consider a "typical ISO company"; then, for each KPA, we will identify the gaps that the organization has with respect to that KPA. As we are considering the "typical ISO organization," we must make some judgments about the processes of an ISO company. Because we cannot make claims at a very detailed activity level, the appendix will focus on major process gaps. For both the CMM and ISO, we will consider the "minimal" implementation—that is, an implementation that has the required items from the model. For ISO, we have also used the TickIT guidelines, as they are the most applicable to software organizations and are used during ISO certification of software companies.

Processes in an ISO 9001 Organization

ISO 9001 is specified as a set of 20 clauses, with interpretations given for software in ISO 9000-3 and TickIT. These clauses can be implemented in different ways by an organization. Thus, before we can find gaps with respect to CMM, we must first consider what processes and structures are likely to exist in a "typical" ISO-certified software organization. These elements can then be assessed to identify potential gaps with respect to the different levels of CMM. In this section, we identify the processes and structures that are likely to result from implementing the clauses of ISO. We therefore discuss the major sections or sub-sections in ISO 9000-3 standards that are relevant for comparison with CMM.

Management Responsibility (4.1)

The management responsibility clauses will ensure that there is a management representative who has authority to implement ISO and report results to senior management. Generally, the head of the group responsible for the processes will play this role. Also, senior management has to periodically review the quality system and its implementation in the organization. Hence, an implementation of these clauses will usually ensure that the organization has a process group and that senior management has a mechanism with which to review the activities of this group.

Quality System (4.2)

The clauses related to the quality system (QS) ensure that the main elements of the management and development processes are documented in a QS. As the organization must ensure that the processes listed in the QS are implemented, implementation of these clauses also necessitates the development of methods for training/orientation on the QS and for disseminating the QS to the people implementing it.

Internal Audits (4.3)

Internal audits have to be conducted by people independent of the team members who are performing the tasks. Implementation of these clauses ensures that an organized independent auditing mechanism is in place in the organization that checks the implementation of processes defined in the QS on projects and that verifies the correction of deviations.

Corrective Action (4.4)

This clause requires that causes of noncompliances be analyzed and actions be taken to correct them and prevent them from occurring in the future. Implementation of corrective action ensures that there are mechanisms to report shortcomings in the QS, correct the shortcomings, and disseminate the changes in the QS.

Contract Review (5.2)

Contract review ensures that a formal, documented contract is established between the supplier and the customer that clearly defines the scope, commitments, and other provisions related to the agreement and that the contract is reviewed and approved (like any other document).

Requirements Specification (5.3)

Requirements specification ensures that all functional and nonfunctional requirements are documented (and subject to document and configuration control) and that the document is approved by the customer. The implementation of this clause is likely to lead to some template or checklist for requirements specification.

Development Planning (5.4)

A development plan for the project is developed and documented (and therefore reviewed and approved) that includes a statement of objectives, organization of the project resources with roles and responsibilities, development phases in the project, development schedule identifying tasks to be performed and resources and time required for them, and more. Implementation of this clause will ensure that

- The development is broken in phases (the minimum is design, implementation, and testing).
- For each phase, formal inputs and outputs are defined, implying that the work products for the project are defined and documented.
- The outputs of each phase are verified/reviewed and approved.
- The development methods and tools to be used are specified.
- Progress reviews are planned (and later executed, with records left).
- The schedule for the various tasks is planned.
- The risks for the project are documented.
- Monitoring methods for the project—that is, status reporting in the project—are planned.
- Interfaces with other groups (within the organization and outside) and escalation mechanisms are defined.

Implementation of this clause is likely to result in some template for the project plan. Detailed methods or guidelines for different aspects of planning, such as estimation and risk management, may not be in place, however.

Quality Planning (5.5)

Quality planning ensures that quality objectives, in measurable terms when possible, and input and output criteria for each phase are specified. Furthermore, the types of testing and verification activities planned are specified. Again, implementing this clause may result in a generic template, but methods for setting quality objectives are not likely to be in place.

Design and Implementation (5.6)

Design rules are created that are used to create a design document (which has to be reviewed and approved). Use of design methodologies and past experience is encouraged. In the implementation of this clause, coding standards are expected.

This effort essentially will make sure that designs are created, documented, and reviewed/approved. Some standards are also likely to be in place.

Testing and Validation (5.7)

The testing and validation clause requires that test plans are created (and reviewed and approved) and that test results and all problems found are recorded (and later resolved). Implementation of this clause ensures that test plans are available, all defects are logged and tracked, and records of testing are maintained.

Configuration Management (6.1)

A configuration management (CM) plan for a project is developed that identifies the configuration items and tools and methods to be used for SCM. Proper version control is done, and changes to configuration items are reviewed and controlled. Some configuration status reports for items and change requests are needed. Implementation of this clause will generally result in some template for CM, basic CM plan procedures, and proper version and change control.

Document Control (6.2)

Implementation of document control measures ensures that all documents are reviewed and approved by authorized personnel prior to their issue, appropriate documents are available to people who need them, and changes to documents are identified and reviewed and approved by original approver.

Quality Records (6.3)

The development of quality records ensures that "footprints" are left for all activities done, so someone can review the performance of the activities objectively. In particular, the implementation ensures that records for the execution of quality tasks (defects found, tracking of defects, and so on) are maintained.

Measurement (6.4)

The measurement clause requires that metrics are reported and used to manage a project. Although it does not propose any metrics, this clause does require that defects and customer complaints are logged and analyzed as metrics. Many suggestions are made regarding the use of metrics. Consequently, implementation of this clause may differ widely. Nevertheless, implementing this clause ensures that defects found by customers and customer complaints are logged. This step will require monitoring of defects. As timeliness is generally of importance to customers, the schedule of activities is also likely to be monitored.

Effort may not be monitored, however, and process measurements (like quality and productivity) may not be in place.

Training (6.9)

The training clause requires training needs to be identified, a training plan to be developed (reviewed and approved), and training records to be kept. Implementation of this clause ensures that some training unit or group identifies training needs, plans training, and delivers training. A few constraints are placed on the contents of the training program.

In summary, an ISO company is likely to have some of the following practices and structures:

- Some QS manuals or documents describing the various practices in the organization.
- A group within the organization that performs process-related activities (and hence can play the role of SEPG).
- An internal audit program, which requires that different aspects of implementation of the organization's QS be audited by personnel who are independent from the ones doing the implementation.
- Some procedures to identify reasons for noncompliance, and to change the processes and disseminate those changes.
- A senior management review of activities performed by the group responsible for the processes.
- Documentation policies and guidelines that require the documentation of all identified work products. In other words, the project plan, schedule, requirements, test plans, and other items are likely to be documented.
- Documentation control procedures that ensure that proper version control is maintained, the documents are reviewed and approved, and the effects of changing a document are understood (and that the changes are made on other documents as well).
- An overall development life cycle specifying the major phases, including requirements, design, coding, testing, and installation. Documentation procedures require that outputs of these phases be documented, approved, and reviewed.
- Project planning policies requiring that a proper project plan be developed that contains the estimates and other relevant information before the development begins. As part of the planning phase, a quality plan also needs to be created.
- Configuration management policies and practices.
- Some training program, with records of training being maintained.
- Some metrics program. In particular, reporting of defects and their tracking to closure are important.
- Quality recordkeeping, which ensures that all quality activities are planned and their outcomes are recorded.

Different organizations will go to different depths in these areas in their ISO implementations. The details of the actual implementation will, obviously, determine the actual gaps for an organization with respect to CMM. For example, one ISO organization might have a detailed measurement program for measuring effort, schedule, and other factors, whereas another organization might just track the schedule and defects. Similarly, a process definition might contain a fair amount of detail, or it might just enumerate the basic stages in the process.

Gap Analysis

The main difficulty in doing a gap analysis study is deciding how to define or characterize processes of a "typical" ISO or a "typical" CMM level-i organization. To aid in creating a practical study, we will make some assumptions. First, although ISO 9001 also looks at the general operation of the organization and its support services, we will focus our attention here on only the software processes. Second, although many things are stated and implied in the ISO/TickIT standards, we will go by what is "generally practiced," "generally audited," and "generally expected" from a "typical" ISO organization. For example, the TickIT guidelines include some statements referring to improvements of the organization over time. These improvements are not defined precisely, however, and, in practice, they are not compulsory for an ISO 9000 certification (although they may be checked in an audit of a "mature" ISO organization). Third, the CMM includes many key practices under each KPA, many of which are categorized under "commitment to perform," "ability to perform," "measurements," and "verification." These key practices focus on policies, authorizations, review, and other aspects of the processes. Here, we will focus mainly on key practices that are grouped under "activities performed." Where necessary, we will include other key practices.

In the CMM, for each KPA, certain goals must be satisfied by the processes of the organization. There are also key practices for each KPA (which are grouped in five groups). These key practices, if implemented, will satisfy the goals. We use the following methodology. We start with the KPA coverage reference sheets provided by SEI, which are used during a CMM assessment. For each KPA, these sheets give the various goals, the activities that should be performed to satisfy the activities for a goal, and the artifacts and documents expected for that goal. These data form the basis for gap analysis. For each goal, we can see whether ISO/TickIT is likely to satisfy the goal. If it is not, we list what is likely to be missing in the ISO company as a possible gap.

Level 2 KPAs

Requirements Management. This KPA has two goals: one focusing on requirements being documented and controlled, and one focusing on maintaining of consistency of other documents (such as plans and designs) with software requirements. Clause 5.3.1 of ISO 9000-3 and clause 4.4.2 of TickIT require that requirements be precisely stated. The general ISO requirement of document control requires that this document be controlled, authorized, and approved. Hence the first goal is likely to be satisfied by an ISO organization. Section 5.3.2 of ISO 9000-3 (4.4.2 of TickIT) requires the existence of a change control mechanism for requirements; it must consider the implications of the change on the project (document control procedures will require a change request document to be reviewed and a change to be authorized). Any reasonable implementation of this clause will require changing the design and other work products appropriately as well. An ISO company is therefore likely to satisfy the second goal also. Thus there are not likely to be any gaps in an ISO organization with respect to this KPA.

Software Project Planning. This KPA has three goals. Goal 1 requires documentation of estimates and derivation of activities supporting the estimates for size, effort, schedule, and critical resources by using a *documented procedure.* In general, ISO does not require effort estimates (although they are implied as part of the plan), and the focus is generally on activities and schedule. ISO also does not require any procedure for estimation. Hence, a **likely gap** could be that a consistent estimation procedure may not exist in an ISO company.

Goal 2 requires that project activities be planned and documented. For these activities, the plan must be controlled and managed, and risks must be identified. Clauses 5.4.1 and 5.4.2 cover these issues, as do the TickIT guidelines requiring risk identification during planning.

Goal 3 requires that affected groups and individuals agree to their commitments and that the commitments undergo review by senior management. Senior management review is satisfied by ISO, as plan documents and commitments must be authorized. ISO does not require any particular group or person to do the estimation. In practice, the project leader is likely to do the estimation in an implementation of ISO. Hence there are no further gaps for this KPA.

Project Tracking and Oversight. This KPA has three goals. Goal 1 requires tracking actual performance against the plans. The effort, cost, schedule, and risks must be tracked, actual measurement data recorded, and formal reviews held at milestones. ISO requires that planned activities be executed (and leave a record of execution), but it does not explicitly require tracking of effort. An ISO company may therefore track only the schedule of activities. A **likely gap** is that an ISO company does not analyze actual effort expended on a project and compare it with planned effort.

Goal 2 requires corrective actions to be taken when the actual performance deviates from the planned performance. In an ISO company, a corrective action is required for any "noncompliances" found in a project. These actions usually focus on activities not done, improper control, and similar problems. Generally, an ISO company may not perform any corrective action based on actual performance. Hence a continuation of the gap mentioned earlier is that an ISO company might not have any procedures for corrective action based on analysis of planned versus actual levels of effort, schedule, or other attributes.

Goal 3 requires that changes to plans and commitments be agreed upon and reviewed. An ISO company will satisfy this goal by approval requirements for its general plan and changes to that plan.

Software Subcontract Management.   This type of management comes under the more general heading of *purchasing* in ISO. Goal 1 requires the selection of a qualified subcontractor; it is satisfied by TickIT guidelines. Goal 2 requires an agreement to be reached with the subcontractor; it is also satisfied by TickIT guidelines. Goal 3 states that there is a regular communication with the subcontractor. This point is not required by ISO and hence can lead to a **gap** in an ISO organization. Goal 4 requires the performance of the subcontractor to be tracked against its commitments. This requirement is only partially satisfied by TickIT, and can also be a **gap.**

Software Quality Assurance.   ISO also focuses on software quality planning and execution, so all four goals of this KPA are likely to be satisfied by an ISO company. One possible gap could arise because ISO does not require the presence of an independent SQA group, although it requires an independent internal auditing group. This omission might create a gap, although it can be argued that an independent auditing group is sufficient to provide the independence desired by the CMM.

Software Configuration Management.   The four goals of this KPA require that the CM activities are planned, what is put under CM is planned and these items are controlled, changes to the items are controlled, and affected groups know the status of the different items. Specifications are given for SCM, which is a support process in ISO. As SCM practices can vary from simple to very elaborate, it is not easy to evaluate an SCM practice. Nevertheless, the ISO practices, coupled with the general requirements of approval, reviews, and document control, are likely to satisfy these goals. A possible gap could arise if the CM audits are not performed. The internal audit mechanism may be looking at CM, however, thereby eliminating this possible gap.

Level 3 KPAs

Organization Process Focus.   This KPA has three goals. Goal 1 states that software process activities must be coordinated across the organization. These activities require that a group exist for this coordination, a process database exist, tools and processes in limited use undergo evaluation for possible use in the rest of the organization (that is, learning), and training be provided. In an ISO company, a group is likely to coordinate all process-related activities. This group may not be trying to identify good practices and tools and may not actively plan to disseminate these practices and tools, and there may not be a process database. This omission can create a **possible gap**.

For goal 2, the process must be assessed periodically and action plans must be developed based on the report. This goal is likely to be satisfied in an ISO company, because an internal audit group is required to audit periodically and all "noncompliances" have to be closed. Some of the noncompliances may require processes to be changed (others might just relate to deployment of processes on projects). Internal audits may not suffice as a process assessment, however, and some process assessment and planning activity might be needed. This problem could lead to a **likely gap**.

Goal 3 requires planning of organization-level process development and improvement activities. ISO has a very limited focus on process management, so this goal is not likely to be satisfied—a **likely gap**.

Organization Process Definition.   This KPA has two goals. Goal 1 requires the development of a standard process for the organization. The activities require that process be developed according to a documented procedure and be documented using some standards. Guidelines and criteria for tailoring of the process for projects must exist. Most of these issues create **gaps**.

Goal 2 requires the collection of information about process use. Activities require that a process database be established and a library of process-related assets be maintained. These activities also promote **likely gaps**.

In other words, an ISO organization may not have procedures for process development, is not likely to have tailoring guidelines, and is not likely to have any process database and process assets. The requirement of tailoring guidelines also means that the processes must be defined with reasonable details so that tailoring guidelines may be built. Detailed process specification is not explicitly required by ISO, so this requirement might create a gap.

Training Program.   Goal 1 of this KPA requires that training activities be planned; it is likely to be satisfied by an ISO organization. Goal 2 states that training is provided. The activities needed for this goal require the existence of procedures for conducting training and standards for courses. This need leads to a **likely gap**. Goal 3 requires that individuals receive training; an activity requires the existence of a waiver procedure for required training. This waiver procedure may not be present in an ISO company and so creates a **likely gap**.

Integrated Software Management.   Goal 1 of this KPA states that the process being used on the project should be a tailored version of the organization's process. Tailoring is not an issue with ISO, so this goal creates an **almost definite gap**.

Goal 2 states that the project must be planned and managed according to the project's process. The activities require that lessons be learned from projects and documented, that a documented procedure for risk management exist, that project effort and critical resources be managed, that thresholds for deviation from planned levels be established for effort, schedule, and critical resources, and that reviews of the project be performed periodically. Although it can be argued that this goal is implied by ISO guidelines, most of the activities are not likely to be performed in an ISO company and hence constitute **likely gaps**. In other words, the gaps here include the lack of a lessons-learning mechanism, proper guidelines for risk management, managing of effort, schedule, and critical resources, and thresholds for taking action based on performance variation.

Software Product Engineering.   The first goal of this KPA notes that software engineering tasks should be defined and performed consistently. Most of the activities under this goal are likely to be satisfied by an ISO company. A **minor gap** could be that the CMM requires the documentation of a rationale for tool selection, which may not be done by an ISO company. Goal 2 requires consistency to be maintained across different work products. It is likely to be satisfied by an ISO company.

Intergroup Coordination.   Intergroup coordination is not a clear issue in ISO, and is not an issue with most software-only organizations. For software-only organizations, however, its omission might mean that intergroup issues between the project team and other groups are not hurting the project. As ISO covers the organization (which CMM does not), intergroup issues are likely to be covered by ISO.

Peer Reviews.   ISO does not require group reviews. It requires only that all documents undergo review. Hence this KPA is not likely to be satisfied by an ISO company, and the **entire KPA can be considered a gap**.

Level 4 KPAs

Quantitative Process Management.   This KPA requires the establishment of goals for the performance of the process on a project, based on the past performance of the process; measurements must be taken during the process execution and the data used to quantitatively control the project. As data collection and analysis are not covered in detail in ISO, much of this KPA will constitute a gap. Specifically, the **possible gaps** are

- Methods for quantitatively managing a project, including making plans, collecting data and analyzing them, and taking corrective actions where necessary
- The process capability of the process in quantitative terms (and use of this capability to set goals for the projects)

Software Quality Management.   This KPA states that quantitative quality goals must be set for the software products, plans must be made to achieve the goals, and the actual progress must be monitored and corrections made, if needed, to ensure that goals are met. Although ISO requires a quality plan and some quality objectives, and it even suggests that goals be measurable wherever possible, it does not require measurable goals and measurable progress. Hence many of the activities under this KPA will constitute gaps. Specifically, **possible gaps** include the quality capability of the process, a documented method for setting quantitative quality goals and developing a quality plan, and a method for quantitative monitoring of progress in achieving quality goals and taking actions based on this analysis.

Summary of Gaps

Based on the preceeding analysis, we can summarize the gaps that are likely to exist in an ISO company with respect to levels 2, 3, and 4 of the CMM. This summary appears in Table A.1.

Where to Go from Here

The gaps given in Table A.1 are those most likely to occur in the processes of an ISO organization with respect to various levels of the CMM. For a particular ISO organization, the exact nature of the gaps will depend on the maturity of its ISO implementation and the kind of processes put in place. Hence, for an ISO organization that desires to move to higher levels of the CMM, it must first identify the actual gaps that exist for that organization, using the general approach outlined here. The gaps in the organization will likely be a subset of the gaps given in Table A.1. At Infosys, the gaps we found were indeed a subset of these gaps.

Table A.1 Summary of Gaps Related to CMM Levels 2, 3, and 4

KPA		Probable Gaps
Level 2 KPAs		
1	Requirements management	None
2	Project planning	Documented procedure for estimation
3	Project tracking and oversight	Tracking of effort and comparison with estimated effort Corrective actions based on actual data on effort (and schedule)
4	Software subcontract management	Regular communication with the sub-contractor
5	Software quality assurance	None
6	Software configuration management	None
Level 3 KPAs		
7	Organization process focus	Method to identify and disseminate usage of new tools and processes that are already being used in some parts of the organization Plan for software process development and improvement activities
8	Organization process definition	Documented procedure for developing and maintaining a process Tailoring guidelines Process definition with sufficient details Organization software process database Library of process assets
9	Training program	Procedure for conducting training Course material preparation standards Waiver procedure
10	Integrated software management	Tailoring guidelines Learning technical and management lessons Guidelines/procedure for risk management Tracking of effort, critical resources, and so on Thresholds for variation of actual performance on a project from planned performance for taking action
11	Software product engineering	Rationale for tool selection Defect data analysis
12	Intergroup coordination	None
13	Peer reviews	All activities and goals of this KPA

(continued)

Table A.1 Summary of Gaps Related to CMM Levels 2, 3, and 4
(continued)

KPA		Probable Gaps
Level 4 KPAs		
14	Quantitative process management	Methods for quantitatively managing a project, including making plans, collecting data and analyzing them, and taking corrective actions when necessary Process capability in quantitative terms (this capability is used in project planning and execution)
15	Software quality management	Methods for setting quantitative quality goals for a project, methods for quantitatively monitoring the progress and taking corrective actions when necessary Quality capability of the process known in quantitative terms

Once the gaps are known, then an action plan is prepared for plugging the gaps. The gap-plugging exercise has two major components: defining what needs to be done for plugging the gaps (that is, procedures), and deploying the procedures defined for projects. As is the case with any process, identifying the procedures is a conceptual activity that requires a good understanding of the current processes and objectives of the organization, so that meaningful procedures can be devised. Deployment is the more difficult part.

For the purposes of planning and execution, we can classify the gaps into three categories. *Process issues* relate to changes in a process definition (and implementation). *Structural or management issues* deal with management structures needed for plugging the gaps. *Metrics-data-related issues* deal with usage of process data. The different gaps under these categories are given below.

Process Issues

Estimation procedure

Process for process development and maintenance

Life-cycle process with sufficient details

Tailoring guidelines for processes

Procedure for conducting training

Course material preparation standards

Risk management guidelines/process

Peer review process

Guidelines for quantitatively managing a project

Guidelines for setting quality goals

Structural/Management/Policy Issues

Collection and dissemination of lessons learned from projects

Identificaton and dissemination of new tools and processes that are already used in parts of the organization

Collection of process assets and ensuring their availability for other projects

Data collection from projects (on effort, schedule, defects, and size)

Communication channels and structures with the subcontractors

Waiver policies for training

Project tracking based on actual performance of the project, and taking of corrective actions if deviations exceed set thresholds

Plan for software process development and improvement

Policies for peer review (and data collection for reviews)

Metrics Data

Process database—which will probably have summary data from completed projects

Process capability—understanding the process capability in quantitative terms

Quantitative analysis of performance of processes on a project

Proper use of these data in project planning

To deal with the process issues, the processes are first defined. One method for process definition is the time-tested method of creating working groups or task forces. For structural/managerial issues, developing the procedure itself is usually not the most difficult part. Structures are needed in the organization to support these activities. For example, for lessons learned, some methods might be needed to identify "good practices" and then some methods created to disseminate these practices. Similarly, data collection in projects is a management issue—how to ensure that good data are collected from projects. Some structural issues can also be considered as process issues, such as project tracking using project performance; we believe that this problem is more of a management issue—that is, the problem is finding effective means of getting this activity done. Data analysis issues usually remain outside the regular project cycle and are therefore grouped separately. Management structures and procedures will have to be defined for these issues.

Once the processes are defined, mechanisms identified, and data analysis procedures defined, piloting and deployment can begin. The mechanism for deploying a process should be defined in the process management process. For example, the process might involve first trying out a new process on a pilot project, followed by fine-tuning of the process, and then by the final deployment. The process management process will define the process for deployment (and thereby fill one gap). It should be understood, however, that deployment structures and resources will be required for any deployment. Unless properly trained resources actively take up the task of deployment, the deployment is likely to be very difficult to achieve.

Two approaches are possible for overall deployment from the point of view of the CMM assessment. The first choice is to fully deploy the new processes and structures in the organization and then go for an assessment. The second option is to provide a limited deployment in some parts of the organization and then go for an assessment. The latter approach is quicker and provides validation of the processes before the big task of organization-wide deployment is undertaken. From the CMM point of view, both approaches are acceptable. The assessment is intended to prove that the organization has the capability of executing projects at a certain level by examining a reasonable number of projects and people. The capability can be proved by a limited deployment. Also, being at CMM level-i does not mean that all projects of an organization are following procedures of level-i—some projects might be following processes that are lower than level-i for customer or business reasons.

Which level should an ISO organization target if it adopts the CMM framework? Although many might suggest that level 3 is the natural choice, we believe that the right "target" is level 4. Reaching level 3 from ISO provides limited visible benefits and the basic process-based approach remains largely unaltered. Level 4 has only two more KPAs; with some extra effort, it should be achievable for an ISO organization. A major advantage of going for level 4 is that it brings about a change in the way the projects and processes are managed—everything becomes data-oriented. This basic shift in operations provides the organization with a quantitative visibility into its processes.

The second major question for an ISO organization deals with how many rounds in which the gaps should be filled. The traditional wisdom suggests that changes should be made slowly and incrementally. We believe that the "big-bang" approach may be well suited, if the gaps are not too wide. In this approach, all identified gaps are "filled" together, resulting in a set of processes that are compliant with level 4. These processes then have to be implemented. A key success factor for this approach is that the entire initiative for reaching a certain level must be treated and managed like a project, which is sponsored and monitored by the senior management of the company. At Infosys, we followed this approach very successfully. Aspects of managing this project are described in Appendix B.

The time required to move to level 4 will vary depending on the severity of gaps, the commitment of the organization to achieving higher maturity levels, and the management of the process improvement initiative. If an organization had a healthy measurement system in place, the processes defined in its ISO-certified quality system are reasonably detailed, and there is enough motivation to handle all gaps together, then the organization can move to level 4 in one to two years.

Summary

A large number of software organizations have been certified under ISO 9001 and now want to move to the Capability Maturity Model (CMM). This appendix, based on Infosys's experience of successfully transitioning from ISO to level 4 of the CMM, discusses the possible gaps in the processes of an ISO organization that might exist with respect to different levels of the CMM.

To identify these gaps, we considered a "typical" ISO organization. The exact nature of the gaps, obviously, will depend on the nature of the organization's processes. This appendix detailed the most likely gaps; the actual set of gaps will be a subset of these issues. The set of gaps given in this appendix can act as a useful guide or checklist for an organization planning to move to higher levels of CMM. The method described in this appendix can be used by an organization to do a detailed gap analysis.

The appendix also discussed what to do after the gaps are identified and the different ways in which an organization can prepare for an assessment. We recommend that an ISO organization shoot for level 4 of the CMM. We also suggest that the "big-bang" approach can be followed for reaching level 4, provided that the initiative of achieving high maturity level is managed like a well-controlled project. We also propose that a limited deployment, followed by an assessment and then organization-wide deployment, might be a more sensible way of proceeding.

References

[1] R. C. Bamford and W. J. Deibler II. Comparing, contrasting ISO 9001 and the SEI capability maturity model. *IEEE Computer,* pp. 68–70, Oct. 1993.

[2] W. Humphrey. Characterizing the software process: A maturity framework. *IEEE Software,* 2(5): 73–79, 1988.

[3] W. Humphrey. *Managing the Software Process.* Addison-Wesley, 1989.

[4] International Standards Organization. *ISO 9001: Quality Systems—Model for Quality Assurance in Design/Development, Production, Installation, and Services.* 1987.

[5] International Standards Organization. *ISO 9000-3: Guidelines for the Application of ISO 9001 to the Development, Supply and Maintenance of Software.* 1991.

[6] M. C. Paulk. Comparing ISO 9001 and the capability maturity model for software. *Software Quality Journal,* 2: 245–256, 1993.

[7] M. C. Paulk, et al. *The Capability Maturity Model for Software: Guidelines for Improving the Software Process.* Addison-Wesley, 1995.

[8] M. C. Paulk. How ISO 9001 Compares with the CMM. *IEEE Software,* Jan. 1995.

[9] U.K. Dept. of Trade and Industry and British Computer Society, 1992. *TickIT: A Guide to Software Quality Management System Construction and Certification Using EN29001.*

Appendix B

Managing the Software Process Improvement Project

In an effort to improve its processes, Infosys, a large ISO 9000-certified software house, adopted the SEI's Capability Maturity Model (CMM) framework, and successfully transitioned from ISO to level 4 of the CMM. A key success factor in this achievement was that the process improvement initiative was treated and managed like an aggressive project. This appendix describes some of the important aspects of managing this software process improvement project.

In its early stages, Infosys recognized that a rapid growth pace cannot be managed without a set of properly defined processes for executing and controlling software projects. To achieve this control, initially it adopted the ISO 9001 TickIT model leading to ISO certification. After the ISO-compliant systems were established, a need was identified for improving the processes further. It was believed that ISO provided little guidance for further process improvement, so the CMM framework [5] for process improvement was adopted. Having implemented ISO, the organization was somewhere between levels 2 and 3 (implementing ISO generally implies that most of the key process areas [KPAs] for level 2 of CMM are generally satisfied and some portions of the same KPAs at level 3 may be satisfied [3]). A limited assessment by an external consultant had also placed Infosys at CMM level 2. Although the organization had been considering the CMM for some time and had developed sufficient in-house expertise in it, due to business requirements and other needs, it decided to move

Based on an article by P. Jalote et al. Technical Report, Department of CSE, IIT Kanpur. Portions also appear, with permission of Addison-Wesley, as a paper entitled "Managing the transition from ISO to high maturity levels of CMM" in Proceedings of 3rd International Quality Week Europe (QWE99).

aggressively on the adoption of CMM in early 1997. This move resulted in Infosys being successfully assessed at level 4 of the CMM.

A key factor in this transition from ISO to a high maturity level was that the software process improvement (SPI) initiative was executed in project mode. This appendix describes some of the most important aspects of this evolution and the strategies that were employed for following a project-management approach to SPI.

Setting the Goal

Two approaches are possible for implementing the CMM (or any other) framework. The first option is to do process improvement and enhancement based on needs and analysis, and then later seek an assessment. In this approach, achieving a particular level is essentially a "side effect" of SPI initiatives. The second approach is to fully accept the CMM framework, set some target in terms of maturity level, and then strategize and plan SPI activities accordingly.

If the SPI will follow a project approach, then—as in any project—the goal or desired end result must be extremely clear. An SEI survey reports that having well-understood SPI goals is a key success factor [2]. Furthermore, everyone involved in the project must be fully committed to reaching the goals. As has been pointed out [7], a shared vision is very important for the success of SPI initiatives. Although goal setting and obtaining commitment are possible with the first approach, they are considerably easier to do in the latter approach because the goal is very clear—achieving a maturity level. Furthermore, demonstrating that goals have been met or that progress is being made toward achieving the goal is much more difficult in the "side effect" approach and can require a considerable period of time to collect enough data to "prove" the case. This exercise is much simpler in the project approach—the fulfillment of the goal can be demonstrated through an assessment.

At Infosys, we followed the latter approach. The lowest level for which Infosys could shoot was level 3. This goal was deemed not sufficiently ambitious, however, and promised to add only a limited value, as the organization already had many of the level 3 processes. As Infosys had been collecting data on projects for a few years, it was felt that the additional two KPAs of level 4 could be met with some extra effort. Level 4 also provided the quantitative visibility and analysis that the organization desired. For these and some other business reasons, the company set level 4 as its target. The senior management of the company, including the CEO, in cooperation with the head of SEPG, selected the target. This action made the senior management and the SEPG partners in the SPI initiative, providing the necessary buy-in by senior management. Such support is important for the success of any SPI initiative [1, 2, 3] and to avoid the potential problem of lack of senior management support [2, 3, 7].

Once the target level was set, the schedule was decided. Because a rough KPA-wise gap analysis suggested that gaps would be manageable, a schedule of about one year was established. A short time span was given to signal the "importance" of the initiative, which is also an important success factor [2, 3]. It was believed that a short duration would also help keep interest in the initiative alive and mobilize people. One year was deemed long enough to effectively complete at least one full cycle of process improvement and to carry out any corrections needed in that cycle. Although moving up the maturity scale is generally considered to be a slow process and many have found that it takes longer than expected [3], Infosys believed that having a focused target and tight project management would make it possible to move up in this length of time. It was also agreed that the head of the SEPG would act as the project leader for this project, with support and cooperation being provided, on an as-needed basis, by the rest of the organization.

Besides satisfying a basic requirement for operating in a project mode, this setting of a target provided other benefits. First and foremost, it stopped all debates about the usefulness of CMM. Any doubts about the usefulness of different aspects of CMM in the Infosys context were laid to rest. Once these debates ended, the task of the SEPG shifted from convincing people about CMM to interpreting the CMM such that maximum benefits could be achieved by Infosys with the least amount of overhead. As we discovered, it is indeed possible to interpret the CMM in a manner that best suits the business goals of the organization.

Second, the task of deciding which SPI initiatives to undertake became much simpler. Without a framework, identifying initiatives is not easy, particularly if extensive data on process performance are not available (which is likely to be the case with an organization operating at a lower level of process maturity). With the target specified, it was much easier to do a gap analysis to select the necessary initiatives. In other words, when the final state to which to take the processes is defined, it becomes easier to determine what must be done to achieve that state. Without a goal like a specific maturity level, which very clearly characterizes the state of the process, deciding upon the SPI initiatives is a conceptually harder task.

Third, an immediate buy-in occurred when senior management set level 4 as a corporate objective. As reported elsewhere [7], one major problem for SPI initiatives is the lack of a shared goal among the various stakeholders. With a goal in place, the entire organization had a shared vision of achieving the target, which made the task of SEPG considerably easier. Without this type of goal, it is much more difficult to convince developers and project personnel of the need for SPI and specific SPI initiatives. Not only do people frequently resist change, but it is also rarely possible to build a watertight case for SPI, particularly in the absence of suitable measurement data.

Fourth, finding people to help in the SPI initiatives derived from the goal became much easier, as it was a corporate objective. Finally, because the initiative ended in assessment, it provided relatively quick feedback on the project and, in Infosys's case, provided a great sense of achievement. Without such a goal, showing the effects of SPI (through data analysis, for example) is usually not easy. A short project duration also helped in keeping interest alive and prevented any disillusionment from setting in regarding the SPI, a factor that has been reported in a survey regarding SPI initiatives [3].

Elements of the Strategy— Guiding Principles

Where some practice is used by some people to plan and execute the project for achieving the goal, it established some guiding principles. Some of these principles are described in this section.

Simplicity

The processes should be kept simple and not very detailed or complicated. Infosys's earlier experience with detailed processes showed that they tend to put off practitioners and are not amenable to "validation" (how do you ensure that the process is being followed?); hence they tend to remain "on-paper" processes. The company had previously simplified its processes by having only a few stages in each process and only a few steps in each stage. Further details about how each step should be done were converted into checklists and guidelines. Applying this principle reduced the description of the processes to a thin, single-volume handbook (whose acceptability among projects was considerably higher). During this project, the same principle was observed—all new processes that were defined were kept simple (and verifiable).

Minimality

Wherever new processes or procedures have to be defined or existing ones enhanced, they should be kept as small as possible. In other words, instead of using elaborate processes, the company had processes that aimed to achieve limited objectives (to satisfy level 4 requirements). This principle aims to reduce the volume of changes in processes, thereby aiding acceptance and simplifying the task of process deployment.

Leveraging of Existing Practices

Where some practice will be used by some people but is not formalized, while defining procedures instead of some "good" method (presumably by finding such methods in existing literatures), we should formalize and build upon the existing practices. This principle reduces the effort needed for process training and increases the acceptability and buy-in value of the processes. This idea ensured that many of the structures and practices that existed due to ISO 9000 were utilized effectively for the CMM.

Relevance to Business Needs

Even though the CMM framework was to be followed, Infosys established that the relevance of its processes to its business needs was not sacrificed. As the CMM allows a fair amount of flexibility in interpretation, this approach ensures that the basic objectives of processes—to support the business effectively—are not transformed to an expedient objective of "achieve level." This point also implied that where it was perceived that some CMM requirement had limited value to Infosys's business, the organization either interpreted it in a manner that it added value to Infosys or did a very "lightweight" implementation. Such an approach provides a solid reason for undertaking the SPI initiative and makes it easier to get the required buy-in from the project personnel.

Managing the Project

Earlier analysis had indicated that Infosys had 8 to 10 areas that needed more attention, most of which related to project management, and many requiring formalization of existing approaches. As the cost of an assessment was high (both in direct costs and indirect costs incurred during assessment and assessment-related activities) and time was short, Infosys decided to follow the "big-bang" approach. That is, it defined all enhancements needed to reach level 4, validated them, and then deployed them all together. This strategy runs contrary to the commonly held belief that process changes should be instituted gradually. The company nevertheless believed that this big-bang approach was better suited. It not only reduced the cycle time, but also considerably reduced the training needs (otherwise, every time changes are made, training will be needed) and kept the focus on the SPI goal.

With this strategy, a project plan was first made and then executed, and the execution was monitored. In short, the SPI initiative was treated like any other project.

Project Planning

The first step in executing the project was to identify the gaps in the existing processes with respect to CMM level 4. This task was done primarily by a group in the SEPG. The main activity was to go over all key practices in the KPAs and identify the missing elements. If a key practice was not directly satisfied, existing practices were examined to see whether they represented reasonable alternative practices for the goals of that KPA. If not, the key practice was listed as a gap. Initially, only gaps at a high level were identified.

Once the gap analysis was complete, what was needed to upgrade the processes to level 4 was known. A project plan was made based on these gaps. The plan divided the project into three logical phases: Phase I to define the processes, Phase II to deploy the processes, and Phase III for assessment. For each phase, the plan specified the tasks involved, the person assigned to the task, the start date, the end date, and the priority. The key tasks in Phase I, which represent the gaps found in the processes, are shown in Table B.1.

Tasks in Phase II included bolstering CMM awareness, providing training in new processes, adding consultancy and "hand holding" for using the new processes, enhancing the audits to check for deployment, and so on. The final stage, Phase III, focused on the assessment. These tasks included forming internal assessment teams, preparing a method for conducting short assessments, performing the assessments, identifying and correcting gaps in projects, and so on. That is, Phase III was intended to ensure that the organization was ready for the assessment.

Although the project plan was for up to assessment, the process improvement activities do not stop once the assessment is complete. The regular structures for process deployment (such as audits, actions of the SEPG quality advisor for projects, and regular monitoring of SEPG by senior management) will ensure that the processes defined during this initiative continue to be used by other projects, and their usage is monitored. The presence of these structures enables such an aggressive schedule to be adopted. Without the process deployment infrastructure, a project might lead to "paper processes" that are defined and used for the assessment but then forgotten. Furthermore, the SEPG's regular procedures will ensure that the processes are constantly monitored and that improvement opportunities are identified and acted upon. That is, the process improvement represents a continuous activity that continues after the current project terminates. This project is essentially one "big" initiative for process improvement.

Initially, only details of the first phase were specified in Infosys's project plan; other phases were specified only at a high level in terms of their duration. Later, detailed activities for the other stages were outlined. Ultimately, the Microsoft Project (MSP) schedule for this project contained more than 200 schedulable activities.

Table B.1   Phase I Tasks

Task Name	Description of Key Activities in the Task
Process database development	Design and build the database; enter data for completed projects; update project planning procedures to employ the database in planning
Process capability baseline	Develop a procedure for capability baseline creation and analysis; create baseline; validate baseline by trying on some projects; update procedures to employ the baseline
Process assets and Body of Knowledge (BOK)	Organize the process assets more effectively; get more entries for BOK; create awareness for increasing their usage
Tailoring guidelines	Decide on the structure of the tailoring guidelines; develop guidelines for development, reengineering, and maintenance processes
Peer reviews	Update existing review procedure to include inspections; institute pilot projects; define a review capability baseline
Project monitoring and control	Determine quantitative measures to indicate the health of a project; enhance existing monitoring mechanisms with quantitative indicators; develop guidelines for performance deviation and for taking action when the performance is out of range
Quantitative quality planning and monitoring	Develop guidelines for quantitative goal setting; setting of intermediate goals; enhance existing mechanisms to include quantitative quality monitoring; develop guidelines for performance variation and for taking action when the performance is out of range
Risk management	Study existing approaches; conduct a survey to find the top risks and mitigation strategies; enhance guidelines for risk management
Requirements traceability	Enhance and formalize the existing approach
Estimation	Do data analysis to develop regression equations; build templates for different types of projects; enhance the use of the process database and capability baseline

Defining the Processes

Proper definitions are a key to the success of processes. If the processes add little value to the projects, they are unlikely to be followed in the organization. To ensure that the processes are reasonable and useful for projects, it is important that the end users of the processes participate actively in the definition step. Processes defined with only limited involvement of the end users are unlikely to be accepted easily by projects. With the active involvement of users in process definition, the buy-in from those users is increased.

At Infosys, to define processes to fill the gaps, the working group or task force approach was followed. For each major gap, a working group was formed; each group consisted of four to five people from projects and one representative from the SEPG. In most groups, the group leader was an experienced person who had dealt with projects.

Each working group was given specific instructions, where possible, about the nature of the expected output. Group members were sensitized about the company's guiding principles. The relevant KPAs that spawned the gaps were also pointed out. The group's charter was to define (or enhance) the process so as to plug the gap and satisfy the relevant KPA, pilot the processes on one or two projects, prepare the necessary training material, and then hand the results to the SEPG for full deployment and training.

All working groups worked in parallel. Because of Infosys's guiding principles and the state of the current processes, in most cases the scope of work was not large. Each group was given two to three months to finish its task. Most people in the groups worked part-time, spending about one-third of their time on this effort. Within about three months, all processes had been defined, and most had been piloted or tried on some existing projects.

Process Deployment

Once defined, the processes had to be deployed on the projects. Because Infosys followed the "big-bang" approach, after all working groups finished their work, the complete set of changes to processes for this initiative was known and ready to be deployed. Deployment is always the most difficult task for the SEPG. In this case, the initiative was a corporate goal, so the task of deployment became easier. Infosys decided to deploy these processes mostly in new projects and let the existing projects continue to use old processes. This decision simplified the deployment task considerably because new projects tended to come in at a steady, slow rate, which permitted the SEPG to "hand hold" them comfortably even with the limited staff.

First, a massive training drive was embarked upon. The company took the view that project people do not need to know CMM—they need to know only the organization's processes. The task of the SEPG was to ensure that the processes were compliant with level 4. Hence the focus of the training was on Infosys's processes. The training material was packaged into two programs: one for peer reviews and one for a comprehensive program having short sessions on each new process element. Whereas the latter training program targeted project leaders only (because most of the new processes concerned project management), peer reviews training was given to developers as well. Within a few weeks, a large number of people had undergone training, as training programs were held multiple times every week.

To aid deployment, the role of the SEPG quality advisor who was usually associated with the project was enhanced. The usual practice was that the quality advisor did not take part directly in any project activities but aided the project's process definition and monitored the project for process compliance. As some of the new process elements required the use of the process database and data analysis periodically, Infosys decided to have support for this function be provided by the SEPG. In addition, the quality advisor received a checklist with which to make sure that processes were being implemented properly.

To further enhance collaboration between the SEPG and other groups, some public relations initiatives were undertaken by the SEPG. A Web site was created, which tried to give high visibility to the people involved with this project. Articles and progress reports were posted on the intranet to keep people informed and interested. Weekly quizzes on quality and CMM were started, with prizes being bestowed on winners, to rally the organization and keep the interest of everyone in the initiative.

Project Monitoring and Senior Management Involvement

Although proper monitoring is critical in any project, monitoring and control were even more important in this project for several reasons. First, the people in the working group were not members of the SEPG; thus they did not report to the SEPG manager and had other tasks assigned to them. Without the existence of direct control and influence on them by the SEPG, proper control mechanisms became very important. Second, the plan for this project depended on the situations in other projects; hence the plan became more dynamic, particularly in Phases II and III. Finally, as the project was intended to achieve a corporate goal, the stakes were much higher.

To ensure that all working groups delivered on time, even though the SEPG was responsible for this project, a steering team was formed. It included many senior managers and was headed by the CEO. The steering team met once per month, and all working groups reported their progress in this meeting. In Phase I, progress on process definitions was reported by the various working groups. In Phase II, the results of different projects deploying the new processes were reported, as was information from the SEPG. In Phase III, the SEPG reported on actions being taken to ensure that the organization would be ready to successfully undergo the assessment. Although the SEPG provided regular monitoring of the initiative, monitoring by the steering team provided the necessary "push" and commitment. Having the CEO as its chair sent the right messages, indicating that the organization was serious about the initiative, which was deemed an important success parameter [2, 3]. It also provided visibility into the initiative to the senior management, another important success factor [2, 3]. In addition, the steering team's meetings and presentations raised the profiles of the working groups with the CEO, which provided an added incentive to group members, as the CEO ultimately controls salary raises, promotions, and stock options. Many people associated with this project ultimately received achievement awards from the CEO.

A CMM orientation program was also initiated for the senior management to give those managers a high-level view of the CMM and the benefits that the organization hoped to derive from reaching a high maturity level. Some senior persons were also roped in to conduct the orientation program.

Risk Management

Once a goal was set and a tight deadline given, it became clear that many things could go wrong during the project. In other words, this project had many risks. To handle this problem, it was decided to do risk management in the same way as was done for software projects. Risk management was typically not associated with SPI projects. Once the goal became clear, however, risk management proved very useful in achieving it.

Infosys followed a simple strategy for risk management. In each steering team meeting, particularly the early ones, team members prepared a list of risks that could adversely affect the outcome of the project. The risks were ranked as high, medium, or low. For each high and medium risk, some risk mitigation step was suggested.

The strategy of presenting and discussing risk management in the steering team meetings was very useful. As many of the proposed risk mitigation steps would be executed by people outside the SEPG, commitments were obtained during this meeting. With the CEO and other senior managers on the steering team, agreeing on risks and executing risk mitigation became considerably easier. Some of the risks that were identified early and the mitigation plans are given in Table B.2.

For example, the early plan was to take only the development and reengineering processes to level 4. A risk therefore arose that there might not be enough new projects of these types that would use the new processes and that would be available for assessment. During the steering team meeting itself, projects were identified and committed to alleviate this risk. Another risk mitigation step for this problem was to expand the scope and include maintenance projects. Again, during the steering team meeting, commitments were obtained and relevant working groups formed for maintenance projects.

Another risk related to the number of entries in the process database. Infosys had set a target of including 50 entries in the process database within six months. From the old project closure reports, about 20 data points were added. The rest had to come from recently completed projects or projects that

Table B.2 Risks and Risk Mitigation Strategies

Risk	Severity	Risk Mitigation Strategies
Number of new development projects may not be sufficient for assessment	High	• Include maintenance projects in the scope • Include other locations in the scope • Identify and commit projects
Not enough data points in the process database	High	• Require all recently closed projects or projects closing soon to submit their closure reports • Include maintenance projects
Process performance variation is too wide	Medium	• Create targeted performance baselines (customer-specific, platform-specific, and so on)
Not enough experienced people available to be on the assessment team	Medium	• Identify suitable people "on the bench" and start training them about the CMM • Select project leaders who are implementing the new processes as assessors
Is our interpretation acceptable?	High	• Discuss interpretation issues with a consultant • Do an abridged process assessment during the middle of the project

were to terminate in the near future. This idea was proposed as the risk mitigation strategy. Once it was accepted, all such projects were asked to furnish their project completion analysis reports, which had been more difficult to collect in the past.

One risk identified early was "is our interpretation acceptable?" Infosys had interpreted and implemented the CMM in a manner that suited the company best. How could it be sure that this interpretation would be accepted by the assessor? This is a very real risk, particularly given that the CMM does not prescribe processes and many different interpretations are possible. The risk mitigation plan for this point was as follows. At the end of Phase I, a recognized CMM consultant was brought to Infosys for a brief period. During this visit, team members presented the company's processes and sought clarification on issues where differences were possible. This discussion focused on processes only, rather than on implementation. During these discussions, some minor gaps and interpretation issues did come up, which were later resolved. This approach minimized the risk that the processes themselves would not be "level 4 compliant" when Infosys deployed its processes. In addition, an abridged assessment was performed once the deployment had started. Similarly, other risks were identified, and mitigation strategies were evolved and then carried out.

Summary

Evidence suggests that software process improvement (SPI) can provide good returns to any organization developing software. Although agreement has been reached on the need for SPI, it is not well understood how implementation of an SPI initiative should proceed.

This appendix proposed that, to rapidly and effectively implement SPI initiatives. these efforts should be treated like projects and should be carried out in project mode. Infosys's successful transitioning from ISO 9000 to level 4 of the CMM was discussed, including the various elements of the strategy followed to complete this transition. These tactics are quite general and reusable in other contexts. Some of the important elements of this strategy were as follows:

- Setting a goal for the SPI in terms of a maturity level. This goal provided a clear and succinct objective that will necessarily require commitment from senior management. Creating an "icon" makes it easier to rally the organization around that "icon." It also provides an easy way of validating whether goals of the project have been achieved—through an assessment.

- Establishing a reasonable duration for the project. This conciseness enabled the organization to maintain focus and interest and to obtain a relatively quick feedback on the initiative.

- Principles of simplicity and minimality, which helped to obtain processes that were likely to be followed. Keeping the focus of the processes on the business objectives of the organization and leveraging existing practices boosted the buy-in by personnel on projects.

- Managing the SPI initiative like an aggressive project. Proper planning was done, followed by proper implementation and monitoring. It helped to have monitoring done by senior management, as these managers gained visibility into the project and were more willing to maintain their commitment and support for the SPI initiative.

- Using risk management techniques to ensure that the goals of the SPI project are met. Infosys used risk management very effectively to continually reduce the risk of failure.

References

[1] M. Daskalantonakis. Achieving higher SEI levels. *IEEE Software,* pp. 17–24, July 1994.

[2] J. D. Herbsleb and D. R. Goldenson. A systematic survey of CMM experience and results. *18th International Conference on Software Engineering,* pp. 323–330, 1996.

[3] J. Herbsleb, et al. Software quality and the capability maturity model. *Communications of the ACM,* 40(6): 31–40, 1997.

[4] W. Humphrey. *Managing the Software Process.* Addison-Wesley, 1989.

[5] M. Paulk, et al. *The Capability Maturity Model for Software: Guidelines for Improving the Software Process.* Addison-Wesley, 1993.

[6] M. C. Paulk. Comparing ISO 9001 and the capability maturity model for software. *Software Quality Journal,* 2: 245–256, 1993.

[7] K. Sakamoto, et al. Toward computational support for software process improvement activities. *Proceedings of the 20th International Conference on Software Engineering,* pp. 22–31, 1998.

Index

The SEI Series in Software Engineering

Introduction to the Team Software Process℠
by Watts S. Humphrey
0-201-47719-X • 2000 • Hardcover • 496 pages

Watts Humphrey provides software engineers with precisely the
teamwork training and practice they need. While presenting a quick
and comprehensive perspective of what team software development is
all about, the book provides practitioners and students in any projects-
based software engineering environment with a practical and realistic
teamworking experience. The Team Software Process (TSP) is built on
and requires knowledge of the author's influential Personal Software
Process (PSP), which details how programmers can (and should) manage
time and achieve quality in their own work. The TSP shows how to apply
similar engineering discipline to the full range of team software tasks,
leading ultimately to greater productivity.

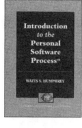

Introduction to the Personal Software Process℠
by Watts S. Humphrey
0-201-54809-7 • 1997 • Paperback • 304 pages

This workbook provides a hands-on introduction to the basic discipline
of software engineering. Designed as a programming course supplement
to integrate the PSP into a university curriculum, the book may also
be adapted for use by industrial groups or for self-improvement. By
applying the book's exercises, you can learn to manage your time
effectively and to monitor the quality of your work.

A Discipline for Software Engineering
by Watts S. Humphrey
0-201-54610-8 • 1995 • Hardcover • 816 pages

This book scales down successful methods developed by the author
to a personal level for managers and organizations to evaluate and
improve their software capabilities. The author's concern here is to
help individual software practitioners develop the skills and habits
they need to plan, track, and analyze large and complex projects
and to develop high-quality products.

Managing the Software Process
by Watts S. Humphrey
0-201-18095-2 • 1989 • Hardcover • 512 pages

This landmark book introduces the author's methods, now commonly
practiced in industry, for improving software development and maintenance processes. Emphasizing the basic principles and priorities of the
software process, the book's sections are organized in a natural way to
guide organizations through needed improvement activities.

The SEI Series in Software Engineering

Managing Technical People
Innovation, Teamwork, and the Software Process
by Watts S. Humphrey
0-201-54597-7 • 1997 • Paperback • 352 pages

This insightful book—drawing on the author's extensive experience as a senior manager of software development at IBM—describes proven techniques for managing technical professionals. The author shows specifically how to identify, motivate, and organize innovative people, while tying leadership practices to improvements in the software process.

The Capability Maturity Model
Guidelines for Improving the Software Process
by Carnegie Mellon University/Software Engineering Institute
0-201-54664-7 • 1995 • Hardcover • 464 pages

This book provides a description and technical overview of the Capability Maturity Model (CMM), with guidelines for improving software process management. The CMM provides software professionals in government and industry with the ability to identify, adopt, and use sound management and technical practices for delivering quality software on time and within budget.

Managing Risk
Methods for Software Systems Development
by Elaine M. Hall
0-201-25592-8 • 1998 • Hardcover • 400 pages

Written for busy professionals charged with delivering high-quality products on time and within budget, this book is a comprehensive guide that describes a success formula for managing software risk. The book is divided into five parts that describe a risk management road map designed to take you from crisis to control of your software project.

Software Architecture in Practice
by Len Bass, Paul Clements, and Rick Kazman
0-201-19930-0 • 1998 • Hardcover • 480 pages

This book introduces the concepts and practice of software architecture—what a system is designed to do and how its components are meant to interact with each other. It covers not only essential technical topics for specifying and validating a system, but also emphasizes the importance of the business context in which large systems are designed. Enhancing both technical and organizational discussions, key points are illuminated by substantial case studies undertaken by the authors and the Software Engineering Institute.

The SEI Series in Software Engineering

Cleanroom Software Engineering
Technology and Process
by Stacy Prowell, Carmen J. Trammell, Richard C. Linger, and Jesse H. Poore
0-201-85480-5 • 1999 • Hardcover • 400 pages

Written by the creators and preeminent practitioners of cleanroom software engineering, this book provides an introduction and in-depth description of topic. Following an explanation of Cleanroom theory and basic practice, the authors draw on their extensive experience in industry to elaborate in detail on the Cleanroom development and certification process and show how this process is compatible with the Software Engineering Institute's Capability Maturity Model (CMM).

Software Design Methods for Concurrent and Real-Time Systems
by Hassan Gomaa
0-201-52577-1 • 1993 • Hardcover • 464 pages

This book provides a basic understanding of concepts and issues in concurrent system design, while surveying and comparing a range of applicable design methods. The book explores two object-oriented design methods for the effective design of concurrent and real-time systems and describes a practical approach for applying real-time scheduling theory to analyze the performance of real-time designs.

Developing Software for the User Interface
by Len Bass and Joelle Coutaz
0-201-51046-4 • 1991 • Hardcover • 272 pages

The authors of this book explain the concepts behind the development of user interfaces both from the end user's perspective and from the developer's perspective. The book provides a categorization of the levels of abstraction of various tools and systems.

Measuring the Software Process
Statistical Process Control for Software Process Improvement
by William A. Florac and Anita D. Carleton
0-201-60444-2 • 1999 • Hardcover • 352 pages

With this book as your guide, you will learn how to use measurements to manage and improve software processes within your organization. The authors explain specifically how quality characteristics of software products and processes can be quantified, plotted, and analyzed, so that the performance of software development activities can be predicted, controlled, and guided to achieve both business and technical goals.

Other Titles of Interest from Addison-Wesley

The Mythical Man-Month, Anniversary Edition
Essays on Software Engineering
by Frederick P. Brooks, Jr.
0-201-83595-9 • 1995 • Paperback • 336 pages

Fred Brooks blends software engineering facts with thought-provoking opinions to offer insight for anyone managing complex projects. Twenty years after the publication of this influential and timeless classic, the author has revisited his original ideas and added new thoughts and advice, both for readers already familiar with his work and for readers discovering it for the first time.

CMM Implementation Guide
Choreographing Software Process Improvement
by Kim Caputo
0-201-37938-4 • 1998 • Hardcover • 336 pages

This book provides detailed instruction on how to put the SEI's Capability Maturity Model (CMM) into practice, and thereby, on how to raise an organization to the next higher level. Drawing on her own first-hand experience leading software process improvement groups in a large corporation, Caputo provides invaluable advice and information for anyone charged specifically with implementing the CMM.

Software for Use
A Practical Guide to the Models and Methods of Usage-Centered Design
by Larry L. Constantine and Lucy A. D. Lockwood
0-201-92478-1 • 1999 • Hardcover • 608 pages

The authors focus on models and methods that help you deliver software that allows users to accomplish tasks with greater ease and efficiency. Aided by concrete techniques, experience-tested examples, and practical tools, the book guides you through a systematic software development process called usage-centered design that weaves together two major threads in software-development: Use Cases and essential modeling. The book illustrates those techniques that have to work and have proved to be of greatest practical value.

Toward Zero-Defect Programming
by Allan Stavely
0-201-38595-3 • 1999 • Paperback • 256 pages

The book describes current software-engineering methods for writing (nearly) bug-free programs. In a precise presentation, it shows how to apply these methods in three key areas of software development: specification which forces the programmer to program more clearly; verification which uncovers additional defects as a team process; and testing which compensates for human fallibility.